THE SPORTING WORLD OF JIM MURRAY

Jim Murray
April 18, 1990

Also by the author:

THE BEST OF JIM MURRAY

THE SPORTING WORLD OF JIM MURRAY

DOUBLEDAY & COMPANY, INC.
GARDEN CITY, NEW YORK
1968

Library of Congress Catalog Card Number 68–25594

Printed in the United States of America

To the Swarthmore backfield, to Unknown Winston, to Dancer's Image, the Harvard Eight with Cox, the son of Frank Merriwell, the Walter who was not camp, Vincent and Al Lopez and every guy who tried to fill an inside straight while behind in his alimony.

CONTENTS

FOREWORD

How do you title a sequel? Better yet, why?

Hollywood has no trouble. Look at the "Andy Hardy" series: the prototype is followed by "Love Finds Andy Hardy," "Andy Hardy Goes to College," "Andy Hardy at War," everything short of "Andy Hardy Dies."

You also have "Son of Lassie," "Jolson Sings Again." You even splice two movies together and get "Frankenstein Meets the Wolf Man" or "The Bride of Frankenstein Meets the Wolf Man." Maybe even "The Bride of Frankenstein Meets the Son of the Bride of the Wolf Man."

With books, it's tougher. What do I call this? *Love Finds Jim Murray?* Would you have *Murray Sings Again?*

I know some people who would buy *The Slow Lingering Death of Jim Murray*. How about *The Son of the Best of Jim Murray?* Say that fast and it sounds as if you've been opening the letters to the editor again.

No, I'm afraid we have to settle for something simple like *The Sporting World of Jim Murray.*

Part of the trouble is the un-cosmic subject matter. Startling exposés are the order of the day. Intrepid journalism wins out. "I Was a Communist for the FBI" gets the *Reader's Digest* all worked up. "How I Found Out the Score of the All-Star Game" hardly gets it done, now, does it? "My Exclusive Interview with Randy Hundley" is hardly in the Louella Parsons category of Great Journalism. No book reviewer will ever say "Stunning in its impact!" of a book that deals with the infield-fly rule.

Even as a personal adventure, a sports writer's effort falls far short. "How I Mastered the Electric Typewriter" is hardly "How I Climbed the Matterhorn." "Because it's there" is heroic to explain why you scaled Everest but not for braving the escalator to the two-dollar window.

Our triumphs are small, our canvas limited. Walter Lippmann would get profoundly depressed. When we talk of "Birds," we mean the ones in Baltimore, not the White House. In our little world, the Cardinals are largely Protestant.

We never get to use words like "escalation," "dialogue," "confrontation." When we speak of "Hawks," we mean the ones who shoot baskets, not pro-war types. John Gunther might spend a year on *Inside Europe* (though I doubt it) but what about *Inside Dodger Stadium?*

Often, 60 million people see the same thing we do. About the only thing we get to see that they don't is Sandy Koufax taking a shower. Believe me, Elke Sommer is an improvement.

The trick is to avoid boredom. "Never go to a sporting event for pleasure!" a colleague warned me when I took the job. You have to be like the bull in a bullfight. They should lock you in the dark for days beforehand so you can treat each event, like the bull, as your first—and last. You have to try to pretend you're seeing Mt. Kilimanjaro for the first time—even though you spend six months a year on it. You have to resist the temptation to nudge your companion in the fourth inning of the World Series and observe "Ball games are like alligators—you've seen one, you've seen 'em all."

Paul Gallico, in his celebrated book *Farewell To Sport,* rhapsodized as follows (but you have to bear in mind he was getting to hell out): "I have for these past years had a ringside seat where men and women have, with their bodies, performed the greatest prodigies ever recorded. I saw the abysmal, unreasoning fury of Dempsey and Firpo fighting like animals and sat in a blinding cloudburst and watched Gene Tunney annihilate an unbeatable Dempsey. I saw Red Grange weave his twisting patterns up and down football fields, and followed in the galleries of Bob Jones as he played his smooth, superb golf shots that have never since been matched. Bill Tilden banged his unreturnable cannon-ball service . . . Babe Ruth stood up to bat on his thin, match-stick ankles . . . Gertrude Ederle rode up Broadway standing in the back of a car with her arms outstretched with joy and happiness . . . What a world! What heroes and heroines!"

Well, mine eyes have seen the glory, too. I saw Frank Howard swing at a wild pitch an airplane had to get out of the way of. I saw Willie Davis drop three fly balls in a single inning. I saw Stan Musial. He only got a hit once out of three tries. I saw Sonny Liston quit in his corner. I saw Brian London bleed, Arnold Palmer bogey.

I saw Willie Shoemaker stand up in the stirrups at the eighth pole and blow a Kentucky Derby. But did I rush to a typewriter to compose "Give me a silly/Guy like Willie? Blowing those finish/lines"? I should say not?!

I can honestly say these old eyes saw Lou Chiozza kick a double-play ball. I saw Maury Wills get thrown out stealing—by 20 feet. I saw Whitey Ford come in with an 0-and-2 pitch that Rocky Colavito hit out into the Bronx. I saw Notre Dame playing for a tie. I saw the Yankees finish last.

The only channel swim I ever went on, the lady got bit by a shark. Sandy Koufax? I saw Sandy Koufax bat. I saw Wally Butts cry. I saw Jim Brown get run out of bounds. Never mind your Graham McNamees, Ted Husings and the greats of the broadcasting world. *I* heard Howard Cosell.

You were there, Gallico, when Ruth called his shot? Pfui! I was there in spring training when Duke Snider did. He pointed to the right field fence—and then hit a foul tip.

You saw Jones? Well, I saw Kermit Zarley. Even the greats showed up in pimples the days I came round. Cary Middlecoff couldn't get out of a sand trap with a shovel. Ben Hogan couldn't get the putter back the last tournament I saw him in. As far as Jones is concerned, if he could hit the ball any better off a fairway or tee than Hogan you should have frisked him for angel's wings, or checked around for the nearest Roman collar and Rosary beads.

I saw Gale Sayers fall down in an open field, Jim Taylor miss a block. Vinnie Lombardi sent in the wrong play. I saw Cassius Clay forget his name and beat up Ernie Terrell because of it.

I saw Louis trying to climb back into a ring. I heard Jess Willard say it wasn't Dempsey who beat him, it was Doc Kearns. You say you saw Tunney, Gallico? I saw Jerry Quarry.

What heroes! What heroines! What nonsense! Maybe it should be "What heroes?" "What heroines?"

Thank goodness, there are a lot of readers who don't need larger-than-life heroics all the time. They can take their sport with a squirt of humor and a twist of irreverence. It's to them that I address this book. Most of it is composed of columns that have won some favor over the years, though it offers some brand new stuff as well. If some of the references seem dated, well, all I can say is that time is an even better rusher than Gale Sayers, but the patterns in sports, like the plays in football, remain basically the same.

And now, if you'll turn the pages—we'll bring you "Andy Hardy at the Old Ball Game."

JIM MURRAY

THE SPORTING WORLD OF JIM MURRAY

GENERAL

Author! Author!

Well, it's that time of the year again. Ho, ho, ho, and all that jazz. Chestnuts roasting on every page. I would like, as a service to you, to cull the best of the Christmas books you might want to give to a loved one, particularly the kids, with especial emphasis on the inspirational volumes.

So, with apologies to Clifton Fadiman and Art Buchwald, not to mention Ralph Henry Barbour and Walter Camp, here are the best of the lot:

"THE FURTHER ADVENTURES OF BLACK BEAUTY." —This heart-warming tale of a lass and her horse should be in every library. It tells the touching story of a horse found in his stall with a broken leg and the trainer wants to shoot it when the young girl of the family (see about Loretta Young for the role) throws herself across the animal and says, "No, no! Let me try to save him!" And she makes a special sling and feeds him sugar for three years and, lo and behold! he can run again even though he has a slight limp. Then one day they put a clock on him and he breaks the track record by 10 seconds; so they enter him in the Kentucky Derby and nobody thinks he has a chance.

And it turns out he doesn't. Because, coming out of the starting gate, his leg snaps again and he racks up the whole field and three other horses die with him and two jockeys get broken collar-bones and double-vision. And the trainer says, "You see! Three years ago I told you to shoot him. But does anybody listen to me? Not when you bat those big beautiful eyes, they don't." And the girl says, "I'm sorry."

"FIGHTING FOOTBALL—OR, 40 YEARS WITH THE FIGHTING FLEMISH."—This tells the story of old Coach

Rockhead and his famous football teams climaxing in the famous locker room scene where the team is behind 100–6 at the half and the coach stands there with tears streaming down his cheeks. He says, "Boys, my sainted grandmother is right now at death's door and the only thing I know of that can save her is for us to go out there and fight! fight! fight! and win this game against the Army!" Just then, the phone rang, and the coach answered it and listened for a minute. Then he hung up and said to the boys, "That was the doctor, boys. He said it wouldn't mean a thing to her condition one way or the other whether we won or lost. So forget it."

"TEN SECONDS TO PLAY."—This is the story of the 97-pound weakling who went out for football and everyone laughed and laughed. So, he lifted weights and built himself up and practiced with the varsity for four years. Finally, one day, in the big game, there were only 10 seconds to play and the coach looked down and saw this kid and said, "All right, son, for four years you've been begging me to let you play and my entire backfield is wiped out. Go in there and show what you're made of."

So the kid went in and fumbled.

"THE KILLER INSTINCT."—This is the story of a tough kid from the slums who came up the hard way and finally became middleweight champion of the world. And one night he was defending his title when the Mafia (they were having their annual parade that day) came in the dressing room and said, "Kid, we've got big money riding on this fight. We'll give you $100,000 to throw it." The kid stood up, a steely glint in his eye and he said, "Big Tony, I was born on the other side of the tracks and I was a tough kid. A lot of people had faith in me, like the warden, and a lot of kids are looking up to me and I don't want to disappoint them. So, could you make it out to 'Cash?' "

"THE HEART OF BASEBALL."—Tells the untold story of "Slugger" McCoy. All the public saw of Slug was the swaggering braggart. Few knew of the many good deeds he performed, but they are all recounted here by his good friend (and press agent) Sick O'Fant. Few knew that Slug was a sucker for a hard-luck story. Anybody who came to him down and out got a loan. At only 8%. And once an old lady's hat blew off and Slug told her which way it went.

Slug never liked to get any publicity on his hospital trips, but the book tells of the time he went to see little Butch Kelly. The kid was dangerously ill and old Slug tried not to blubber as he looked at the wan little face and said, "Kid, just for you, this afternoon against the Cardinals, I'm going to hit three home runs." And little Butch looked bravely up at him through his tears and said "Mr. McCoy, how could that possibly help me?"

Also big this year are the "How To" books. "How To Play Polo." "How To Crocodile Wrestle." There is also a book modelled after jockey Eddie Arcaro's "I Ride to Win." It's written by Jockey Con Artist and it's titled "I Ride to Lose." Its chapter headings include "How to Pull a Horse," "Favorites I Have Gotten Beat On," "How to Signal Your Bookie in the Post Parade," "How to Steer Horses into Trouble," "How to Arrange a Betting Coup," "Shopping for a Price and How to Get It" and "Boat Racing on Dry Land" or "Do You Really Need Every Rider in on It Or Are Four Enough?"

"SUNDAY'S HERO."—This tells the fictionalized story of the regeneration of a football hero set down for betting on games he was in. The book's most moving scene comes when he tearfully promises the commissioner "If you reinstate me, you won't be sorry. Incidentally, neither will I." So the commissioner reinstates him and he says, "Do you mind if I use your phone, Commissioner?" And the commissioner says, "Go ahead" and the hero calls his bookie and says "It's O.K., Joe. Same deal as two years ago."

"SILVER BOY."—The story of a fighter whose mother wants him to be a violinist. So he sneaks out at night and fights, and he's up for a shot at the championship when his mother finds out and says "Lowlife! For this, I scrimped and saved! So you could break your hands fighting with a bunch of loafers!" And he says "But, Ma! my hands are all right! Look!" But she makes him go back to Carnegie Hall and give up fighting and the night of the big concert his accompanist accidentally slams the lid of the piano down on his hand and all his fingers are broken. Now he not only can't play the violin, he can't even fight. So he's working in a liquor store.

By the way, you can't get any of these through the Book-of-the-Month Club.

Mamie Knows Sports

Mamie Van Doren is an interesting little collection of statistics—37-23-34—an actress whose dramatic forte is taking a bath. She is built like something you'd time eggs with and the kind of clothes she wears you'd think she'd catch her death of cold.

Her pictures not only don't need sub-titles, they don't even need dialogue. They run to such searing social documentaries as "Teacher Was a Sexpot," and "3 Nuts in Search of a Bolt" and some Frankenstein opuses where her longest dialogue is a scream. She has also starred in the center fold of *Playboy* magazine with a wardrobe of a cheek mole. It is unlikely they will ever name any Broadway theater after her.

You would not think to look at her that Mamie has very much of an athletic background, but she is second only to Casey Stengel—whom she does not otherwise resemble—in her years around athletes.

Her first date was Jack Dempsey. Some of her later ones were Art Aragon, Bo Belinsky, a Grand Prix driver named Graham Hill, a hydroplane racer or two, an occasional jockey. She has intercepted passes on 49er end, Monty Stickles, and knew Sandy Koufax since the days when he was studying architecture, largely hers. There is some notion that she, and not baseball, is the real national pastime. She thinks coaches and managers encourage their players to go out with Mamie because she doesn't smoke or drink. Also, she says, she goes to bed early. Also doesn't ruin her eyes reading.

I approached Mamie with a problem of some concern to the Republic: How come the American girls got beat by the Russian girls in the USA-USSR dual track meet at the Coliseum recently?

Mamie was startled to hear American girls finished second in any competition. "In what?" she wanted to know.

"Well," I began, "in the javelin—"

"The javelin!" Mamie screamed. "What in the world would any woman be doing with a javelin?"

"Well," I guessed, "perhaps in case they had to take the subway home—"

"In heaven's name, what other things are they trying to compete in?" Mamie interrupted.

"Well," I told her, "they throw this big heavy iron ball and this round wooden-and-metal platter and they jump over bars and into sand pits."

I thought Mamie was going to faint.

"Why, the poor, addled dears!" she murmured. "What do they have next, a rock fight? Good heavens! They don't let the men see them in these warlike activities, do they? What do they think they're getting ready for, an Indian uprising?"

"Well," I said defensively, "they've got to get in shape."

"In shape!" Mamie screamed. "Do you mean to tell me I'M not in shape! Do you see me throwing an iron ball around? Or jumping in piles of sand?" She shuddered. "They'll get muscles even a girdle won't be able to fix. When I walk down the street with a date I want them to be able to tell which one is the man. As for javelins, they don't make the javelin that's as good a weapon as perfume."

She paused. "They got it all wrong. What they should do in these things is have more feminine things."

"Ah," I said, catching on. "You mean, pie-baking, a sew-off, canning preserves, quilt-making?"

Mamie made a face.

"Darling," she purred. "I mean, like seeing who could get dressed for dinner in under six hours. Like putting two adorable men downfield and seeing who can get them to take her to the Cocoanut Grove first. There will be certain conditions. Bikini bathing suits will be OK, like an allowable wind. But the topless will have to be out, right?"

I nodded. "Khrushchev frowns on even ankles showing. You will remember he objected to the Can-Can and Shirley MacLaine the last time he was here. Of course, he had his wife along."

"Maybe we should have a contest to see who could read the most fan magazines under the hair dryer. Who can dye her hair the whitest without getting the ends split. Maybe we should see who can run up the biggest charge account at Magnin's?"

I shook my head. "Department stores are out," I explained. "They had some trouble with an Olympic athlete one year. She got her specialty confused. She was taken on a team as a 'shot-putter' but she must have thought they said 'shop-lifter.' They made her put the dresses back because it was a non-Olympic event but she still holds the unofficial world's record."

"How about a contest for endurance telephone conversations with your next-door neighbor? I think we can break the 16-hour barrier if one of them has had a recent operation."

I frowned. "I don't think they'll go for it," I advised her.

Mamie looked unhappy. "What's the matter with them," she snapped. "Are they Communists or something?"

One Day in April

One-minute interviews:

CASSIUS CLAY, the well-known heavyweight champion: "Am I the greatest? I'm surprised at you. Of course, not:

"First, you have to consider Jack Johnson or Jack Dempsey. Then, there is Joe Louis. Frankly, any one of them could knock me kicking. I doubt I could last a round with any of the three. Between you, me and a couple million readers, I couldn't fight any one of them in a dark room.

"How would I rate myself among heavyweight champions? Well, I would say I might get a draw with Marvin Hart and I think—I repeat, I only think—I might hold my own with Tommy Burns. But, honestly, I don't rate with the great champions like Floyd Patterson, Primo Carnera or Jack Sharkey. I'll tell you the truth: there are nights when I couldn't lick Pete Rademacher.

"But I'm learning. If I were better looking, or had more self-confidence, or wasn't so shy, I might rank with some of the heavyweights of the past—say, Tom Heeney, or Unknown Wirston or Salvatore Ruggierello. I'm pretty sure I could go the route with Johnny Paychek or Johnny Risko. On the other hand, I can't be positive. I hate to tell you but I wouldn't lay a glove on Paul Berlenbach if we fought for two years.

"Would I fight Cleveland Williams, Ernie Terrell and Doug Jones the same night? Don't be silly: I might not even fight 'em the same year. If you want to know the truth, I wouldn't even fight Doug Jones again for Europe, tax-free.

"But, then, I don't really have to fight for a living. I could always turn to nuclear physics. Or brain surgery. If you'll excuse me, now, I have to go lecture at Harvard. I'm explaining Einstein's Theory."

SANDY KOUFAX: "How much am I getting this year? Too much. Frankly, I'd play baseball for nothing. I kept telling Buzzie, I'd play if they just mended my uniform from time to time. O'Malley wanted to give me part of the concessions but I told him to turn it over to the Red Cross. To me, playing baseball is a privilege, not a business. Just put down $1 a year and I'll play, I told them. After all, what else would I do with my summers?"

FRANK HOWARD: "So I says to my wife, 'Honey, you just take care of the dishes and I'll make the living around here.' The way I look at it, a woman's place is in the kitchen and a man's place is in right field. Right? I just don't understand these guys who let their wives run their lives for them. Women have too much to say in this country as it is. Me, I wear the pants in my family. My wife just irons them. When I tell her to."

YOGI BERRA: "Which team do I consider will emerge triumphant this season? Really, old fellow, I haven't given it a great deal of thought but the vagrant notion does occur to me that our athletes have a decided edge—talent-wise, that is. We also have more money, if you want to consider the crude aspects of the thing. After all, this is not an eleemosynary enterprise we are engaged in.

"I don't wish to indulge in any fanciful thinking but I should say from a conservative estimate we might win the mythical pennant by anywhere from 10 to 15 games depending upon a number of variables, the juxtaposition of Mars with Venus, the horoscope (I'm a Scorpio, you know), the presence or absence of a high pressure area over the Northwest Pacific and whether an occluded front moves in during July. Now, if you'll hand me my monocle, I have to get back to my translation of Ovid. I'm working for my Ph.D. in Latin and Greek. Casey Stengel is helping me."

LEO DUROCHER: "The knockdown pitch is a barbaric throwback and should be outlawed. There's too much brutality in sports, as it is. Why, only the other day I saw a fellow try to trip a base-runner. When I was managing, we didn't permit this sort of thing. My object has always been to win fairly and squarely and to be a good sport about losing. After all, it's not whether you won or lost, now, is it?

"That ruffian who said 'nice guys finish last' just didn't understand the situation at all. As for throwing at a batter's head, my gracious, a person could get hurt: I always say, on the ball field, don't do anything your mother would be ashamed of. Of course, mom was always very broad-minded. So am I, frankly, if you don't think so, just look at all the broads' husbands who are suing me."

SONNY LISTON: "I have always tried to model my life after Albert Schweitzer and St. Thomas Aquinas. In the next war, I'm going to apply for chaplain. I have always tried to respect the law, womanhood, and I address policemen as 'sir' and remove my hat in the presence of traffic cops. I drive carefully, try to keep good company, go to church regularly and give temperance lectures. I also try to give good example and I was saying to my Boy Scout troop only the other day, 'Boys, no matter how tough the going gets, hang in there. Even if your shoulder gets thrown out of joint, just remember you've always got another one. Think of all the people who have to go through life with only one hand. Never give up.'"

What's that you say? You don't believe it? Why? Just because it's April first? Don't be a fool.

Machine over Mind

I got nothing against television except they ought to let the guys in the white hats lose once in a while. But what's bugging me is the way they're lousing up our elections.

Democracy, you know, is dull. We don't have coronations or elopements with commoners and when you say "presented at court" in this country, you don't curtsy, you bring bail.

The nearest thing we have to a royal family is the Kennedys. And they're not only commoners, but if they keep winning elections they'll get even commoner.

So, we have to get our kicks out of elections. That is, we used to. You could always lay in a stock of beer, a bowl of popcorn and turn on the "Eye" on election night and settle back for some laughs and suspense.

Not any more. Now, some joker in a sincere suit comes out five minutes after the polls have closed with a slip of electronic tape in his hand and announces: "On the basis of incomplete returns—3 votes cast in the little town of Shakespeare's Hamlet, N.H.—Univac now is able to predict positively Sen. Bustgut has won overwhelming re-election."

Even when one pork barrel specialist is leading 2,000,000 to 0 at midnight, Univac sniffs the wind upstate and announces he hasn't a chance. Candidates tearfully concede when they're still millions ahead because you can't argue with science.

My fear is this action will slip over into athletics. For instance, let us take you now to Chavez Ravine for the opening of the season for the Dodgers where our ace forecasting team of Nutley and Drunkly have set up their computer machine and are busy analyzing the game, which hasn't started yet. Drunkly speaks: "On the basis of incomplete returns from the dressing room where Sandy Koufax just broke the shoelace of his right shoe and someone put piranha fish in the whirlpool, we are now able to estimate the Dodgers will go down to defeat, 11–0. Don Drysdale will not be able to appear. Someone stole the greasy kid stuff from his medicine chest and the equipment manager has discovered the bubble gum won't bubble. The Dodgers will bar the room to the press after the game until the Coke is all gone."

When Lew Burdette is on the mound, Univac will positively predict, "The first pitch will be a spitter. The game will be held up while Durocher argues that either Burdette is wetting them or they should call the game on account of rain."

On a ball hit to the outfield, the machine will announce, "On that ball going to right field, Frank Howard will drop it."

When Frank Robinson comes to bat, there will be a conflict. Univac will predict he will get hit in the ear. CBS' computer will hold out for the temple. Both will agree his head will be numb. Whether he gets hit or not.

In an early inning, the machine will concede a post-season playoff game to the Giants. "Manager Walter Alston will put in Stan Williams in the 9th inning," it will announce, "to save Drysdale for spring practice."

When Willie Davis comes to bat, Chet Drunkly will call in David Nutley. "Davis will hit an apparent triple," he will announce, "and Umpire Jocko Conlan will call him both safe and out. *The Sporting News* and Commissioner Frick will back up the umpire. 'Davis is safe and out,' Frick will announce. 'With an asterisk after it.' *The Sporting News* will put out an extra calling attention to the number of times this has happened beginning with Ed Delehanty and Chief Bender."

When the Mets come to town, the networks won't bother with the expense of a computer but just feed the notes to a vacuum cleaner. Someone will suggest they feed the Mets to it, too.

On All-Star golf, the machines will spoil the suspense when Snead and Palmer come up to the 18th tee all tied. "Snead will hook in the rough," the machine will predict. "His right hand's too far over on the shaft."

Boxing will be a shambles. In the 5th round of a slam-bang battle between Take-It McCoy and Quits McGillicuddy, the machine will announce McGillicuddy will take a dive in the 8th round and ringsiders will be advised to wear life preservers. They will arrive at this prediction by feeding it Frankie Carbo's notebook.

The Rams will have a 2–0 lead at the half, but the electronic monster will shake its head. "According to data assembled from the backside of his uniform, Zeke Bratkowski will be thrown for 11 straight safeties in the 4th period, two on the same play, and the Rams will lose, 20–2. Elroy Hirsch will blame the press."

The Rose Bowl game will be a duel between two cybernetics machines which will predict the Long Beach float as winner of the Rose Parade. Physics profs will be hanged in effigy.

At Indianapolis, when the starter says "Gentlemen, start your engines," the machine will cough discreetly and advise "Tell

Nos. 12 and 14, not to bother. Tell the Ajax Rear Axle Special to check its rear axle. Tell No. 11 to check his insurance."

There is a ray of hope. In July, the networks will announce one of the machines has had a nervous breakdown: it will be found predicting the Yankees will NOT win the world's championship and will be hauled off to have its tubes checked for cirrhosis of the circuits or hardening of the antennae.

"We began to suspect something was wrong when we caught it rooting one day," the medics will admit. " 'Strike the bum out!' it was yelling. All the time, right there in its mouth was the tape: 'He will hit a home run.' It had become a fan. It is useless to us and was last heard firing off messages to 'President Thomas E. Dewey.' "

Poor Jim's Almanac

And a Happy New Year to all . . . !

This is the time of the year to look forward not backward but I have come across a magazine piece by my friend, Chuck Champlin, in which he merely looks askance.

Chuck's outlook on 1963 is printed in my favorite magazine of any year, *Los Angeles Magazine*, in its current issue, in an essay titled "A 1963 Almanac."

Readers of this daily brochette of trivia will recall Chuck as the highly inventive young man who restored to the literature of our time such items as the Wind-Up Doll ("The Liz Taylor doll—you wind it up and it breaks up your marriage"), the all-purpose commercials (for baseball he had "Thrill to the pulsating excitement of two bull pens in action"), and the broken tibia in touch football which awoke him to the dangers that if the President continued to play it while his phone (to the Kremlin) was ringing, World War III might be the direct result of a dropped pass.

Chuck's Almanac for 1963 avoids such obvious predictions as the weather and a new triangle for Liz and plunges into such fearless foreseeing as a Cassius Clay-Sonny Liston fight which he envisions as the "first million-word gate in history" and sees the new Dodger watchword as "Wait Till Last Year!"

But, by and large, he skips the, so to speak, underworld of sport for the more cosmic predictions like the one that January will see Hollywood announcing Hayley Mills has signed to do a remake of "Rain" and October will see Clete Roberts fresh out of wars and his passport expired. I think a sporting version of Chuck's (and Los Angeles') Almanac is in order this first day in the Year of Our Lord 1963:

Jan. 2, 1963—Blue Cross declares, after paying Rose Bowl disability claims, that cowardice be a condition of insurability and anyone challenging a Big Ten lineman be automatically ineligible by virtue of demonstrable courage, which is in Paragraph 10, Clause 7 on the exempt list. In invisible ink.

Feb. 1, 1963—Cassius Clay announces he will fight Sonny Liston for nothing, later reports he was misquoted by AP and what he really said was, "Nothing will get me to fight Sonny Liston."

Feb. 15, 1963—Spring training starts. Twenty major league managers predict pennant. Walt Alston warns, "Don't sell the Mets short." Four Mets owners call a press conference to announce they will sell them any way they can.

Feb. 20—Dan Reeves submits sealed bid of $20 million for the Mets. "Money isn't everything," he announces.

March 1—Buzzie Bavasi announces no deals for Dodgers. "They want the moon," he complains. Walter O'Malley gets him on the phone. "If you mean Wally, give him to them. If you mean the other, I will try to get the government to give it to us if we will promise to put up a playground with swings."

April 1—Dan Reeves gets the Mets, announces he will transfer them to Disneyland.

April 2—Branch Rickey accuses Bavasi of not dealing in good faith. "We offered him a season pass and a framed photograph of Gussie Busch for Don Drysdale." Bavasi explains he was holding out for Green Stamps. And anyway, the Mets offered Elio Chacon for Drysdale.

May 1—The Rams trade Dan Reeves to the Giants.

May 3—Sonny Liston and Cassius Clay sign to meet. "I'll be

glad to meet him anywhere so long as we don't fight," explains Cassius Clay.

May 15—Maury Wills is reported missing between second and third at Candlestick Park. The Coast Guard is searching and ships in the area have been diverted.

June 10—Sam Snead won't win the National Open, as usual. Arnold Palmer will, as usual.

July 5—Ford Motor Co. will announce new car, "Son of Edsel."

July 22—The bull wins a bullfight in Tijuana. Aficionados split over whether he gets matador's ears.

July 22—Hunting is paralyzed by announcement that henceforth every hunted animal will be guaranteed a public defender, a rifleman assigned to shoot to kill every hunter licensed to shoot and kill him. The hunting trophies on the wall in future will all have glasses on them and extinct species will be two-legged hunters instead of four-legged animals.

Aug. 10—Sonny Liston will successfully defend his heavyweight title against the Bulgarian standing army. Cassius Clay will announce he will join the Foreign Legion. Floyd Patterson will suggest elimination match with Adlai Stevenson.

Aug. 12—Skindiver announces try for world underwater endurance record, submerges off Catalina.

Sept. 15—Skindiver announced as world's underwater endurance champion. "He went under at 4 p.m. Aug. 12," announce officials. "As of 5 p.m. today he has not surfaced, thus breaking the old record by 1 month and 3 days."

One of the Best

Know what they're doing now? They're bringing out pool tables in "tangerine, blue, white, gold and gray-beige" if you can believe such a thing.

I ask you! Next thing you know, they'll be putting doilies on the cue racks and coasters under the spittoons. Dammit, is NOTHING sacred any more?

You know the decor a pool table is supposed to have—green felt, worn in spots, a naked bulb hanging down by a frayed cord with a green shade at the end. Whiskey rings on the rails. Anything else, you can't possibly play the game properly. It's like baseball on horseback.

It's the time of the year again when I always think of pool and Ed—St. Patrick's Day and all.

Ed was my uncle. If he ever saw a tangerine pool table he would have sworn off drinking on the spot.

Ed, you see, was the athlete of the family. If you count pool, that is. Ed was a hustler—a pool and dice hustler. Maybe you saw the movie? Well, Paul Newman, THAT was Ed. Only Ed was a five-and-ten-cent store hustler. Newman they made out to be a big deal.

I guess Ed was what they used to call in more innocent times "the black sheep of the family." As if there was only one to a family. At that, Ed did embarrass the family. He was the only one who ever made night court. He made it regularly.

They were pretty tame arrests. Just Ed and a pair of dice—sometimes, both of them loaded. The vice squad didn't have much else to do in Hartford. A crap game was a crime wave in that town. Here in L.A., the cops would be relieved if that was all that was going on when they busted in.

But in Hartford, there was so little else doing, you could have sold tickets to the game if you got out handbills. Only Ed didn't want a crowd. You see, Ed cheated.

You can see where this unforgettable character of mine will never make the *Reader's Digest*, more's the pity. But I used to come downstairs in the morning and there would be Ed boiling dice and eggs in the same pan. The eggs he ate. The dice he squeezed in a wooden vise until they got in a shape they wouldn't come up a "6" or an "8" if you rolled them down Wilshire Boulevard all night long.

These were for putting up your sleeve until the sucker, alternately known as the "mark," came up with a point that was a "6" or "8." Then, you palmed the play dice and rolled the shirred eggs back to the shooter. Sometimes, of course, the three-minute dice slipped out when you didn't want them to. This was known as "leaking" and when it happened, the table usually looked like it was suddenly growing dice. On nights when this took place, Ed came home all beat up. Once, his eyes were swollen so shut I had to lance them with a razor blade so he could see to get out of bed.

He never cared for work—he couldn't even stand to watch it—or school. Not enough action. He got all the way to the sixth grade before he swaggered out to get on his knees behind a trash barrel for a dice game. In a sense, he never got up.

He never married. He was always in too big a hurry—going nowhere. He looked a good deal like Jimmy Cagney—fast, stocky, tough. He could do tricks with a pool cue—put the ball in the side pocket—or YOUR pocket. If he'd been born 20 years later and 20 grand richer he might have tried golf and respectability. "Snooker with a sun tan," he called that game.

He did his hustling in his own joint in his best years—the "Parkville Young Democratic Club," a name that was a howl. There wasn't a guy in it that ever voted. Ed and his partner, Johnny the Polack, didn't even know who was President. The only thing they read in the papers was the race results. There was never any campaign literature, just scratch sheets. The only "campaign" posters said "Don't Spit on the Floor" and "No Sitting on the Tables, Use the Bridge." The only political appointees who ever hung around there were the members of the vice squad.

Ed ran his poke up to $11,000 once—during the Depression when this might have made him the richest man in town. In liquid cash, anyway. He never trusted banks because they were dropping out the game like swatted flies those years. He kept his loot in a stove in a hot dog joint on Main St. where he could get it out in a hurry at all hours of the night. He got it out in too big a hurry one night, went to Florida and the big leagues where they sent him home in a barrel. He didn't even get a tan.

But Ed liked the life. I don't think he would consider that Jack Kennedy has any fun.

Ed cashed out about eight years ago this time. He might have lasted longer—he was 52—but he kept crashing out of the hospital because he thought the doctors were putting the con on him. Besides, I don't think he really wanted to outlive the pool halls.

I got handouts from Ed all my life—when he had it. But his greatest legacy was a list of mottoes he used to embroider on my mind:

Never bet on a dead horse or a live woman . . .

Never take money from an amateur—unless he insists . . .

Never play a house game whether it's a racetrack, roulette or just a tired guy cutting a small pot . . .

Never play cards with a man with dark glasses or his own deck . . .

Don't ever make change for a guy on a train . . .

Never play a man that's better than you . . .

Never buck a slot machine—they don't make them for YOU . . .

Take your time chalking your cue—they'll wait . . .

His headstone just says "Edward Murray, 1902–1954" but a better epitaph was the one the character in the blinding suit and phony diamonds gave my sister Eleanor at the funeral: "They was better crapshooters and better pool hustlers. But for one man for two events by one player, I'd have to take Eddie. He was one of the best."

Mom Sez

Let's see now . . . where were we?

Oh, yes. You may remember in our last, I was just about to go on vacation. With the kids. As a result, you have before you today a total wreck. I am in no more condition to begin writing a sports column than to knit an afghan.

Accordingly, I am going to bring to you a guest columnist. She's inexperienced and weak on spelling and she licks cake frosting off her fingers and hits her little brother when he doesn't mind but she's finally begun to let her hair grow thanks to Hayley Mills, of whom she has 81 photos by last count.

Before Hayley Mills she had a hair-do that ran more to Frank Howard than crinoline and old lace but now it's gotten to the point where you can put a bow in it without Scotch tape. She is 4 ft. 2, eyes of blue, not very old and answers to the name "Pamela" unless you're calling her to do the dishes. This is her story of our vacation:

Dear Diry:

Last week we all went to Apple Valley and Hesperia (speling?) In which are in California but not by much and we had a luvly time.

We cudn't go on Mondy as Mother sed who is going to do the washing and Daddy yelld I cud move the Germany army quicker than this family.

It was hot when we started out and Daddy sed we will drive through the town of Pear Blossom only he cudn't find it and he started to yell and got all red in the face and he yelld at some driver who he sed cut in front of him and Daddy was hollerin and carryin on until Mom sez OK, Floyd Patterson, do you want to start your vacation with a nosebleed or are you going to act your age which is a lot older than that young bull your yellin at? Daddy kind of hunched up in his seat and mumbled but I caught him sneakin looks at the other man who had tattoo marks on his arms and a bad temper, too.

It was fun in Apple Valley. They had this swimming pool that turned Tony's hair green and Ricky's lips turned blue but Daddy ran off and played golf with Mr. Bass who owns Apple Valley and has a house with a mountain growing in the living room it is so high.

Daddy came back, he was much happier and Mommy sed, Well, how many rounds of golf did you drink? and Daddy sed, You mean play, and she sed, You heard me the first time. And Daddy sez, Oh, Newt and I played nine. Newt is Mr. Bass and he is a big man in a cowboy suit with kind of sad eyes. Mom sed, Newt looks kind of sad to me, and Dad sez, Oh, any man that ain't married looks sad to you women and the oney thing Newt is sad about is there's 200 million dollars in the county and he's oney got half of it. And Mom sniffed that, Well, money don't buy happiness, and Dad sez, That's right, but it'll sure start the bidding off on a nice note.

We went to a Lu-Wow (speling?) at the Apple Valley In that

night and Hilo Hattie was there and we kids got to stay up and Daddy sed, Ain't this great! that air tastes just like wine and Mom sez, I bet.

We went horseback riding, all except Daddy who sed, I don't trust no horse, and Mom sez, How come you bet money on them, then? and Daddy yelld, Because otherwise you'd spend it on some sappy lamp to clutter up my workroom.

We went to Hesperia and Daddy got lost going there one night and went up the wrong way on the freeway before everybody got honking at him and he caught on. I was wonderin why those truckdrivers were wavin, he sed to Mother and she sed, They were probably waving good-bye.

It was fun in Hesperia although Daddy sed when we got there they would probably have to change the name to Hysteria. Ricky and I went swimming in the pool and Ted & Tony playd golf with Daddy and Daddy also playd golf with Bill Lane and he was cross when he came in. Know what that Bill Lane sed? Daddy yelld at Mom. He sed, I know how you can take 9 strokes off your game, Jim, just don't play the last hole. I think that's a good idea, Mom sez. That way you can take some inches off your waste, too, by not playing the 19th hole, neither.

We stayd up late and Ricky and Mom danced and Dad did the Twist with Mrs. Wood but the next day when we were driving home and the boys put the Watusi on the radio Daddy yelld, What kind of noise do you call that? Why don't they play Guy Lombardo any more? and Ricky said, Who is Guy Lombardo, Mommy? and Mom sez, He was kind of the Civil War Chubby Checkers. General Grant was a big fan.

Daddy was steaming but didn't say nothin until Rick sed, Who started the Civil War, Dad? and Dad sed, I don't know but I bet it was some sappy woman. Mom sed, Hump! and then Dad sed, Pam, I want you to write down this vacation just as it happened and Mom sed, Are you going to get your child to do your work for you now? and Dad yelled, If it's good enough for Ring Lardner, it's good enough for me! and Mom pretended to faint and sed, Ring Lardner! Get a load of him. You should apologize to his memory, and Dad sed, That is a good idea. Put that at the end, Pam. Apologeez to Ring Lardner.

More Mom Sez

Well, I'm back. Had a nice vacation, a "rest" that combined the best aspects of a daily golf tournament, nightly marathon dance, an Air Force survival test to see how long a man can go without sleep, afternoons of a camp counselor or a channel swimmer. Two more days and this column would be coming to you from an iron lung.

Accordingly, I have brought along a guest columnist, the third baseman of the Malibu Inn Little League team, in his own way one of the ablest historians of our day. Ricky got the simple uncomplicated view from the back seat of our vacation. His narrative begins here:

Well, we went down to Disneyland and Dad sez, Did you see the Long Beach turnoff as I thought it would be right here? and Mom sez, No, Parnelli, but you better slow down or that cop will show you the way to Long Beach, and Dad hollered, Now, don't start that or I will turn this car right around now. And Mom sez sweetly, OK, children, don't anybody breathe loud or we will not have the joys of seeing Disneyland with an old grouch.

And we staid at the Disneyland Hotel and it was so beautiful Pam wanted to trade our house for it and even Daddy sez, Well, it's OK if you don't mind being up to your hips in kids with Mouse hats on, and Mom sez, At least, their happy kids. And Dad sez, Dammit, I'm thirsty, and Pam sez, Daddy, I'll buy you a Coke, and Daddy got this choking look. And Mom sez, Oh, no, what Daddy means is he wonders why they don't have a Peter Pan Bar and Grill or Snow White's Saloon, and Daddy sez, Oh, shut up.

Then, Mom and Dad went to Hawaii and they put these flowers around their neck and it made Daddy sneeze and Mom sez, Daddy gets hay fever from a flower pressed in a Bible for two centuries, the oney place he shud spend his vacation is the Sahara Desert and, if they had a floor show, he wud. And they were gone two weeks and when they came back Dad was all peeling and his eyes were running but Mom looked nice and brown.

We sure had a wonderful time in Hawaii, children, Mom sez, we staid at this beautiful hotel, the Sheraton Maui, which is build right in the side of a hunk of volcanic rock and ever room has vines growing over the wall like a big flower pot, and Daddy growls, It looks like the Maginot Line which I bet they bought at war surplus, and Mom sez, Oh, Daddy goes over to Hawaii and they have lovely volcanoes and they burn the sugar cane at night and it rains and they have rainbows and places where maidens leapt to their deths and what does Daddy do? He heds right out for a golf course. To him, Hawaii is just one big sand trap. In the evening he has a drink on the terrus and he looks out and sez, Look at that crimson hibiscus over there, did you ever in your life see anythin so lovely? And the next morning hits a golf ball over there and I say, Where is it, dear? and he sez, Over in those dam red weeds.

What was Hawaii like, Daddy, Pam asks him and Daddy sez, Well, they give you an orkid with everything and, if you do not happen to be crazy to have orkids with your fried eggs you just better not order any fried eggs. They apparently kill off all the baritones at birth becuz the oney baritone I heard the whole time in the islands was your mother. They call white men "haoles" which is pronounced "howlies," probly in honor of the sound they make when they get the bill. The Queen of England would of have to took in washing to live there. They put weeds in all the drinks.

They have a lovely island drink called a "My Tie," Mom contradicks him, and it has a lovely orkid and some mint and a pineapple and sugar cane in it. And Dad sez to the waitress, I will make a bargain with you, young lady, leave out all the horticulture and I will not report you to the Better Business Burro for the outrajus prices you charge. Besides, I want to git diabetes in my own good time.

The hula dances were lovely, Mom sez. I did not see a one under 200 lbs., Daddy contradicks, except on the posters.

Then, one night, Mom sez, they had this volcano errup and this couple wanted us to fly over and see it and Dad sez, Fine, leave us go. How much? And the man sez, Oh, not much. Oney about the cost of 35 Martinis apiece. Look at it that way. And Daddy turned kind of funny and blue in the face and I knew the man sed the rong thing. Oh, Dad sez, the thing about volcanoes is, ya seen one, ya seen 'em all. I will wait and see it in the movies.

Oh, shoot! yells Daddy, the language. Everything is "Nooey, nooey" or "Umma, umma," or "Ahney, ahney." I thot the whole country stuttered. They have 13 letters but they use only four of five of them—u's, p's, i's, and l's. Every place is named "Ooey, nooey, nooey, papouli." You cannot talk it unless you hiccup.

Din you like nuthin, Dad? Pam sez, and she sounded kind of sad. And Dad thort a minute and he sez, Well, yes. I notice everybody smiles over there. I never see so damn much smiling in my hole life. And then he got quiet.

And then, he sez, we went out to see the Arizona. This is the battleship that was sunk in Pearl Harbor and part of it is sticking up out of the water and they is 1,102 American boys still aboard her down in that water. And they still raise and lower the Flag over her every night as if she were still in commission and the crew still waiting orders. And I got this big lump in my throat cuz I remembered suddenly what an old lady sez to me in Beverly Hills the day Hawaii became a state and I din know what she ment. She sed, Now the boys on the Arizona have come home.

Yes, Dad sez, I have to say all us Americans have to be proud we have Hawaii. She didn't come cheap.

Fingers of Dust

There must be a no-limit crap game going on in the Great Beyond today. Or a high-stake poker game with a marked deck. Or some kind of a grift. Otherwise, Doc Kearns never would have left here.

Maybe there's a nice little town that should be bilked. Or a nice guy whose pockets are leaking money and he trusts people.

Maybe some fight manager out there has been careless enough to leavc his boy's contract lying around unsigned.

Maybe there's a gold strike some place and Wilson Mizner needs someone with goose grease in his hair to make change for the miners and then pass his hand through his head and deposit a week's salary worth of gold dust in with the dandruff. Doc didn't have much hair the last time I saw him but when he was a kid he had lots of it when he used to wash the gold out every night. He had the cleanest hair and the biggest bucket of illegal gold in the Klondike. He was the only guy in the territory who could claim jump with just a head scratch.

Maybe Doc heard there's a young hobo kid riding the rods with a sledge-hammer for a left and an anvil for a right who could make a million bucks and history if he had the right guy figuring the angles for him.

Whatever's going on, Doc is on his way. He never was one to sit still. Death caught him in his sleep because it was the only way it could. Doc never stopped long enough to die when he was awake. He was, to use his own words, "Always moving around, moving things. You can't sit still. Life ain't no escalator."

I hope they put a nice suit on Doc. Something ochre with a border of cerise on the shirt and a diamond stickpin and a nice gloss on his patent leather shoes. Doc always liked to be noticed. I hope they slipped a double-sawbuck or two in his pocket. Doc liked to buy wherever he went. And, as the song says, a fellow likes to die standing pat.

I hope Dempsey cries a little. Doc would pretend to be furious but each of us hopes somebody cries a little when we die. Maybe Mickey Walker will dab his eyes a little and remember the weekend in Paris that lasted 30 days. It emptied one whole vineyard and broke the one-day record for hotel room rubble set by the Zeppelins in 1917 and not broken again until the Luftwaffe in 1941. The Parisians were happy to see Doc and Mickey go. They would have gladly exchanged them for an enemy occupation.

Kearns didn't make Dempsey champion. But he gave him the opportunity to make himself champion—which is the same thing. Doc always figured it was his biggest hustle. That was the trouble with Doc. He dealt with mirrors so much he couldn't tell a legit deal when it came up. If he sponsored a sunset he would have wondered what God's angle was or if it was really two guys with a paint brush and a backdrop.

Dempsey could have beaten Willard with face slaps. But the Doc loaded the gloves just to be sure. Doc never copped out just how. But he had taken the price Willard would go out in the first round and he would have stood Jess in front of a moving train to collect. Willard got lumps in his head you could lose your finger in to this day. And that was 44 years ago.

Maybe Dempsey would rather remember one hot afternoon in Shelby, Mont., the little town that wanted to be put on the map. So Doc almost wiped it off. He closed more banks there than the Depression. Shelby didn't know it, but its promotion was just an elaborate way to transfer its assets from the First State Bank of Shelby to Texas Guinan's. "A dead game stake," Doc allowed as he left town with coattails flying, the money in a satchel and a lynch mob in hot pursuit.

Fight managers always deal in the editorial "We," as in "We wuz robbed," or "We win easy." Not Doc. Doc cut the fighter in for half the purse but none of the glory. "I win the championship in 1919," he always used to say as if Dempsey wasn't even there. Very occasionally, he might add, as if an afterthought, "with Dempsey." But the fighter was never more than a partner. Doc figured they were an entry—1 and 1A.

Doc was never a mob guy. He was his own man. He split with the fighter—period. But he spent so much, so fast, there was a time he was running neck-and-neck with the Marshall Plan.

Doc was always after me to write his book in the last years. But I always told him I was too busy. We always are. I regret it now. The eyewitness stuff Doc took with him when he went to sleep in Miami the other night is more precious than a mountain of warmed-over clippings. It was the raw ore of a life and gaudy times we shall never see again. Doc Kearns was one of a vanishing breed of American, still hustling around at the age of 81 and searching his few remaining locks for one last fingernail of gold dust.

Who's in Second?

Someone once said the only vice connected with the Vice Presidency was the anonymity that comes with it. That comes, in fact, from finishing second in anything. "The only thing worse than finishing second," the late Red Sanders used to say, "is to be lying on the desert alone with your back broke. Either way, nobody ever finds out about you."

No one calls up to ask, "Who came in second?" Nice guys might finish last, but at that they're luckier than the cats who finish second.

Accordingly, I would like to pause to pay tribute to these brave bulls of sports—the born losers, the all-time place bets of history—via a quiz program to see how many of these accident prones, or prone accidents, you can recall?

Only those who can correctly identify Herbert Hoover's Vice President (or Herbert Hoover, for that matter), Tommy Manville's first wife, Zsa Zsa Gabor's last husband—or the guy who held Paul Revere's horse—can qualify.

The name of the game is "The Price Is Wrong," and if you score 85% or more, you're sick.

First prize is a pair of tickets to the next major league game at the Coliseum or a win ticket on the bull at the next corrida. Second prize is two weeks in Philadelphia. Third prize is Philadelphia.

Honored players get fitted with the emblem of the society, goats' horns on a custom dunce cap and a gold pass which entitles them to lose the ticket the next time they win the Irish Sweepstakes, be in the wash room when the house buys a drink or have the cops raid the joint the first pat hand they get that night.

We will begin with current losers. Everybody knows Roger Maris hit 61 home runs, the all-time high in that department. But did you know that Mickey Mantle's 54, good only for second place, was the all-time high in that department for a man who did NOT win the league championship?

Don Larsen pitched the only perfect game in World Series history. But did you know what happened to the guy who pitched the NEXT most perfect game? Bill Bevens had a no-hitter going with only one more out in the ninth inning of the fourth game of the 1947 Series. He was pitching for the Yankees against the Dodgers when the following things happened: a slow-footed pinch-runner stole second on a close play that might have ended the game. The manager ordered him to walk the next man—who turned out to be the winning run, a refinement of the game which was to cost the manager, Bucky Harris, his job the next year even though he won the Series. A banjo hitter named Lavagetto then swung late but hit a bad pitch to the wrong field—and Bevens had not only lost his no-hitter, he had lost the game, his chance at the Hall of Fame for the first World Series no-hitter, a small fortune on the winter banquet circuit and all chance ever to forget the game. A year later, he was down in the bus-stop minors still talking to himself.

Bill Terry of the Giants was the last National Leaguer to hit over .400—.401 in 1930. But consider Babe Herman of the Dodgers, who merely finished second with the highest batting average in the history of his team and the highest ever to finish second in that league—.393. The result is all everybody ever remembers about Babe are the occupied bases he stole and the good, game tries he made to catch routine fly balls.

Jesse Owens won the 200-meter race in the 1936 Olympics and set a record that stood for 24 years. But the American who was second to him was Matthew (Mack) Robinson of Pasadena. Mack, it so happens, is unfortunate enough to have another second to his name. He is a brother to Jackie Robinson. Jackie Robinson made the baseball Hall of Fame. Jesse Owens made the track Hall of Fame. Mack has spent the intervening years pumping gas or acting as custodian at Warner Bros., where he is now. One-tenth of a second faster on that day in Germany and Hitler might have turned his back on HIM, history might have been changed and somebody might now be sweeping out Mack's office instead of vice versa.

Gene Tunney and Rocky Marciano are the only two retired

undefeated heavyweight champions in history. But James J. Jeffries was a close second. He had retired once and might have stayed there. But one day he answered the door and Tex Rickard was standing there with a blank check and a good idea. "Jeff," he wanted to know. "How'd you like to fight a guy named Jack Johnson?" Looking back on that day, all things considered, Jeff would rather it had been his mother-in-law come for a visit.

Hugo Weislander of Sweden won the 1912 Olympic decathlon—it says in the book. But Jim Thorpe, who won four of the 10 events in it, was third in four others and fourth in the rest, did not even get second. Weislander even got Jim's medals because Thorpe had once played baseball for lemonade money on a hot afternoon. Jim makes the losers because he had to give back his medals. But Hugo may make it, too, because he got to keep some that didn't belong to him.

Harvey Haddix and Lew Burdette are another duo in a close race for the shadows. Haddix qualifies because he pitched 12 innings of no-hit ball and then finished second when he lost the game in the 13th. But hardly anybody remembers that Lew Burdette allowed a lot of hits (13) but pitched pretty near-perfect clutch ball himself for 13 innings.

The moral is—the race is always to the swift, the battle to the strong, the bull is a longshot, but let's have a moment of silence to those who lost by an inch when it might as well have been a mile.

ROUGH STUFF

Introduction

Here, in this section which we choose to call "Rough Stuff," are the sports in which man does violence to man. These are the sports in which "Love" is no part of the scoring and in which the watchword is "an eye for a tie, a tooth for a touchdown, a life for a lap."

This is the world of carburetors and conflagrations, where the bleacherite doesn't shout "Lovely shot, Joe!" but rather "Get that other eye, Louie!" or "Hit 'em again, hit 'em again! Harder!" or the simple "Kill 'im, Arch!"

This is a world of knee-wrappings, collodion, encephalograms, fire engines on the track. This is the "More plasma!" side of sports. This is where the bull goes out with his feet in the air—or the matador—or the lightweight champion does. This is the limp-off or stretcher side of sports.

It sometimes seems as if all this violence will end up doing violence to the sport itself. I mean, how many fatalities can boxing endure? Or auto racing? Will there be a sound knee left in the country if football continues to grow? And how many bulls do you watch bleed to death before you get disgusted?

But Americans—much as they protest to the contrary—worship violence. Their television programs are a clatter of gunfire, a miasma of men pitching to their death clutching their abdomens. Some people almost slaver when they see a savage block. I have watched men who booed Cassius Clay when he was introduced, then would scream at him, nay, implore him, to "Kill 'im!" when he gets his adversary goggly-eyed and poised on the brink of unconsciousness. Blood is the real hero of this crowd. Anybody's blood.

It is, quite simply, what made pro football a billion dollar business, ranking right along with the oil industry as a major source of wealth for young Texans—or Californians. Bigger and faster men, bigger and harder plastic armor, an injury toll greater than the Battle of Waterloo. Scouting reports in college football often read "Doesn't like to be hit; so, let's hit him hard and see how he likes it." Or, "If we can wipe Pellegrini off the cob, we will have removed their one good football player and the game is ours." In a court of law, this might be assault with a deadly weapon or assault with intent to do great bodily harm. Here, it's "sport."

"Sport" it may be. "Sportsmanship" it is not.

The object of football, after all, is to score points, not fractures. Boxing is the only "sport" whose objects is to hurt the other fellow, to put him on the point of death, if necessary. After all, the title is at stake, isn't it?

The title of murderer.

It's the public's fault. Let a skilled boxer take the ring, a man who seeks to win by scoring points, who treats the game the way the English "fancy" treated it—as the manly art of self-defense—and the crowd will begin to sing "Let Me Call You Sweetheart" or to sneer "Why don't you sign his dance card and kiss him, Slugger?"

They don't want art, they want gore.

Target shooting is way down in the list of spectator sports in this country. But let a group of shooters line up in a Coliseum and let the target be each other and you'd sell out. Draw a ring in the ground and put two men in it with knives in their teeth and you could scalp tickets.

Football can save itself. A loosening of the rules can bring the contest more nearly to a ball game and less of a 22-man wrestle. But there are coaches who feel that if they cut down on the nose-bleeds they cut down on their victories. A coach in a celebrated declamation some years ago told his squad they were no damn good because they all had all their teeth. A prizefighter who doesn't have a cabbage for an ear and the Aurora Borealis for an eye is scorned as "an agony fighter," a "dancer."

Still, you have to come to terms with it. The conspiracy is one of silence. A boy gets clobbered and an ankle or a jawbone shattered as he waits under a downfield punt and the chances are later he will murmur (through wired jaws or crutch-supported legs), "It was just one of those freak things—Butch didn't mean it. He just made a clean tackle."

The chances are better that Butch used a tactic he learned in 10 years on the practice field—the "shiver arm" or the bringing up of a plaster-of-Paris blackjack on an "injured" arm into the opponent's jaw line. Or the surreptitious twist of the leg at the moment of rolling over on the tackle. This is known as "intimidating" the opponent. It has the seeds of the destruction of the sport in it.

Even basketball, that YMCA game, intended more as a ballet than a dock fight, looks more and more like a rumble in sneakers and shorts. Stitches are no longer found only in the basketball. They are found most nights in the basketball player. A sharp elbow is as important to a guard as a good foul shot. For some, it is their only good foul shot.

But basketball and football cynically practice their unnecessary and unjust form of mayhem. Boxing is saddled with so many semi-skilled workmen—the sport is so barnacled with practitioners who have never even been taught the rudiments of self-defense but instead have been rushed to matches in which they would be better off tied to a railroad track—that sometimes hardened old-timers cannot bear to look. No matter how hard and muscled the body is, the skull is only a fracture of an inch thick. And filled with blood. Sometimes, at the end of a fight, so is the ring.

But the stadia are filled. The blood lust is present. The score can be kept in compound fractures as well as touchdowns. We are a violent people. If you don't believe it, get two tickets on the 50-yard line. Or at ringside. Or on the shady side of the Plaza. Or at courtside at a Laker-Celtic game. We haven't come so far from the days of the Romans and their gladiators as we like to keep telling ourselves we have.

The crowd gets hotly in the act. In Madison Square Garden you are in much more danger from a flying bottle than a right cross in the ring. Violence begets violence. Violence attracts the violent. It poses a dilemma for a promoter. Does a $6 fight ticket entitle a guy to bust up $200 worth of chairs, the eyeglasses of a ringsider (who will sue) the ring lights and anything else that comes to hand? As I have written, the promoter decides on it in a moral manner. He passes it on to the insurance companies. The insurance companies, dear reader, is thee and me. The motto of the day is, I got mine, too bad about you.

Thus the sports page aspects of "Rough Stuff" in the sixties.

A Taste of Rubble

CINCINNATI—Well, here we are again in lovely Cincinnati, a city once maligned as the only municipal rubble heap this side of occupied Germany.

But I've reformed. Either that or I've acquired a taste for rubble, which is kind of like the fish sandwiches they serve around here. They're all right if you can keep them down.

It's the home of the Cincinnati Reds and the Beautiful Ohio, although I'd hate to see the wife of the guy who christened it that. It's called the "Queen City" but what the hell, royalty isn't what it used to be anywhere. Only with Cincinnati you have to wonder if it ever was.

They put a new coat of paint on old Crosley Field, a kind of gangrenous green so that you can't be sure whether it's a sight for sore eyes or just an eyesore. The announcer announces before each game that suggestion boxes have been placed around this unreal estate inviting your suggestions. I have one for them: Burn it.

Between the Yankees last year and Frank Howard this year they may not have to. Two more Howard line drives—Elston or Frank—and the Cincinnati outfielders will be up to their hips in rubble, which is only fair. I mean, why should they be any different from the rest of the neighborhood?

They still haven't finished the freeway outside the ballpark. I guess the workmen put away their spoons early each night. Either that, or it's Kentucky's turn to use the cement mixer.

You may remember the Reds from the 1961 World Series. On the other hand, you may not. They weren't in it long. They were the ones chasing the balls to the fences and dodging the flying cement chips.

They were owned by a charitable foundation, which came as no surprise to anyone who came to see them play. The Yankees contributed one game so they could take it off their income tax.

The chief beneficiary of the charity so far seems to have been the new owner, Bill DeWitt, who seems to have got the club for eight books of green stamps and a promise to keep a light in the window. As I get it there was almost a million bucks in the Treasury but to get at it you had to take the Reds. And not everybody needed money that bad. There's a politician looking into the deal but it sounds like a fair exchange to me. DeWitt had to promise to stay in Cincinnati at least till the freeway's finished. By that time it'll be the most unfreeway in the country. The trouble is they had to change all their designs in the midst of construction. The original plans were for horses.

But don't get me wrong. I love Cincinnati. It's Pittsburgh that's declared war on me now. I just left there where I stayed long enough to give a shot in the arm to capital punishment.

The mayor there got real mad and called me and Los Angeles some awful names. In fact, I have to say this is a very Uncivil Servant. I think Sam Yorty should answer him but Sam is one mayor who doesn't take me very seriously—an attitude, I might add, that doesn't make him unique.

The TV station there phoned me and offered to pay my way to Pittsburgh if I would go on the air to explain myself. What made me suspicious was they didn't say anything about return transportation. Under present conditions I prefer Cincinnati. But the offer is good only for 30 days.

In addition to that, I can't stand excitement. That's why I ordinarily like baseball. But with the Reds and Dodgers they'd raise the blood pressure in a crocodile.

The Reds are the dumbest ball club I have ever seen. They just can't seem to get the idea through their heads they don't belong in first place. They do everything wrong in one game and then turn around and pull the Dodgers' hats down around their ears in the next.

The first baseman got hit by a ball that he swung at the first night and thereby got to share the league lead in his unusual category with Frank Howard.

Their pitcher kept throwing over to first base to get Maury

Wills and I will say this for the first baseman: He caught most of them. Jim O'Toole picked up a bunt off the bat of Willie Davis, but then threw to the wrong base—first base. As it turned out, the play was to third. Because that's where Davis was when the dust cleared. He set the world record for the 270-ft. dash. Hereafter, the Reds will throw to second even if he fouls one off.

Frank Howard hit one ball so hard I had to cover my eyes when I saw Frank Robinson reach up for it. If he ever got it, they would have had to cut the baseball out of his hand. If they could ever find the hand.

The next night, the game was won by a local boy they booed out of town two years ago. But Joe Nuxhall came back. And looked like the hottest prospect of either staff—or either league—for the Hall of Fame. This is one team that will never get goiter.

As for me, I very well may get it—from a rope. But until hizzoner in Mr. Pitt's burg cools off, I'll take comfort in the experience of Bugs Baer, who put the knock on Bridgeport years ago. If you've ever been there, it's hard not to. They got mad but after hotter heads prevailed they had a reconciliation banquet where the mayor got up and said magnanimously to Baer, "Bugs, we want you to know you're welcome to Bridgeport," and Bugs, bless him, got up and said, "Oh, no, your honor, you're ALL welcome to Bridgeport." And walked out.

Florida & Dodgers

VERO BEACH—And now for a word about Florida.

Florida is a body of land surrounded on three sides by sharks and on the fourth by Alabama and Georgia if you like to think of that as any better.

The architecture is a skillful blend of the vulgar and the tasteless. It's as artificial as a banker's smile and as flat as a bride's first cake. It's a geographic afterthought and so low in the water—early navigators didn't see it till they ran aground. A cigar butt is a hill and you can bring up water with a spoon.

The rivers are tidal and so are the tourists. They flood in the winter and ebb in the summer. The alligator is the only true native and he's an improvement on some who came later.

It has more thunderstorms than a British mystery movie and so many swamps its state anthem should be "Chloe." I won't say the climate's bad but, when I tell you even Texas cattle couldn't stand it, I don't have to. They brought over Brahmas from India to cross-breed and keep the Herefords from dying of heat and wood ticks. This produced a breed which both scratches and sweats, which makes them right at home in Florida. The human breeding is a little more complicated.

It's a Disneyland for hypochondriacs. You qualify for residency on the West Coast of Florida if you have flunked two blood pressure tests and have one or more hardened arteries. When they say "traffic accident" they might mean wheelchair. At a funeral it's often hard to tell the guest of honor.

Miami isn't a city, it's a self-governed clip joint, Coney Island with delusions of grandeur, where people spend $100-a-day to get together and compare symptoms.

The men wear white ties and the women wear transparent shoes with no heels or toes, thus exposing the two parts of a woman's body which have to be the ugliest.

Florida has had several real estate booms. The first one proved to be several miles out to sea to the extreme discomfiture of buyers who needed a visa—or a shark repellent—to visit their property. Palm Beach considers Miami common and Miami considers Palm Beach stuffy and they're both right.

Major league baseball trains down here because the only competitive sport is shuffleboard and lobby-sitting, which gives baseball just enough of an edge to be able to make the nut.

The Dodgers train at Vero Beach, a case of arrested municipal development Stephen Foster somehow overlooked.

It gives you fair warning because you come into it via an airport that is a wind-sock stop about as up-to-date as the Spad. It hasn't been painted in so long you have to think the Union Army interrupted the first coat. The only way to redecorate it is with a match but you'd have to paint it to burn it.

Other teams train in the lap of luxury—gaudy hotels that give them a rate because in our advanced society ballplayers attract customers. In the benighted days of the past they chased them out. At Lakeland, the Tigers live better than Louis XIV, and at Clearwater, Tampa and Ft. Lauderdale press and athletes have modern motels, room service digit-dialing, swimming pools, television and a wake-up service.

At Vero, we have a few of our own. Oh, you don't have any phone in your room or radio or TV but you can sign up for fly-paper if you want. You can smell the oranges or listen to the crickets any time you want. You can go swimming in the creek if no one's looking.

The others may have wall-to-wall carpeting, air conditioning, picture windows and muraled walls. But we have wall-to-wall flooring, real glass in the windows, genuine plastic drapes with roses on them and shades that you can (what will they think of next!) raise and lower by means of a string with a loop on the end.

We have genuine, 100% air, filtered through a screen which sometimes permits some of Florida's first citizens to fly in. The windows actually are stained glass in some of the rooms. The murals are surrealist, which is to say they are formed by swatting flies with inky sports sections.

The quarters are tastefully furnished with particular attention given to open spaces and the uncluttered look. The furnishings are not exactly Danish modern. They have running water. Sometimes that's just the trouble. It has no respect at all for a spigot. Not all the water comes out of the plumbing. Some of it comes down from the roof and there are nights when you need a pail more than a pillow.

I have a very famous room in Barracks B. There is a hole in the door—the Sandy Koufax-Walt Alston-Larry Sherry memorial hole in the door which may someday be given a historical marker with suitable ceremonies.

It is notable historically because it commemorates in its own peculiar way the night Alston broke his own curfew. So did Sherry and Koufax but this was considerably less of an upset. They had been out getting pizza but the acoustics are bad in this plywood stockade and Alston misunderstood. Besides he was pounding on the door so hard he couldn't hear well.

He crashed through but not before somebody loudly sounded out "you better stop all that pounding or you'll wake up the Skipper and Koufax and Sherry are trying to sneak in."

The Skipper was understandably on edge that night because on a previous night Duke Snider and a crew had beaten the curfew by coming home by railroad. They were not in a Pullman, they were in a Volvo. It's not impossible to put a Volvo on a railroad track, just inadvisable.

The point of all this is Alston's troubles would be considerably lessened if the Dodgers moved into, say the Fontainebleu, the only roundhouse in the world you can't wear overalls in. At least there, you can get the pizza sent up and get valet parking even if you drive up on a railroad track.

As you can see, a very complicated place, Florida and Vero.

Baby, It's the Yanks

WASHINGTON, D.C.—Headline: "CBS Buys Yankees."

Establishing shot: Interior of oak-paneled office of J. B. Culturevulture, executive vice president of the network, a job he won when, as the trainer of the only all-gorilla band in captivity that could play Beethoven and ride bikes at the same time, he smashed every Nielsen rating in the country and ran the Republican convention right off the air one summer when the viewers rioted. He has so much cologne on he smells like a ripening corsage and he is smoking a cigar and getting a pedicure as the phone rings. He picks it up. An excited voice comes over it:

"J.B.? Baby? Solly here. J.B., you've been looking for something for Huntley and Brinkley to do between conventions? Well, your boy done it. J.B., we have just bought the Yankees."

J.B. (as girl cuts toenail too fine): "Ouch! Solly? The Yankees? Swell. We'll rope off Rhode Island and use it for a parking lot. Boston will have to go. We'll call it 'Yesterdayland.'"

Solly clears his throat.

"No, no, J.B., the ball team. The New York Yankees. You know. 'Take me out to the ball game.' Lissen, Baby. We now get into the World Series, never mind if the other guys paid for the package."

J.B.: "Sounds swell, Solly. Now, tell me, what do these guys do?"

Solly: "They play baseball, boss. You know. Three strikes, you're out. The game is never over till the last man is out. That kind of thing."

There is a silence.

J.B. (irritably): "Well, I mean, like—what else do they do? Ride one-wheeled bikes? Wrestle bears? Play the kazoo? Baby, you can't just stand there and hit ground balls. This is TV, Baby. What I mean is, will they dig it in Dubuque? How long does a game last?"

Solly: "Two hours, J.B. Sometimes, three."

J.B.: "Tighten it up, Solly. You can't sell a three-hour show. What I had in mind was a half-hour segment. With commercials, that comes to 12 minutes a game."

Solly: "But, boss! A game is played till you get a winner. It takes time."

J.B.: "Nonsense! Get Walter Cronkite and one of those machines and he'll give you the outcome before two men have batted. You have my word for it. We predicted Goldwater would be the nominee before he had his first pair of long pants. The machine is hung up on the 1996 election right now. What kind of costumes does this act wear?"

Solly: "Well, they have these kind of pin stripe suits."

J.B.: "Pin stripes! Solly, tell me you're kidding! What do they think this is, radio? From now on, they come on like Liberace. They got a broad in the lineup?"

Solly (miserable): "No, boss."

J.B.: "Then, get one. (He puts the phone down.) Miss Allen! Get me Arlene Francis on my other phone. Ask her first if she does live shows. (Picks up first phone.) Now, Solly, can these guys do imitations? Bird calls? Any of them do Cagney? Cary Grant? Bette Davis? Can they even yodel?"

Solly: "Boss, all they do is stand there and play baseball."

J.B.: "Well, maybe we can get Ed Sullivan to stand there and point. Don't they even tell jokes?"

Solly: "Well, the manager is kind of funny. Yogi Berra."

J.B.: "Too risky. He'll have to change that name. That cartoon character copyrighted it. Well, now, let's see. The team isn't funny, can't dance, sing or tell funny stories and dresses like a road company Guys and Dolls. Solly, what did we pay for them? Or did they just come as part of the agency package?"

Solly: "Eleven million dollars, J.B."

There is a shocked silence. J.B.'s face purples but he speaks softly.

J.B.: "Solly, baby. Sweetheart! For $11 million I could have bought the 'Howdy Doody Show,' 'Life Can Be Beautiful' and 'Sing Along With Mitch.' For 1% of that, I had 15 apes on bicycles playing the Moonlight Sonata on sweet potatoes. Have you got anything that can top that? The Weather Report will have a better Nielsen than these guys. More people will watch test patterns than pitchers warming up. Solly! $11 million will buy 50 lunches at '21.' I just figured it on this pad. What do you have to say for yourself?"

Solly: "But, boss. These guys win! I mean, like all the time."

J.B.: "That's another thing I been meaning to speak to you about, Solly. You remember Perry Mason? What happened? I'll tell you what happened. He won everything from double-parking to spying on the government. I don't have to tell you how tired the public got of this. Solly, the first time I get letters from Daughters of the American Revolution or the Confederacy or the Society for the Protection of Everybody Born West of the Hudson River, these guys lose, I don't care if I have to re-read the entire life of Arnold Rothstein and Sport Sullivan."

Solly: "Boss, you can't tamper with baseball."

J.B.: "Baby, do you know who you're talking to? I personally gave the answers to Charlie Van Doren through a hole in the isolation booth. You remember when the little old lady from Pasadena who was the expert on doves' wings was sweating in that box? Solly, she wouldn't know a dove from a condor. You can fix doves' wings, you can look up the king of Ethiopia in 1880 and slip the answer with 60 million people looking on, you can fix a lousy little ball game. For $11 million, you don't have the right to tell a guy to strike out if it'll mean a happy ending?! Solly, what do you think we're in this for—sport?"

Solly: "But, boss, baseball is sacred—like the Flag or Democracy and the Farm Vote."

J.B.: "Humbug, my boy. Who was it made a musical out of

Shakespeare's 'Hamlet'? Who cast Abbott and Costello in 'MacBeth'? Why, I'll cast Martin and Lewis at shortstop and second base, if I want to. First prize in 'Queen for a Day' will be to pitch for the Yankees. And, by the way, Solly. About that name. It's sure to offend the good folks down in Georgia, Alabama and around there. We'll have to think of something more universal."

Solly: "How about the 'New York Rioters'?"

J.B.: "It lacks what I like to call 'zotz,' Solly. I mean, I'm just dropping this out the window and letting gravity take over—just putting it in a bottle and seeing where the tide takes it. Maybe it'll get off at Bridgeport. But how does this grab you, Solly? We call them the 'New York Nobodies.' That ought to get everybody. Stamp on that for a while and see if it comes up wine."

Solly: "J.B., you've done it again! Words can't express—I mean, you're magnificent, boss."

J.B.: "Nicely put, Solly. Now, the next time you draw money out of petty cash, don't come back with the Yankees, come back with the Roller Derby. I've got to get those apes of mine out of the house. All they do all day is sit around and watch television. And, by the way, I'm having a few of the agency people over for a barbecue Sunday. Tell Mickey Mantle to come over and hit a few home runs for us, or Whitey Ford to throw a few spit balls. Maybe Yogi Berra can tell us how to change pitchers. Meanwhile, let's get our heads together and see if there isn't one way we can jazz up the infield fly rule. We'll get Walter Cronkite to do a documentary on it—or on pitching. We'll call it, 'The Hell It Curves.'"

Bats in the Image

The scene is the plush Madison Ave. office of "Image Makers, Inc.," a high-powered public relations firm whose slogan is "The 'Impossible,' We Do By 11 O'clock," or "We're No. 3, We Try HARDEST!"

Lester I. Smart, the executive vice president, is on the phone. Lester I. is trying hardest at the moment to make his secretary kiss him. Reluctantly, he picks up the gold French phone which a brass plate identifies as the one Marshal Petain used to surrender France in 1940. Vichy France was one of I. M. Inc.'s earliest accounts.

"Ralph Houk? Ralph, baby, how are you? How's the old CBS subsidiary? Pancake makeup for the infield this year eh, baby?

"What? It's about the image? The Yankees' image? Pish, tush, Ralphie, a mere bagatelle. Can we handle it? Ralphie, can a Sicilian make pizza? Can Bette Davis smoke?

"A tough job? Ralphie, don't make me laugh. Who do you think got Benedict Arnold on 4th of July fireworks? Recall who it was almost got Hermann Goering named grand marshal of the Rose Parade? Ralphie, we could get Nasse into Hillcrest! Who do you think it was got the 1919 Black Sox on bubble-gum cards? Ralphie, baby, we could get Cassius Clay elected governor of Alabama. IN THE PRIMARY! I may point out with pride who it was who got Count Dracula honorary chairman of the blood bank drive. Ralph, with a big-enough budget, we could get the maneating shark for the national emblem. Al Capone could have been head of the FBI if he came to us. You got nothing to worry about, Ralphie. The Yankees will be the most lovable team since Laurel and Hardy before we get through."

He hangs up. "All right, Miss Higgenbottom, straighten your lipstick and get off my knee. Enough of this silly lovemaking, we got work to do. Get me my assistant, Poison Penney, and tell him to bring the Yankee file—not all those kooky farmers, the baseball team."

A few minutes later, there is a knock on the door, and a furtive little character with a pointed nose, beady little eyes and sharp pointed teeth enters. This is Poison Penney who is married to Lester Smart's sister and is thus known in the industry as "Brother-in-Law Rat." He works for 10% of the gross, and all the cheese he can eat. He simpers into a chair, looks around to make sure no cats are about, and opens a folder.

Lester takes off his glasses wearily, pinches the bridge of his nose between his thumb and forefinger and sighs. "All right, what's the bad news, what have these guys been doing, campaigning for cancer?"

"Almost, Boss," Poison agrees quickly, "I have gone over the files and, believe me, this crew could improve their public image by going out and painting moustaches on George Washington, pushing Little Orphan Annie into traffic, or drowning her dog Sandy. Boss, if these guys died, not even George Jessel could think of something nice to say. These guys wouldn't accept a collect call from their mother if she was kidnapped. Boss, they make Central Park muggers look like public benefactors. It's my guess they sleep in caskets."

Lester puts his head down on the desk and starts to sob. "Other guys on the street get Albert Schweitzer, Lady Bird, Perry Como and the Good Ship Lollipop. Me, I get gangrene, the Black Muslims, the White Citizens Council and the Purple People Eaters, and now, the New York Yankees. All right, tell me the worst."

Poison clears his throat. "Well, it goes back to 1928 when their manager, Miller Huggins, died. Lovable little fellow. Fellow named Christy Walsh had to phone up the management and tell them for God's sakes to send some flowers."

"Great, great!" moans Lester.

"Then, they have this great star, Babe Ruth. I mean, boss, a sweetheart. You know. Big, lovable, fat guy with a positive genius for hitting home runs. Not an ounce of harm in him. Goes around to hospitals visiting sick kids and old ladies. Boss, next to Santa Claus he's the most popular image in history."

Lester shudders. "And when he was through they just gave him a minor job, eh?" he fears the worst.

Poison sighs. "Boss, they kicked him right out the door—RIGHT OUT THE DOOR! And I don't think they even opened it. They wouldn't even let him sell peanuts in their ballpark."

Lester groans. "Go on," he sobs.

"They got this lovable old character of a manager. I mean, Boss, like he's right out of Hans Christian Andersen or a Disney movie. Little old gnarled fellow, makes you smile just to look at him. He's got a way o' talking could make the phone book seem like Joe Miller, y' know what I mean?"

"But he was a loser? I mean, he couldn't win pennants—World Series?" Lester guesses hopefully.

Poison shakes his head." Every year, practically, he won. He won the year they fired him."

"Fired him!" moans Lester, covering his eyes. "Oh, no! Good Lord, why don't I get an easy account—like the Benedict Arnold account? Why does Dull, Dim and Burnup get all the cushy whitewash jobs—like the Mafia?"

"There's more," says Poison Penney grimly. "There's this character they had catching for them over the years. Boss, are ya ready? His name is Yogi Berra. Right! The one they made that lovable cartoon character out of. They kid him around the league. Bring him comic books and bananas. He's got ears out to here. He's got this kind of sad face. He walks funny. When I tell you kids love him, it's only half of it. He takes his hat off in the presence of ladies. He's a family man, a churchgoer. And how he can hit that old apple! He personally wrecks the careers of a half-dozen Yankee-hating pitchers. They're thinking of giving him Don Newcombe to hang in his den. And he's Italian. Boss, I don't have to tell you what that means in New York City."

Lester eagerly: "So they make him a manager?"

Poison: "Right!"

Lester looks relieved. Then, apprehensive. "He doesn't blow the pennant?" he fears.

Poison looks grim. "No. But they fire him anyway."

Lester turns white. His lips tremble. He slides open a desk drawer, pulls out a handful of pills, pops them in his mouth. He pushes savagely on a buzzer.

"Wait a minute, Boss, there's more!" yells Poison, alarmed. "There's Vic Raschi and Ed Lopat and Herb Pennock and Lefty Gomez. Boss, there's . . ."

But Lester isn't listening. "Miss Higgenbottom," he is barking into an intercom. "Get me Ralph Houk! Quick!

"Hello, Ralph? Ralph, this is Lester. Ralph, there are two kinds of accounts Image Makers, Inc. won't take—the Devil and the New York Yankees. Are we clear on that? No, Ralph, not even for a piece of CBS. We can handle traitors, murderers, gangsters or graverobbers. But an outfit that trifles with shiny faced kids and baseball—really, Ralph! My advice to you is to wait till midnight some night with that club of yours and get this thick wooden spike and drive it into their chest. Either that or change the name to the 'New York Bats.' No, Ralph, not wooden bats. The kind with wings on them . . ."

A Child Shall Lead

I have to say Maury Wills gets all the best of it. When he wants to go on a pitch, does he have to wait till the ball passes the batter? No. He can take off the minute the pitcher's back is turned if he wants. No wonder he steals all those bases.

Also, what's so hot about Duke Snider? The pitcher's 60 ft. 6 in. away from him, isn't he? Let him try to get a hit off Don Drysdale if he's only 46 ft. away and as out of control as a truck going down hill with the brakes out.

You think it's tough to throw Willie Mays out at first? What if he had only 60 ft. to go? How'd you like to try to score on a passed ball when the backstop is only 20 ft. back?

I know a ballplayer who has all these handicaps to put up with. He doesn't get paid. He even has to buy his own bubble gum. He's got his mother's big brown eyes and he laughs a lot and he's the only person I know can sit in a bathtub for an hour and a half and come up dirtier than he went in. But he's finally learned to stop eating with his fingers and his ears are cleaner than they used to be and he hasn't thrown anything down the toilet in a year and a half. He holds the listed league record for peanut butter sandwiches, which sometimes means the piano keys stick.

He's kind of the Jim Gilliam of the Malibu Inn team which is kind of the New York Mets of our Little League.

If Ricky gets on base, which he occasionally does if the pitcher is wild enough, he has to stay there until the pitched ball is hit or caught. And he can't spike the 2nd baseman. No spikes.

Ricky is one of 1,250,000 kids playing Little League in 6,000 leagues in 25 countries. And I caught up with the biggest Little Leaguer of them all over at Lakeside Country Club the other day, Peter J. McGovern, 6 ft. 3 in. president and chairman of the board of baseball's biggest little enterprise. It is Pete McGovern's job not only to administer Little League but to defend it. You see, the sociologists brought their copies of Dr. Freud out to the foul lines about ten years ago and, as soon as the game was explained to them, they decided that Vienna would disapprove of Little League. For one thing, they made the shocking discovery that losers cry.

Of Course, 10- and 12-year-old kids cry when they lose their marbles, play hide-and-seek, get the smallest slice of cake at a party or can't find sox that match, but sociologists can't be expected to know everything. Competition, they said, was bad for kids. They might grow up aggressive and self-reliant.

Most of the hair-raising indictments of Little League—the kid who ran away from home because he struck out, the boy who sat up in the tree all night because he walked in the winning run—proved, on investigation, to be the fault of the parents, not the players. Papa put undue stress on excelling. He wanted his kid to be Babe Ruth even though he himself wasn't even Smead Jolley. But Pete McGovern points out that this kind of a father would want his son to be Jascha Heifetz if he bought him a violin or Caruso if he bought him some sheet music. The trouble with Little League was parents who were bush league.

Little League has been a proving ground for all baseball. It had five fatalities in 25 years, less than two-tenths of one per cent. And most of them were not the fault of the game. The most publicized was where a boy was struck over the heart with the ball. But it was a bad heart. The ball didn't kill the poor little fellow, the excitement did.

When Little League found that most serious accidents were cranial, it quickly devised safety helmets—first, plastic earmuffs, now, radial suspended helmets. Big league baseball, after first hooting at the idea, followed suit. Steel spikes will be the next to go because Little League has shown a composition spike is just as useful—unless the use you have in mind for it is blood-letting. It is just as good for the sole and much better for the soul.

Little Leaguers' reaction time is a fraction of a second slower than a big leaguer's. So, when they found a ball thrown from

44 ft. at 75 m.p.h. arrived at a Little League home plate exactly as fast as a big league ball thrown from 60 ft. at 95 m.p.h., they moved the mound back 2 ft. They have a resident physiologist and staff (something baseball could save itself millions of dollars a year if it employed one to screen players) constantly exploring to improve and safeguard the game.

The safety device they need most now is a rubber stopper for the wig-flipping, ear-smoking, parental popoff or a plastic gag for the big mouth that yells "You can't do that to my kid!"

There's nothing wrong with Little League that a gross of Tootsie Rolls won't cure. But there's plenty wrong with fathers and mothers who take out their aggressions with little kids. So McGovern plans seminars to teach parents to be good sports. Lots of luck.

Who Needs It?

"Oh, boy!" the mother of my kids sighed. "Just think! No Little League this year! Isn't that heavenly?"

"Sure is," I told her fervently. "Just think: no carrying loads of kids down to the field. No long afternoons sitting in those drafty seats."

"Yes," she sighed. "Jane said she had to bring her little Mikey down to practice today. And Tom has to help fix the centerfield fence."

"Boy, I'm glad we're out of THAT!" I told her.

We fell silent.

"Remember the day Tony threw the fourth ball and lost the game to the Colony A's and he cried right there on the mound?" I asked her.

"Do I?!" she said. "I don't like that man who was umpire to this day."

"The ball was a strike," I told her. "It was right over the plate. How many years ago was that? Lord, Tony was just a little shaver, wasn't he?"

"And the time Teddy got that triple, the first hit he ever made? Did you ever see anybody so excited?"

"A long time ago," I told her. I got the book down, the one I used to score games in. There was The Big One right there. Ricky pitched. A pitchers' battle all the way, 29–21. "Rick's control was pin-point perfect that day. Only walked 20."

"He was so cute in that hat that looked 20 sizes too big," she said.

"It WAS 20 sizes too big," I told her.

"Yes," she sighed again. "We're WELL out of THAT. Took up all your weekend, those long doubleheaders. We DID meet some nice people, though. Wasn't it Phil's dad who wrote 'My Mother, The Battleship' on TV?"

"No. It was the show where the wife was a troll. Or a Martian, or something," I said. "Say! Do you remember the father-and-sons game where I hit the home run?"

"No. But I remember Pete made you pop out one year with the bases loaded. And Bert caught the ball."

"Pete's in the Marines now. I think he's in Vietnam. Or was. So's Bert."

"They're big boys," my wife murmured. "Turned out quite good looking."

"Their nose was always running in those days," I remembered. "Remember the infield-fly rule arguments?"

"Yeah," she said. "I bet you're glad THEY'RE over with."

"You bet I am!" I told her.

I drove over to the Little League field. There they were—hordes of kids, dropping flies, throwing balls over the catchers' heads, sneaking out to the soda pop counter. The umpire was arguing with a manager. They had a rule book out. A guy with a hammer was shoring up the left-field fence. A guy was touching up the "Busch Realty Supports Little League" sign.

"Hey, Jim! You wanna umpire?" someone shouted.

Well, I thought, I DO know the rules. And a fellow ought to help. I noticed the guy they had STILL wasn't giving the kids the corners.

"My kid lost a game once and cried because they didn't give him the corners," I told the guy next to me. He was a stranger but he had THE LOOK—the one where you try not to show the strain. I KNEW it was his kid at bat. His wife was glaring at the ump.

"Hey, Jim! I bet you're glad you got your last kid through Little League, eh?" the manager of my kid's last year's team yelled.

"Yeah," I said. "Who needs it?"

Break Up the Yanks!

I went to the Yankees-White Sox game the other night with my fingers crossed. Frankly, I couldn't stand the suspense. It was the first time in a long while I have rooted for the Yankees and I was afraid for them.

In the first place, the second-baseman had warts. The center-fielder had bubble gum caught in his cavities. The pitcher forgot to wash behind his ears and the catcher's mother forgot to bring his mitt.

As if that wasn't bad enough, the first baseman brought the bad news that his brother had chicken pox. It was clear the league would have to invoke the disaster clause. Warts you can cure. By tying a dead toad on them. But chicken pox can wreck a good ball team.

The Yankees, of course, are the Beverly Hills Yankees and, unlike the New York Yankees, they are holding up their league instead of heading it up.

The Beverly Hills Little League is the only one in the world where the bleachers at game time look like the first three rows at Academy Award night. The starting infield all have braces on their teeth and when the pitcher gets to first base, they don't put a windbreaker on him, they put mother's mink stole. There are so many Lincoln Continentals parked around the field it looks like the Ford factory has sprung a leak.

The teams don't have a trainer but a direct line to their pediatricians who are standing by with sugared aspirin and marked copies of Dr. Spock.

Dorothy Lamour's son is the manager of the Beverly Hills Yankees, to give you a rough idea. I mean, if he kicks dirt on the umpire he'll ruin a pair of $100 bench-made alligator shoes. The kids' uniforms are cut by Dior.

I went to the game as the guest of the celebrated recreation director of the Holmby Hills Rat Pack, otherwise known as "The Clan." Dean Martin had a son in the game, Dino Jr., a blue-eyed, tow-headed kid with a sneaky fast ball, a lot of control and a big weekly allowance.

Dean was accompanied by his wife and the rest of his family (who outnumber the starting lineup) and "Killer" Mack Gray. Killer Gray is a member in good standing of the Warner Bros. underworld and a veteran of the Metro-Goldwyn-Mayer gang wars who earned his ferocious nickname holding George Raft's tommy-gun between takes of "Scarface." The evidence is he has killed nothing more dangerous than a fifth of whiskey in his time, which was not recent.

Martin, on the other hand, has had more serious duties because forming a Little League for the Clan is a lot more complicated than baseball. He bestirred himself frequently during the game to implore "Somebody hit the ball to my kid!" but otherwise spent a nail-biting evening like every other parent present.

"Little Dino is going to be the greatest player in the league, perhaps in history," Killer Gray loudly assured me. This is impeccable Little League behavior. Little League rooting, as you know, reverses every trend known to baseball. In the majors, when a guy strikes out, you yell: "Ya bum, ya couldn't hit it with a tennis racket!" In Little Leagues, you murmur, "Say, that boy has a nice swing, doesn't he?" That's because you never know whose father is sitting next to you. Laugh at the wrong time and, in Beverly Hills, your career could go into total eclipse.

Dino's lovely mother, Jean, on the other hand, turned pale when she saw her heir on the hill. "Oh, dear," she said, upset. "It's so much more fun when he's on third." You have to know that almost the worst thing that can happen to a mother in Little League is to come and see her son pitching. This means your heart constricts 150 times a game instead of only 20 or so.

Dino pitched well. His sinker sank—sometimes halfway to the plate. But the game was a pitchers' battle—8–6. For Little League, this is the tightest kind of ball.

The Yankees held on to win even though Dino—to the distress

of his father and the glee of his mother—got transferred to third base in the fifth inning. He had exceeded his quota. In Little League, a pitcher can pitch only until he gets hungry which is usually about four innings.

The White Sox had the tying runs on second and third when the last batter hit a sunk sinker off the hands to the infield. The umpire dashed to third. Umpires in Little League have a habit of guessing wrong. The play was at first. The umpire had his back to it. So Manager Bill Howard called the play—in his team's favor. "He's out," he told the umpire. "Y'er out!" shouted the umpire. And the Yankees had won again. No one argued. In Little League, you're just glad to get home in time for late dinner. Besides, umpires sometimes call them worse when they get to see them frontward.

But Jean Martin was disturbed. "Was he really out?" she wondered. Her famous husband arched an eyebrow. "Of course, dear," he chided. "It was in our favor, wasn't it?"

On the ride home, Dean Martin Sr. was philosophical. "These kids today," he mused. "They got everything going for them. You punish them, you say 'Okay, go upstairs to your room.' In their room, they got three television sets and an electric train.

"When I was a kid we had Little League for the Mafia. You don't get any uniforms, you just learned to steal in your regular clothes. To tell you the truth I'm just surprised they don't have Little League polo."

The Ghost Goes East

Headline: "Star Pitcher To Cover Series For Wurst Deadline Service. Prosit Poofax To Give Readers Of 'Daily Equivocator' View From The Mound. See These Pages For Daily Startlers On Series."

We take you now to the mound and the thoughts going through the mind of the eminent journalist and left-handed pitcher, Prosit Poofax. There are two out and Mickey Mantle is at bat.

"Wow. So that's Mantle. Lord, I wonder who cut the horns

off? If I get him out, they oughta give me the ears. Well, here goes. If he gets me, it'll be on my best pitch. The smoker. If it's close, I just hope he gets out of the way of it.

"Oh. Where's that going? Good Lord, I believe it hit on the roof. Brother. Is this gonna be a long Series. Remind me to tell my readers it was a hanging curve-ball. I don't want Mantle to think he can rap my hammer like that. There, Mick, that's the last off-speed pitch you get till spring training. He's laughing. The bum knows it was my screamer.

"Oh, oh. Here comes the Skip. Looks like he wants to cry. Well, how does he think I feel. What, Skip? Naw, naw, that wasn't my fast one. A slider, Skip. Got it out over the plate. What? Do I have good stuff, he wants to know. What does he think Mantle hit? A change-up? Of course, I got good stuff. If Mantle got around on that ball a little more he woulda hit it to Bridgeport. Go back to sleep, Skip, and be sure to bunt.

"Who's this comin' up? Elly Howard. What's the book on him? Slow stuff in and out. I ought to bust him one right in the ear. Maybe I'll just break this nice little curve over—here, Elly, break your back on this one.

"Whew. That was close. That ball didn't miss my head by more than two inches. Helluva note. Throw the ball in there at 90 miles an hour, it comes back to you at 110. I get a laugh at that infield of ours. Waving at the ball like they had a chance. Why, you clown, you couldn't stop a medicine ball.

"Oh, oh. Here comes old Iron Wrist our third-sacker. Lookit him sweat. I know what he's thinking. He's praying I don't get one down and inside to Mantle or he'll be eating through a straw till Christmas. What's that he's saying? 'Let 'em hit it, Prosit, we're behind you.' Is he kidding? With this infield I don't dare give up a foul tip.

"Lord, here comes Maris. Better get the catcher out here. Hey, Thornboro. C'mere. Whadda ya say we put this guy on? Throw it by him? That's gotta be the funniest line of the year, Thorny. The last guy that tried that was his high-school coach. I'm gonna wet one. Try and hold onto it for a change, will you? That umpire's blind anyway. You could dip a ball in a bucket and he wouldn't catch on.

"O.K., Maris, get your umbrella out. They're gonna call the

game if the wind blows anything off this ball. Oh, my word. There it goes out to right field. Big Rank hasn't moved out there. Play it on a bounce, big Rank. For heaven's sake, hold it to a double, son. Oh, oh. He's under it. He's got it surrounded. Please, Rank, catch it in the glove just once.

"Oh, no! Right off the helmet. And he's still looking up. He can't feel a thing. Behind you, Rank. No, no. Let Willie get it. Get your hands off that ball, Rank. Lordy. Where's that one going? What's the ground rule on a ball thrown from right field into Central Park?

"Here comes the first baseman. Man, this is no time for Frank Merriwell-at-Yale lectures. What? 'We'll get these runs back,' he's saying. Where do you get that stuff you're smoking, you pop out with the bases loaded. This team won't get three runs the whole Series. Why, if this club was in that fixed World Series in 1919, it'd still be a scoreless tie in the 20,000th inning. They couldn't put a run in a silk stocking. Just go back there and try to hold the ground-outs to a one-base hit.

"Who's that up there? Yogi Berra? Either that, or there's a leak in the Bronx Zoo. All right, Yogi, miss this and I'll buy you a banana. Pull your ears in or they'll get cauliflowered. The only way you're gonna hit this pitch is with the back of your hand. Even then, it'll get through this infield.

"Oh (sob). How did he ever get a bat around on that ONE? That's right, Rank. Fall in the seats. And while you're at it, stay there. You oughta pay to see this World Series. Hey, Yogi, where do you put your tail when you get in that pin-stripe?

"Oh, oh. The Skip is standing on the top step. O.K., Skip, tell us again how the Yankees only put their pants on one leg at a time like the rest of us. Only this ain't a dressing contest. They eat with forks, too, do they? Don't make me laugh. Our only hope is that war's declared.

"Atta boy, Skip. Take me outta here. But, first, get on that phone and check with your bull-pen. I gotta clue for you. If there's no answer, it ain't out of order. If those guys haven't gone over the wall, they're dumber than I thought they were and, believe me, that's DUMB. Tell 'em if they throw a fast ball to Mantle they're gonna have $100,000 worth of damage to that roof out there. You were worried about Ronny Mavis playing left field? Don't worry, Skip. Where these guys hit it, he can't get hurt. He'll need a ticket to catch a ball where that Mantle lands 'em. If I were you, I'd station my center-fielder on the Merritt Parkway.

"What's that, Skip? You wanna make a change? Don't apologize. Here's the ball. I'd give it to one of your infielders but they'd drop it. Lots of luck, Skip. I just hope these guys don't win the Series in three games. But I'm betting that's the way it's got to be.

"Oh, oh. Here comes my ghost writer. Lemme take a shower first, will ya, buddy? What? You're on deadline? O.K. here's what ya say: 'The Yankees can be taken,' says Prosit. 'I made one little mistake to Mantle.' (One little mistake. Yeah. I threw the ball to him.) 'The Yankees draw their pants on one leg at a time. They are suckers for a National League curve ball. We will win this thing in six.' (Six! I just hope we last four.)

"Tell our readers not to give up on us. We're in this thing to the end. I got a great team behind me and I know we can do it. Put a headline on it 'Yanks Lucky, Says Prosit. Should Have Thrown Mantle My Fast Ball.'"

Baseball's Finest

In a World Series, a pitcher can bring his best pitch. A hitter is not asked to hold up his swing. A base runner can take all he can get. The second baseman can cheat a step towards the bag if he wishes.

There's only one class of performers who go out there in handcuffs—the umpires. They are without their most potent weapons in the umpiring arsenal—the "run 'em" or the "you're out of here, mister."

The umpire in a World Series can eject a player only if he (a) draws a gun; (b) votes Communist; (c) gets caught phoning his bookie between innings. Anything in between and the chances are he'll get to play the full nine innings. The only person who can knock a player out of the game is a batter.

The only really-important player ever kicked out of a World Series was Joe Medwick in 1934. And it took the commissioner of baseball to do it. The score was 11–0 in his team's favor at the time, and the crowd was showering him with fruit. Their team had the zero. It was a question of getting him out of there or finishing the game in the world's biggest pile of garbage.

The umpire is the most on-the-spot guy in the Series. No matter what he does, he's going to have half the 50 million audience mad at him. He feels the pressure as much as the rawest rookie up from Spokane. He can lay a bigger egg on television than a talking car. They have a little refinement of the electronic era now called the "instant replay." You can put the donkey's ears on an umpire by the flick of a switch.

Umpires can blow calls in World Series, just as they can in spring training. But it's significant that Arnold Rothstein didn't try to bribe the umpires in 1919 even though he could have saved money. There were only three of them in those days. Moreover, they got just enough money then to tide them over till they got a winter job.

Things are little better today. For where you will see a headline, "Willie to Demand $150,000," you'll never see, "Ump Holding Out for 25 G's" or "Bonus Ump Signed for Record Sum."

In a World Series, they get $4,000. Now, that may seem like a munificent sum—until you realize that a utility catcher, whose only contribution to the winning team effort is apt to be handing one of the regulars the soap in a shower, always gets a full share. And even the losers' share hasn't been below $5,000 in a dozen years. And won't be this year. "We feel we ought to get at least as much as a loser's share," two umpires told me privately the other afternoon.

The importance of honesty in umpiring in a World Series can be illustrated by more stories than you would care to listen to in the press room after a long game. In 1928, it was a National League umpire, Bill Pfirman, who made possible Babe Ruth's second three-homers-in-one-game feat. In the seventh inning of the final game that year, the Cardinals' Willie Sherdel had apparently just struck Ruth out. But the ump ruled Ruth had stepped out of the batter's box and, even though the "quick pitch" was legal then, it had been outlawed for the Series. Ruth hit the next pitch, a fourth strike, over a roof in right center. Later he hit a third home run.

In 1953, the Dodgers played the Yankees, and, by the seventh inning, the score was 5–4 in favor of the Yanks when the Dodgers rallied, tied it up with three straight hits. With Gil Hodges on second, Carl Furillo on first, the batter, Billy Cox, bunted. Yogi Berra, the catcher, chased the ball and threw to third. By the time he had caught up to the ball, the runner, Hodges, was already into his slide. The third-base umpire, Art Gore, was a National Leaguer, but he unaccountably flashed the "out" sign.

To say it was a surprise is to put it mildly. The Yankee third baseman was as shocked as anybody. Along with everyone else, he didn't know why Yogi had bothered to throw to third when Hodges already had the play beat. In the press box, the writer, Harold Rosenthal, supplied the explanation: "The reason Yogi threw to third," he said, "was because he saw that Gore had already called Hodges out."

The "quick" call is something that Edwin Henry Hurley, the senior umpire in this year's World Series, avoids. A broadcaster (Mel Allen) once asked him to speed up his calls. "Mel," Ed Hurley said, "if they ain't fast enough for you, call your own. But don't be surprised if I contradict you." It was another famous umpire who was cogitating one day over a close play and was hotly pressed by a manager for a decision. "What is it? What is it?" the manager demanded. "Son," the umpire drawled. "It ain't nuthin' till I say it."

Ed Hurley, who practiced umpiring in front of a mirror the way Ted Williams did batting, has put a son through Notre Dame umpiring, and a daughter through an exclusive girls' school in the East. His favorite reading will never make the best-seller list—the Book of Baseball Rules.

To his mind, baseball would do as well to scout the minors for iron wills as for Maury Wills. "The umpire who will fold under pressure can do more damage to the game than 50 ballplayers who will."

And pressure is not always a three-and-two-count in the ninth inning with your brother-in-law at bat, and the game and the Series on the line. Pressure for Ed Hurley Monday was a fly ball over his position (second base). Sandy Koufax had what promised to be a no-hitter. Centerfielder Willie Davis backed up on the ball, then charged. It hit his glove. Ed Hurley flashed the "out" sign. Then he noticed the ball trickle off the end of Davis' fingers. He swept his palms down in a "safe" sign. Fifty-five thousand people groaned. Millions others muttered curses. A no-hit World Series game, as rare as rubies, went down the drain. Only Willie Davis and Ed Hurley and two guys with telephoto camera lenses knew Willie Davis hadn't caught that ball. But even if only Ed Hurley knew it that would have been one too many for Ed Hurley. That's why baseball can be as proud of its umpiring as its no-hit games.

Lot of Character

As this is written, it is Lincoln's Birthday and I have a great idea for a way for baseball to celebrate the anniversary of the Great Emancipator. It can emancipate Emmett Littleton Ashford from the cotton fields of baseball—the leaky bus circuits and back alleys of the minor leagues.

Emmett Ashford is a Negro. As if life weren't tough enough, he is also an umpire. He does not, it should be noted, however, hit himself over the head to go to sleep.

Emmett would be the last guy in the world who would want to be taken into the big leagues on race alone. He wants to be considered not because he's a Negro but because he's good.

No less a critic than Bobby Bragan, who has always been able to restrain his enthusiasm when discussing umpires, considers Emmett one of the five best he has ever seen.

Ashford did not show up at the Fair Employment Practices office one afternoon, pass an eye test and demand he be made an umpire by nightfall. He has been practicing his trade for 13 years. Los Angeles-born and raised, he was not an athlete, he was a bookworm. He was also a collegian and a postal clerk when the city recreation department first put a chest protector and mask on him, promised him $1.75 and told him to be sure and call the corners.

Some people in the world enjoy lying on a bed of nails. Others walk airplane wings or high wires. Emmett Ashford loves to umpire. On the field, he's like a kitten with a ball of yarn. He frequently beats the baserunners to second base. He can go backward as fast as Steve Bilko can go forward. Lively and inventive, his "Safe" or "Out" are right out of Shakespeare or grand opera.

He has memorized five sets of rules from girls' soft ball, where he got his first big national chance, to basketball, where he is unaccustomedly melancholy when he has to "officiate" at the clown games of double-headers.

But it is baseball which brings the sparkle to Ashford's eye and quip to his lips. He has umpired from El Paso to El Salvador. He has called a man out in the Dominican Republic when even the rival team was begging him not to because 16,000 armed men in the stands didn't want him to. He has left games under police escort and in disguise but he would call a strike if it split the plate even if the only sound he would ever hear after that would be the firing squad.

He has been told by a whole rooting section in Texas to "Go home, we don't want you doing a white man's job." But he stuck it out, and, two years later, the same people were giving him a testimonial dinner.

He maintains a sense of humor with a sense of discipline. He has to: he has seen half a dozen umpires he broke in go to the major leagues. He was on the base paths in L.A. and San Francisco long before there were Dodgers and Giants on them and if the Angels were playing the "Senators" they met Sacramento.

But when they came, Emmett had to go—back to the minor leagues where he tries to maintain a standard of living and conduct so impeccable that the league salary and expenses leave him slightly in the hole at the end of a season. "I think it is important in my case to live well and dress well and go first class at all times," he says. It is inconceivable to him that his personal loss ledger won't pay off in a big league profit one of these years.

At 44, Emmett hopes it will happen while he can still see without bi-focals. He has been patient—even when the criticism went through the league that he was "Showboating" for doing the same thing other umps were called "colorful" for.

It took baseball almost as long as Mississippi to catch up with the Emancipation Proclamation. To its credit, it made up for a lot of lost time when it did. Now that Dusty Boggess has retired, it has a chance to make up for a lot more, behind the plate as well as at it. If it will contact Dewey Soriano, president of the Coast League, it can buy up Ashford's contract, make itself a lot of character—and get itself one, too, in Emmett Ashford.

Feller & His Team

It didn't surprise him a bit, but Bobby Feller made the Hall of Fame in his first whack at it this week, along with Jackie Robinson. Bobby got 150 out of a possible 160 votes but this show of popularity didn't exactly please him. You see, Bob wants to go in the Hall of Fame as an entry. He wants to bring his own team with him.

Feller made this clear in an article he wrote for the *Saturday Evening Post* this week in anticipation of his election to immortality—or at least what passes for it in the world of baseball.

Bob writes like he pitches—straight and fast. But his control is as wobbly as ever. He knocks a few guys down and sticks the ball right in the ear of a few other people. Whitey Ford, for instance. Bob teases Whitey with a slow curve ("Whitey Ford is the best money pitcher I have ever seen") and then, wham! He blazes one right at Whitey's head. "Ford does not have anything like a Hall of Fame record . . . let me back this up with figures. When I won 26 games in 1946, I started 42 games and finished 36. Last year, Ford started 39 and finished 11."

Bob suggests that instead of a Ford in its future, the Hall of Fame settle for a bicycle built for two—Ford and his relief pitcher Luis Arroyo. Because Luis saved so many games for Whitey, Feller thinks Luis ought to get in the glass case with Ford in case Whitey starts to get shaky after the first seven years. Otherwise, he intimates, Whitey shouldn't even be allowed to go through Cooperstown on a fast train.

Bobby is not even particularly enthusiastic about Jackie Robinson passing through the portals with him. He thinks Satchel

Paige should be the first Negro to get to Cooperstown. For one big reason: Satch is a pitcher. And Bobby is partial to pitchers. He is miffed because only 20% of the modern players in the Hall of Fame are pitchers. Of course, the last time I looked, only 11% of the players on a team were pitchers, and of the 76 players in the Hall of Fame, 23 of them are pitchers.

But after Bobby leaves Jackie Robinson lying in the dust of the batter's box, shaking his head to clear the beanball out of it, he turns his attention to who SHOULD be in the trophy room with him.

His first nominee is George Blaeholder. That's right, B-L-A-E-H-O-L-D-E-R.

Now before you leap to the conclusion Blaeholder is Feller's brother-in-law, you should be advised he too was a pitcher. In his lifetime, he won 104 games and lost 125. Hardly Hall of Fame stuff, but George pitched for the St. Louis Browns, baseball's version of the OUR GANG comedies. But when I tell you that George had only one season in his career over .500 you may be pardoned for thinking he should get arrested for staying in Cooperstown after dark.

Not so, says Feller. Blaeholder qualifies because he is the inventor of the slider.

The slider—also known as the "nickel curve," the "curve ball after taxes"—is most famous as a pitch that breaks so little and goes so far. "Blaeholder makes the Hall of Fame because he invented a pitch that enabled Roger Maris to hit 61 home runs," is Fresco Thompson's raised-eyebrow evaluation.

It's unclear how Blaeholder invented the slider—whether he had a blister on his throwing finger or just decided the Browns weren't entitled to a full 10-cent curve or a full day's work is not revealed by Feller.

Feller would also like to bring Red Ruffing along with him because Red won seven more games than Feller did. Of course, pitching on a team with Ruth, Gehrig, Dickey, Lazzeri, Rolfe and Combs on it, as Ruffing did, should make a 20-game winner out of a balloon dancer. Feller wants Fred (Firpo) Marberry with him, too, because he was a fine relief pitcher although Feller scorns the modern trend to relief pitching generally.

But Bobby may have an idea at that. We all may have been

paying too much attention to run-of-the-mill things like RBI's and ERA's in our selections. We may have been overlooking the more inventive kind of ballplayers. Like a few I have right here.

Let's put Dick Stuart in for pioneering the practices of fielding fly balls and swinging at curve balls on one bounce. Maury Wills should make it for keeping his home run production at one in an era when even drag bunts go in the seats.

Elio Chacon makes it for perfecting the stagger system of playing second base and revising the old verse to put the Chance in the middle of the double play instead of the end. Chuck Connors qualifies for learning to shoot a rifle one-handed, or the same way he used to strike out, and the guy that invented the trapper's mitt gets a special room paid for by all the five-thumbed first basemen who managed to stay in the major leagues only because of him.

As for Bobby Feller, now that he's made it, he should learn people in glass cases shouldn't throw spitballs.

Pilots or Profs?

It is the belief of those who make their living off it that baseball is a science at least as difficult to master as a cyclotron—a belief not necessarily shared by the rest of the civilized world.

When the rest of us think of a baseball manager, we tend to think of a guy in charge of turning off the showers or seeing to it the decks aren't marked for the airplane poker games. On the field, they wake him up occasionally when the pitcher is in a jam and he wanders out to the mound and imparts the deathless advice "don't give him nothing good to hit, but don't walk him."

Legend has it the late "Uncle" Wilbert Robinson was once similarly stirred into consciousness one afternoon and when his eyes were opened wide enough, he saw the bases were loaded. Naturally, he assumed it was the other team. So he waddled out to give the rival pitcher the benefit of his deepest thinking on the situation and it is the only time on record a pitcher got the side out after a word to the wise from Uncle Robbie. Of course, it was his side.

But, regardless of what the majority of us ignoramuses think, the resident master-minds of the game are of the fixed opinion it would perish without them. It's for sure their families wouldn't eat so well. Accordingly they have devised a series of tests to give to their literate ballplayers, some of whom, they suspect, are as ignorant of the refinements of the grand old game as sportswriters.

They can't give sportswriters tests as we are protected against this kind of unlawful seizure of our drinking time by the bill of rights, a fundamental cornerstone of which is the right to remain stupid if you so desire. But there is nothing to protect baseball rookies who have already waived large sections of their civil rights when they signed a baseball contract, an extraordinary document which, one must remember, after all, was drawn up by the forefathers of a sport which didn't even get around to reading the emancipation proclamation until 80 years after it was written.

The examination, when given to a literate ballplayer, is in the form of the multiple choice question. You know, the "mark one answer only" kind. Typical question: "A baseball is (mark one) a—round; b—square, c—neither," a question only one out of 10 flunks.

More favored, however, is the oral examination because this lets everybody in. Baseball has had only one player in its history who couldn't talk. And it missed the golden opportunity to make him a manager.

Of course, .350 hitters are exempt from this examination. All they have to be is all square with their parole board and able to sign an "X" on their contract. They should, however, be human and relatively sane—although these conditions must not necessarily be met and often aren't.

The trouble with the answers in these training camp examinations is they are not always strictly honest. When they ask the rookie "with a man on first, do you hit to right?" the rookie will usually answer correctly "yes," the honest answer more often would be "No, I hit it back to the pitcher."

Our examinee, then, is the honest answerer—an all-purpose utility man, Joe Cretin, who is known as a "ballplayer's ballplayer" which means he is no threat whatever to anybody's job. Joe never passes the manager's tests but it doesn't matter since he can't hit major league pitching anyway and would be on the Keokuk roster by May even if he had the answers on his sleeve. His answers have the virtue of frankness, however, and are for that reason worthy of reproducing. Here is his latest term paper:

Q. What must you keep in mind at all times?

A. Not to get caught stealing.

Q. Second base?

A. No, no. Wallets and wrist watches.

Q. When the ball bounces off your knees and rolls behind you into foul ground with a runner on first, what must you do?

A. Buy the official scorer a drink so he'll call it a hit.

Q. When a fly ball comes into right center with a runner on third, what do you do?

A. Let Snider take it.

Q. Better arm than you?

A. No. He makes more money than I do.

Q. If you see you can't catch up to a fly ball that is going to carom off the wall, what do you do?

A. Fall down and pretend I got a sprained ankle. I never could play that carom.

Q. If your throw goes wild and the guy on third starts for home, what should you do to protect yourself?

A. Tell the manager I just got a long-distance call from my grandmother that she is in bad shape and can I be excused for the day. If he says no, I pick a fight with the umpire.

Q. What is the rule on the infield fly?

A. Let someone else take it.

Q. What do you say to calm a pitcher down in a jam?

A. You tell him that blond he's been making eyes at is the umpire's wife.

Q. When you throw home over the catcher's head with a man on second, what's the first thing you should do?

A. Tell the pitcher you're sorry.

Q. If you do happen to get sent back to the minors, what should you be determined to do?

A. Call up my brother-in-law and see if he's got an opening at the laundry.

Q. If Eddie Mathews comes into the bag with his spikes high, what should be the first thought to cross your mind?

A. To ask the skip if you can switch to the outfield.

Q. If Willie Mays came up with men on base, is it wise to walk him?

A. Is the pope a Catholic?

3-Star Baseball

Well, I see where baseball has popped up with the bases loaded again.

They have picked the Mystery Guest as commissioner of baseball. Will you come in, Commissioner, and sign in, please? Now, is there a product connected with what you do?

The gentleman in question is a retired three-star general. You can see this is exactly what baseball needs. Beset by pro football (over 60% of the age group between 21 and 34 consider THAT the national pastime), rising costs, the demise of the minor leagues, the threat of anti-trust, they have decided that what they need is a man who can compute the trajectory of an artillery shell, lecture learnedly on the importance of air cover, recite the arms manual from memory and chronologically list Napoleon's campaigns and Lee's mistakes at Gettysburg.

If that's what they wanted, what was the matter with Bruce Catton? If a military man was needed all along, why not Audie Murphy?

Why did they pick Judge Landis after 1919 instead of Von Moltke? Did anybody contact De Gaulle?

I won't bore you with the general's name. Matter of fact, I keep forgetting it. He's so anonymous, someone in the East suggested he might be the Unknown Soldier. It's for sure he's the Unknown Baseball Commissioner. He might be the game's first unlisted commissioner. If you need him, you leave a message with his answering service—Walter O'Malley.

I don't know how he stands on the important issues of the game. Like the infield-fly rule. Or, how is he on World Series rainouts? Does he know the hit-and-run play? Who does he think was the greatest, Ty Cobb or Babe Ruth?

I do know he was checked out by a screening committee of Walter O'Malley, Bob Reynolds, John Galbreath and John Fetzer. I don't suppose they bothered him with any messy little particulars like franchise-shifts which, as everyone knows, are league matters. It took baseball 50 years to move its first franchise but it has been moving them so fast and in so many directions since that you're in danger of getting hit with one on the freeway. Some of the franchises seem so sure to move the team bus double-parks when they arrive in town.

The general did display one outstanding qualification in his first press conference. Someone asked him when was the last time he had seen a game and he said that if he had seen one in the past year, he didn't remember it. That was a wholesome start. He might have added, "The trouble with baseball games is, you've seen one, you've seen 'em all."

One member of the screening committee, sent to check on the general's interest in sports, so to speak, generally, later confided with a perfectly straight face, "He's a great sports enthusiast. He plays a damn good game of tennis and squash."

In this spirit, allow me to present my own candidate for commissioner of baseball, Field Marshal Gerhardt Von und Zu Nichts, head of the ground crew of the Luftwaffe and much-decorated commanding officer of the Unter den Linden recruiting office. Field Marshal Von und Zu Nichts holds several of his country's distinguished service medals including the Order of the Double Cross and the Army-Navy umlaut for stepping up production at the Krupp works which he did by first stepping up production in bull whips.

Reporter: "Marshal Nichts, can you tell us what plans you have for your executive administrator, Lee MacPhail, and your staff of four?"

Commissioner: "Yah! Vun vill shine my shoes, anudder vill drive der Mercedes und der rest vill decode messages from Valter O'Melley. Ve vill keep vun orderly to swallow messages ve don't vant to fall in der hands of der enemy."

Reporter: "Marshal, what do you think of the Braves' move to Atlanta?"

Commissioner (enthusiastically): "Absolutely first class maneuver. I haf studied der campaigns of General Sherman and I must say our campaign is superior in every respect. Ve vill bring Atlanta to her knees. Ve vill not leave vun dollar in der whole verdammt town!"

Reporter (dismayed): "But what about Milwaukee?"

Commissioner (scornfully): "A billeting area, my poy! An army must live off der land. Ve did not mistreat der good burghers dere. No reprisals. No shooting. Ve chust plundered dem a little bit. Vot do you think var is, er, I mean baseball—a love affair? Dis is total var! You cannot haf silly little sentimental attachments. Victory, my poy!"

Reporter: "What about the Mets? Don't you think they have to start winning pretty soon? Are you going to help expansion clubs?"

Commissioner: "A mere matter of propaganda, my goot man. Ve nefer says 'Der Mets lose!' Ve say, 'Der Mets inflicted heavy casualties on der enemy—der San Francisco Chiants.' Ve must add der time guard against unrest on der home front. In Chermany dere are still zum people think ve are vinning Vorld Var Two."

Reporter: "But what if they get '*The Sporting News?*'"

Commissioner (snapping his fingers): "Ve confiscate *Der Sporting News*, ve hold der families of der sportswriters hostages. Ve attack, attack, attack! Today baseball. Tomorrow the vorld. If I advance, follow me. If I retreat, kill me. As Mussolini said."

Reporter: "But what about the basic traditions of baseball? You know, the game's never over till the final out, 'Take Me Out to the Ball Game,' may the best team win—all that jazz?"

Commissioner: "Bah! Bourgeois nonsense. Zis is der new order. From now on it is, if it moves, salute it! If it doesn't move, paint it! Understood? Now, square dot hat und click dose heels und repeat after me, 'I vill nefer do anything detrimental to baseball if I hope to zee my family and loved vuns again.' Disobedients vill be sentenced to a lifetime of press box hot-dogs, coffee in cardboard cups and 24 hours a day of Leo Durocher recordings in a Vero Beach cell mit der screens off and der bed under der main shower pipe."

Reporter: "But you can't do that! This is the United States of America!" Commissioner: "Donnerwetter! Den vot do they give me dis job for? That's all I know."

The Grand Old Stand

Baseball is a game played by nine athletes on the field and 20 fast-buck artists in the front office. It must have a constitution like iron. They can't kill it. They've kicked it downstairs, dumped it in the river with cement on it, cut holes in its tires and poisoned its tea.

It won't turn up its heels. Cities have gone in hock for it, poets sing of it, intellectuals adore it. Only its own try to slip it a mickey.

Which brings me to the fact that baseball is having its winter meetings in Houston right now. They got together to compare mistakes. I'd go but my doctor says my heart won't stand the pounding boredom.

Accordingly, I'd like to bring you, as they say on radio, a résumé of all the non-action:

9 A.M.—Meeting convenes. Rumor of big trade brewing. Press alerted.

9:30 A.M.—Joint press conference between New York and Milwaukee. They have traded an overage, overpaid outfielder who can't hit a curveball for an overage, overpaid pitcher who can't throw one. They throw in a catcher who can't catch one. "This trade will help both clubs," the managers announce. "Those boys need a change of scenery." Those boys need a change of occupation but the story goes on the A wire all the same.

9:45 A.M.—Milwaukee, which will transfer to Atlanta as soon as the process servers let go of its sleeve, is approached to move to the Okeefenokee Swamp. The Seminole Indians have promised them exclusive television coverage at a fabulous sum to every Indian reservation in the South. Milwaukee loses interest when it finds out Indian television is smoke signals and the payoff is in beads.

10 A.M.—The Pacific Coast League takes in Cairo and Nairobi.

10:15 A.M.—The New York Yankees announce they are optioning out the centerfield statues of Ruth and Gehrig to Richmond to make room for CBS erection of statues of Major Bowes and Mary Margaret McBride. And two pay phone booths. The Del E. Webb Construction Co. is awarded the contract at a low bid of 800 million dollars.

10:30 A.M.—The New York Mets announce they will take the statues of Ruth and Gehrig for Shea Stadium. They will send Yogi Berra, Casey Stengel and George Weiss over to get them.

10:45 A.M.—Buzzie Bavasi offers Ken McMullen for Mickey Mantle. "You have to take chances to keep ahead in this game," he announces. The Yankees agree, offer to take a chance on Sandy Koufax. They offer Phil Linz and a mouth organ for him.

11 A.M.—Charles O. Finley calls on baseball to start World Series at 2 in the morning so interstate truckdrivers can see it. "My Uncle Louie was an interstate truckdriver," he explains, "and the only World Series he ever got to see was in Denver once when he got a flat tire outside of a TV store window. It was either the fourth inning of the third game of the 1952 World Series or the third inning of the fourth game. Uncle Louie was never sure which. But he says it was a great thrill." Survey shows 1.7 truckdrivers in a sampling of 18 key states never saw a World Series, 1.2 of them said they didn't care, said they went to the racetrack anyway and they would rather have racing at 2 A.M.

11:14 A.M.—The Yankees announce the signing of Mickey Mantle with the proviso that any game he is too injured to play in, he will have to pay to see like any other spectator.

11:15 A.M.—Mets offer to let Mickey Mantle see their games for nothing.

11:30 A.M.—Kansas City Athletics request permission to move to Perth Amboy. Commissioner of baseball turns them down. Perth Amboy turns them down.

11:45 A.M.—Yankees announce statues of Miller Huggins and Col. Ruppert will be torn down to make room for one of Myrt and Marge and Garry Moore.

12 noon—Yankees announced as winners of the annual "All Heart Award" given to the baseball employer who has demonstrated the most sympathetic handling of the problem of the older employee. The award is in the form of a bronzed ship. With a plank sticking out the side and a figure shown being pushed off it. Del Webb accepts the award on behalf of CBS. Del Webb gets

the contract to build the trophy case at a low bid of 3 million dollars.

1:05 P.M.—Houston announces new name for team, the "Astros." Pardon me!?

1:10 P.M.—The Cubs and White Sox announce a trade of a pitcher who didn't win a game last year for a catcher who didn't get a hit. "The trade will help both clubs," said the announcement. "These boys need a change of scenery." In this case, from Chicago to Chicago.

1:15 P.M.—The commissioner of baseball announces the leagues will open their own van and storage business. "There are times when we have to move franchises and can't wait till morning." A hot line will be maintained from the trucking office to 20 front offices and some trucks will be on the highways at all times in the event of a red alert. Machinery will be set up so as not to move some franchise by mistake and have to return it to its home town with apologies.

1:30 P.M.—Rumors denied that the Yankees shot Santa Claus. CBS announces it is buying all baseball for use as a summer replacement show for Dobie Gillis.

Goof Balls Find Niche

If Babe Ruth were alive today, what do you think he'd be most famous for? His pitching? Wrong. His homers? Wrong.

His strikeouts. There were more of them than anything and the way things are going nowadays, they'd be more valuable to him.

A curious thing is happening in the world of baseball. It's not how you play the game, but whether you lost. The most celebrated player of our day is not Mantle, Maris or Mays, really. The "M" boy in the hearts of our biggest metropolis is "Marvelous Marv" Throneberry, the first baseman—if you use the term loosely—of the New York Mets.

The Mets themselves have crept in the heart of the populace by setting an all-time losing season of 120 games. They have had the ultimate salute—a book written about them by Jimmy Breslin titled (from the original Stengelese) "Can't Anybody Here Play

This Game?" Books used to be titled, "The Pride of the Yankees," "The Spirit of Notre Dame." That kind of thing. But now, "The Mess of the Mets," "The Shame of the Senators," "The Phlop of the Phils" are hotter box-office. Good authors, too, who once knew better teams, now only do four-letter teams (if Cole Porter will forgive me). To the rhetorical "Can't Anybody Here Play This Game?" the answer, circa, 1963, is "Who Cares?" or even, "Let's Hope Not."

Accordingly, in the context of the new times in sports, I'm going to let you tune in on a conversation between George Dumm, the general manager of the New York Messes, and the head of his farm system, beloved old "Pop" Fly. As we fasten our ear trumpet, Pop is talking.

POP: Have I got a pitcher for you, boss? A doll. He can't do anything, boss, not anything. You heard what happened to Koufax when he lost circulation in one little finger? This guy hasn't got any circulation in the entire left side of his body, boss. And he's a southpaw.

DUMM (coldly): Wait a minute. We got a reputation to maintain. We almost won a game the other day and that would ruin us. That last double-crosser you sent up—the first baseman with a club foot? He had an operation and can now field as well as Frank Howard. What kind of publicity can we get from that? Who's gonna write books about guys who field .900? This pitcher's liable to have brains.

FLY (thunderstruck): Brains. Boss, he was a kindergarten dropout. To him 2-and-2 is logarithms.

DUMM (unconvinced): How is he on balks?

FLY (ecstatic): Boss, he has a balk motion you can see from Staten Island. He may never throw a legal pitch. He balks passing you the salt at dinner.

DUMM (interested): How's his control?

FLY: Boss, he couldn't hit the ground if he dropped a ball from an airplane. I will guarantee you. He's so wild when he rears back to pitch his own second baseman ducks.

DUMM (still looking for a catch in this bargain): Can he throw a curve?

FLY: Only on the bounce, boss. On the fly he can't get it past his chin.

DUMM: How about infielders? We got to get rid of two.

They've started to beat out outfield hits. The fans are beginning to boo.

FLY: I got an infielder in Wichita not only can't go to his right or left, he can't even stop a ball standing still. He gets nosebleeds bending over.

DUMM: Can he steal?

POP: Only watches. I had to sign his parole to get him, but you can't let a hot prospect like this get away. He's worth 40 games a year to us, losses, of course. If it comes to running, he couldn't steal chickens on a blind man.

DUMM: But he might hit a home run.

POP (reproachfully): With cataracts in both eyes? Boss, don't you trust me? Would I send you a guy who would hit a home run? Just ask yourself. I made a solemn promise to my dear mother that no Fly would even put a speck on the family name by fobbing off a whole ballplayer on you. My word of honor, boss. This guy would need a seeing-eye dog to even find home plate.

DUMM: He sounds perfect. I'll get the newspaper guys in here early to do a story on him in my office. Don't let me down, now.

FLY: Boss, I'll guarantee you he'll bump into the wall and try to shake hands with your portrait of Miller Huggins. Just don't leave any elevator doors open or we'll lose the biggest loser in the Messes' history.

DUMM: How about that outfielder you recommended from the Coast? Will he break the strikeout record this season?

POP: If he lives. Just be sure to have his oxygen tent close by. And, by the way, tell the guys not to smoke too close to it. And room him alone. The guys get awful tired of hearing him reminisce about the Civil War and his friendship with Lincoln.

DUMM: How old is he?

POP: Boss, he's been pronounced dead so many times there are doctors in this town who believe in ghosts when they see him up and around.

DUMM: We need a new catcher. "Freight Train" Woodman stopped two curve balls with his feet yesterday and caught a pop foul on one bounce. Destroying the image. Sometimes he goes several innings without passed balls.

POP: Boss, I got a catcher who gets two passed balls before the National Anthem. He drops the ones the ump gives him and they roll to the backstop. He not only gets passed balls, he trips on them running back to catch up to them. Can you see Dick Young's story right now? Is this guy our kind of guy? Is he in the book? Can an Italian sing?

DUMM (enthusiastic): I can see Dick's story now: "So-and-So leads the league in self-fractures inflicted by stepping on rolling balls he couldn't get a glove on."

POP: Boss, it's only the beginning. We've got the greatest farm system in the league. I got one-legged pinch runners, one-armed pinch hitters, I got a trainer who flunked pharmacy and a manager who's got sleeping sickness. A first-sacker who's got the gout and every time he kicks the bag he screams in pain. You think by mid-season he's going to keep inflicting that pain? Boss, this team will go into the cellar at Cooperstown en masse. And there ain't a one of them won't fall down the stairs. Relax, boss. The team is so bad they shouldn't even let them watch the Yankees shave on television and the bubble-gum people pay 'em not to chew it. I tell you, it's the perfect team, boss. Your dream team.

The Making of a Met

News Item—New York Mets say they're sick of their clown image. "It's funny only to guys in the press box, but not to us," complains veteran player. Front-office opening drive to improve caliber of play on the field. "Need a winner here. Moneymoon is over," avers spokesman.

We tune in now on a phone conversation between that wily old ivory hunter, baseball scout Pop Fly, calling from somewhere in the wilds of the Deep South to the front-office management, George Weisenheimer.

"Boss? Lissen, boss, have I got a find! You've heard about the $100,000 infield? Well, I got the 10-cent infield. There isn't a one of them could get off a dime. I spent the afternoon fungoing grounders at them and it added up to eight black eyes, four split lips and 107 went-right-through-the-legs. There isn't a one of them who knows what the ball looks like closeup. Boss, they'll make Elio Chacon look like Mr. Shortstop. I haven't seen so many fumbles since the Harvard backfield. The only way a batter could make an out against them is the infield fly rule. It's a cinch they can't catch the ball.

"What's that? Boss, just a minute while I adjust my ear-plug and tune up the sound. I thought you said you wanted an infield like Tinker-to-Evers-to-Chance. What? You did? Boss! Are you kidding? Those guys could make double plays. We want guys who could turn double-play balls into doubles to the centerfield fence, right?

"Now, lissen to me and stop with the jokes. I had a little bad luck the other day. You know that kid I said was the clumsiest human being I'd ever seen? Well, he drowned taking a shower. Too bad. Could've been a regular Smead Jolley.

"And that fresh busher I told you about? The one I said looked as if he was born with a hangover hasn't made a curfew since he left the playpen? Well, his wife caught him kissing a waitress. He said he was just giving her mouth-to-mouth resuscitation till his wife pointed out there wasn't enough water for miles around to make a cup of tea.

"But the busher is a regular Met, boss! He said he dragged her out of the way cause he didn't want to collect a crowd. He collected one anyway. Turned out she had eight brothers, all crack shots. That busher won't be dropping any flyballs for us for a couple of years. He'll have air going through him till Christmas.

"Boss, I'm on the trail of the biggest thing of my career. How does a catcher with cataracts grab you? But, wait! That's nothing. You've heard of guys with two left feet? Boss, I think I've found him! If this guy doesn't have two left feet, he has two right ones. What? Why, I tracked him through the sand. He only left one footprint all the way from Baton Rouge to Bay St. Louis. I see him as a natural for first base. There'll be no way he can make the tag. Boss, he has to buy two pairs of shoes and throw two of them away! Now, is that a natural Met?! Just asking, boss. We know he is.

"What? Boss, you can't be serious! You were thinking of somebody more along the lines of Billy Terry for first base? Boss, it's about the image. Bill Terry was one of the greats. I see a kid looks like Bill Terry and I get my hat right away. I get the Yankees on to him. They're going to ruin that franchise with the talent they're picking up. Who can wave a banner for Mickey Mantle?

"What? What do you mean, now I'm talking? You WANT the Mickey Mantles? Boss, it must be the heat back there. What about those signs, 'We Don't Want to Set the World on Fire, Just Ninth Place'? What about the New Breed? You wanna turn Casey Stengel into a push-button manager? Boss, do you want robots or characters?

"All right, all right, don't yell! But I can tell you something right now. I give the best years of my life to this organization. No telling how many kids I taught to balk. Who was it interviewed every cross-eyed kid in Florida? You said yourself I was the world's best at spotting a sorearm pitcher 200 yards away. How many outfielders with 20-200 vision did I send up to the majors?

"Just ask yourself, and then yell, Ya old walrus. Who's been filling your ball park all these years? Me and Casey Stengel? Or do you think Tinker-to-Evers-to-Chance will? I tell ya, one year with real ballplayers on that club and the only bats in Shea Stadium will be ones with wings on them. I've devoted a lifetime to spotting a loser.

"I wouldn't give Babe Ruth a bus ticket. Who was it recommended posion ivy for the outfield? Right now I'm working on the biggest deals of my career—a 78-year-old pitcher with hangnails and an AA dropout. I'm a perfectionist, boss, I'll never be satisfied till we drop them all . . . Tinker-to-Evers-to-Chance! Bah! Tinker-to-Evers-to-No-Chance, that's the ticket. Otherwise, it's Tinker-to-Evers-to-Bankruptcy."

Big Frank "Boxed"

Frank Oliver Howard, the well-known right-fielder and stage personality, wrapped a towel big enough to dry the Queen Mary around his massive naked shoulders and sat down heavily on the dressing table. The wood groaned and sagged several inches.

He had just jogged several laps in the outfield, causing tidal waves as far away as the Red Sea. Seismologists in the Chilean Andes began to systematically check cities and off-shore islands to see if one of them had disappeared.

Frank Howard already leads the league in retirements. Casey Stengel is still going strong at 74. Warren Spahn will be pitching strikes at 50 but Frank has given up the game for good several times.

Of course, they gave Frank $108,000 before he ever drew on a pair of spikes and I know a lot of people who have retired on a lot less. Some guys they have to cut the uniform off, but Frank is the first guy to retire while the flowers are still fresh from his debut.

Retirement, of course, is the dream of all of us. The full-page, full-color ads by the insurance company, showing a gray-haired man and his blond wife leaning over the rail of the Lurline and sailing into a palm-lined harbor with native boys diving for pennies, has beguiled premiums out of several generations of dreamers.

But Frank Howard was not putting to sea or planning to sit under a coconut palm with a straw hat and a banjo. Frank was going to work in a box factory.

Somehow, this would take the bloom off retirement for most of mankind but Frank's war with baseball had reached a stage where a career with a broom following a horse would seem preferable.

His troubles stemmed over an honest difference of opinion with Walter Alston. Alston thought he detected a hesitancy over Howard's manner of swinging at a curve ball. So, as a matter of fact, did most National League pitchers. Whitey Ford was the first pitcher of note to come up with an innovation—fast balls. There are still holes in the outfield at Yankee Stadium to show where he was in error. If the ball Frank hit in Dodger Stadium hadn't hit a chair, it might not have come down yet.

"I am tired being a part-time player," Frank Howard announced as he tested the dressing room table for tensile strength and gameness. "I am tired of playing only 80 games a season."

It was pointed out he had played 123 games last year and 141 the year before, or more than double the number of games Mickey Mantle regularly appears in. But Frank was in no mood to be swayed by facts. "If I am a horse-drawn ballplayer, I want to find out about it," he announced. "I would like to play every day even if I have to do it for a second division team."

Rumor had it that Frank was quitting baseball because his wife wanted somebody around to empty the trash and take down the screens in spring, but Frank sees it as a basic clash of philosophies with the manager. Alston would like Frank to change his stance. He would like him to be standing closer to a curve ball when it comes over the plate and preferably not have his back to it.

Alston, of course, has never consulted the major league pitchers. To a man, they would have contributed a sizable part of their income to the Frank Howard Retirement Fund. They voted Mrs. Frank Howard the Wife-of-the-Year.

You would think that when a man shows such a marked passion for swinging at bouncing curve balls, the pitchers would be more inclined to take up a collection to keep him IN the league. But the catch is that when Frank does get a piece of wood on a breaking pitch, more often than not he hits it straight back at the pitcher.

It is the opinion of more than one seer that Howard is going to hit a ball back through the box some night and where there once was a 200-lb. pitcher standing, there is only going to be a pair of shoes.

Several pitchers have seriously considered retiring themselves as Howard line drives whistled past their ears and even Whitey Ford's instant reaction over the two bagger Howard lined in the World Series was one of relief that the ball went OVER him instead of through him.

Pitchers would be resting a little easier this season if Buzzie Bavasi had panicked when Frank originally announced he was retiring to a life of ease in a box factory. The conversation went something like this:

Frank Howard: "Buzzie, I have decided for the good of everyone concerned that I will retire from baseball."

Bavasi: "Good, Frank. I think you are doing a wise thing. If I were in your shoes, I would do the very same thing."

There was a pause.

Frank: "Well, okay, Buzzie, see you around. Give the guys

my best and if you're ever in Green Bay, look me up in the box works."

Buzzie: "I'll do that, Frank. Give my best to the wife and remember to follow through when you're pasting those boxes up."

Bavasi hung up. Around him, owner Walter O'Malley and veep Fresco Thompson needed smelling salts. They were all for calling out a company of Marines, the White House, the U.N. or the Red Cross and have Howard brought to camp in irons, if necessary.

But Buzzie had seen 27-year-olds "retire" before. Billy Loes used to retire several times a season. "Don't rent Frank's bed out just yet," he advised the owner.

It is a matter of record Bavasi did not even bite the nails off one finger before Howard was back on the phone. "I don't want to come back to baseball," he cautioned, "but I do feel I owe it to you to discuss it."

"Sure, Frank," soothed Buzzie. "Any time. I think I'll have some free time about the All-Star break, if you're in the vicinity."

Frank, as usual, bit for the curve ball. He didn't even send it whistling back around Buzzie's head. As Buzzie hung up the phone, he sent instructions down to the front office.

"Make up Frank Howard's bed and call down to the commissary and tell them to run in another herd of cattle and a pipeline from the dairy. I think I've got the count up to 3-and-2 on Frank Howard and he's looking for a fast ball.

"Who does he think I am—Whitey Ford?"

The next day, Big Frank was back in camp. He had gone down swinging once again. And the box industry lost a great prospect.

Worker of Art

If you want someone to play piano for you, get Horowitz.

Need a doctor? Get Jonas Salk's exchange on the phone. You want to win a golf bet, get Sam Snead for a partner.

If you want a conductor, try Leonard Bernstein. Heifetz will do on the violin. If you want to dance, see if Fred Astaire is busy. Want someone to sing nice, just hand the music to Andy Williams.

But if you want to win a pennant or a World Series, you hand the ball to Sanford Koufax. He gave a performance here Thursday afternoon that should go to Carnegie Hall. Or Westminster Abbey.

A Koufax-pitched game is a work of art, a tribute to the craftsmanship of Man—like the Kohinoor diamond or a Greek statue.

There have been lots of good pitchers. Even a few great ones. There are lots of diamonds, too. Quite a few people paint pictures for calendars. Just owning a curve ball doesn't make you a great pitcher. Just like an easel doesn't get you in the Louvre.

If such a word is possible in what is, after all, just a game, I would have to say Sandy Koufax is a "genius" at pitching. I think he rolled out of bed one morning with his fast ball, just the way Sam Snead did with his golf swing. You can't teach a guy a fast ball. If he's not born with it, he has to learn a knuckle-ball or a spitter—or take up parcheesi.

Sandy Koufax has long fingers, tremendous pride and back muscles that enable him to propel a baseball 60 feet 6 inches as fast or faster than anyone in history. The same physical attributes enable him to break off a curve that drops over the plate like an Indian falling off a horse.

He has now won 142 baseball games in his career. He has pitched four no-hitters. You can't hit his curve ball. You can't even hear his fast ball. He has now struck out 2,138 batters in his career. He struck out 29 of them in the past seven days.

What makes Sandy Koufax great is the same thing that made Walter Johnson great. The team behind him is the ghostliest-scoring team in history. They pile up runs at the rate of one every nine innings. This is a little like making Rembrandt paint on the back of cigar boxes, giving Paderewski a piano with only two octaves, Caruso singing with a high school chorus. With the Babe Ruth Yankees, Sandy Koufax would probably have been the first undefeated pitcher in history.

The manager of the Dodgers, Walter Alston, woke up Thursday morning with a terrible problem: he didn't know whether to go with Drysdale or Koufax. This is the kind of terrible problem every manager in major leagues would like to have. It's like trying to decide whether to date Elizabeth Taylor or Jane Fonda, whether to buy a Cadillac or a Continental or Imperial, whether to take a million dollars in cash or stocks.

You are not exactly handing the world championship to the Minnesota Twins if you go with Don Drysdale. On the other hand, it's fun seeing their lips turn white when they see Sandy Koufax taking his turn in batting practice with the starting lineup.

It's no disgrace to Don Drysdale to say that Drysdale with three days rest is not as good as Koufax with two days rest. Jim Grant, the Minnesota pitcher who won 21 games himself in 1965 and two Series games, cheerfully placed himself, among the also-rans when talking about Koufax. "You," he said, "are talking about the greatest pitcher alive. And maybe dead. I would say the only thing I can do better than Sandy Koufax is sing and dance. If it's pitching you want, I'll wait till he's through."

On reflection, one wonders why Alston ever hesitated. "It was," he said, "one of the toughest decisions I ever had to make."

One imagines Walter in his embarrassment of riches weighing the imponderables—like the curvature of the earth, the mean annual temperature of the Galapagos Islands, the position of Venus and Mars and the gold market.

Don Drysdale is very probably the second-best pitcher in baseball—for one game that you have to win. It's not his fault that Sandy Koufax is the first best. If Alston had started anybody but Koufax, management probably would have demanded a psychiatric examination.

The Dodgers, who were picked to finish seventh in the National League, now have finished first in the world. A castoff outfielder who has played this game in a lot of towns where the trains just whistle when they go through played this series like a guy who owes money. Lou Johnson goes through life like a guy catching a bus. He went through Minnesota like a guy kicking in the front door. Eight hits for 16 bases, two home runs, five runs-batted-in. His home run was all Koufax needed. The only time Minnesota scored off Koufax this series was in the rain.

Ron Fairly, who recovered from a wrist sprain just about the time the team plane took off for Minneapolis, led or tied the regulars in everything but larceny—home runs, hits, runs, runs-batted-in. Wes Parker whom the Twins thought was just a shy kid who was good on foul pop-ups, turned into Rogers Hornsby. "Parker," said Twins manager, Sam Mele, in the understatement of the year, "surprised us." That's nothing. Parker surprised Parker. "I thought those guys couldn't hit," puzzled the Twins' Jim Grant. "I think they been censoring their statistics all year like in war."

Since this is the third straight World Series the American League has lost, the outcry will once again go up that they ought to retitle the league to "Bush."

But the Twins weren't inferior to the Dodgers. They were inferior to Koufax. Who the hell isn't?

All baseball, like Caesar's Gaul, is divided into three parts, the American League, the National League—and Sandy Koufax. It is the view of the hitters that he ought to be declared illegal—like poison gas, the spitball, and firing on lifeboats.

Koufax the King

Sandy Koufax belongs in baseball about the way Albert Schweitzer belongs in a twist joint. After midnight.

You get the feeling when you see him in the monkey suit that someone is going to change the gender of that old bromide and demand, "What's a nice young fellow like you doing in a place like this? Now, get out of those sweat clothes and into medical school."

In a game historically dominated by extroverted young roughnecks from the oil fields or the cotton patches, Sandy comes from a nice Jewish family in Brooklyn. Scholarship and good manners were revered. He has never worn a pair of overalls in his life. He had the kind of childhood where someone probably cried when he got his first haircut.

He is shy, considerate. He prefers his music great, not loud. On plane trips, he plays word games with the press, not Hearts with the boys. There are many intelligent, well-educated boys in baseball today, many of them on the Dodgers, but almost every major league ball player has violence somewhere within him. They are a throwback to a long line of warriors. Sandy, on the other hand, seems a captive of baseball, trapped by his talent, not his instincts.

You never see him in the bars. The Baseball Annies, forlorn, adoring little creatures who jump in elevators with the single boys on road trips and hang around lobbies in their best dresses and perfume and wobbly high heels, look at Sandy longingly as he hurries by after a game, as if they'd like to take him home and chain him there. But Sandy ignores them. His tastes do not run to grown-up autograph hounds. He wants a wife, not a fan. It's going to be difficult to find her now.

The plain truth is Sandy might not even follow baseball if he weren't in it. He is probably the only guy in the league who not only understands what is going on in Vietnam but cares. The team is proud of him and he is popular—but in the special way that a brother who went away to become a lawyer is looked up to by the family in which not everybody could make it.

He is baseball's pampered child, but it has never given him a day's temperament. They never let him ride the leaky buses or play in ball parks so dim you couldn't even play cards. Sandy never spent an hour in the minor leagues. You don't send a Rembrandt around to drug store galleries to languish among all those prints of pooped Indians slumped over dying horses. They wanted Sandy right where they could see him, not out playing in traffic with all those ruffians where he might get hurt.

Anyone who ever watched him pitch could understand why. Only a handful of men in history could put the spin and velocity on a thrown ball that he did or have the wildness. Sandy never threw at hitters. But sometimes it would have been better if he did. Where Sandy was aiming the ball was the safest place to be.

But the Dodgers were as patient with him as a poor family with a relative with lots of money and a bad heart. The only suspense was whether Sandy would care enough for the game. There was always a lurking suspicion that, once he took the bonus money, the attitude was "Baseball, Schmaseball, as long as you got the money." But this was the opinion of the know-it-alls who didn't know Sandy. Sandy had a strong sense of duty and even when the duty lay with the odd little world of baseball, Sandy discharged it.

Gradually, almost imperceptibly, Sandy became a pitcher instead of a refugee from a white collar. He began to pitch victoriously instead of brilliantly. He pitched two no-hit games. In baseball, one can be a freak. Two establishes a trend.

Pitchers are one-purpose human beings. But in Sandy's case, it's ridiculous. He can field a thrown ball like a guy groping for a towel with soap in his eyes. He could run faster on snowshoes. On a team that beats out infield hits, he has trouble beating out outfield hits. He hit one to Frank Robinson in right field in the Coliseum and by the time he turned around to the umpire to say, "What do you do next?," it was a routine out from the rightfielder to the first baseman. They have to drop paper to show him the way from first to third. He got a home run off Warren Spahn one night and they say they had to pull Spahnie down off a hotel ledge later.

They rub Sandy down for hours the day before he pitches. They'd probably get him a butler and a footman if he held out for them. He is the Dodgers' Man With the Golden Arm.

But being a great pitcher does not always add up to being a good one. Despite his glittering career and statistics that glow in the dark, Sandy had never won a BIG game. Sometimes, an invisible gremlin of fear plucks at the sleeves of the best of them when the stakes are high and the hour is late and there are no second chances. The league had long since discarded the canard, "with Koufax, stay close to him and you beat him." But no one was ready to bluster that Sandy would run neck-and-neck with the cool-heads like Hubbell and Ford. With 30,000 people screaming at him to drop the brush, even Rembrandt might come out with a picture of a pooped Indian.

The pressure on Sandy Tuesday was about what it is at 40 fathoms without a snorkel. It was a baseball Battle of the Marne with reporters from all over the league looking up synonyms for the word "choke" and trying to think of ways to shorten "collapse" for headline purposes. It was a night for throwing hysterical curves that bounce, for shooting fast balls over the backstop, for ending up the night kicking the locker and drying your eyes instead of starring on the postgame show.

Sandy Koufax threw 87 pitches. Fifty-seven of them were fast balls and 47 of these were strikes. He threw 30 curves and 20 of them were strikes. The St. Louis Cardinal "attack" up to the 7th inning consisted of one hit batsman and an errored (by Koufax) bunt. With men on second and third and only one out, it was a time to listen closely for the hiss of gas. Koufax reared back and the next two batters just aimed the bat where they thought they heard the ball go by. One of them managed to hit it all the way back to the pitcher's mound. Sandy trapped it as deftly as a guy chasing soap around the bottom of the bathtub but it was so tame, not even he could misplay it. That, it so happens, was the old ball game.

Sandy Koufax stood calmly in the locker room later explaining patiently how it had been a routine night. There was no suggestion that this night he had become a professional pitcher and that the prophets who sneered at him as Little Lord Fauntleroy with a cannon for an arm could now claim "I knew it all the time." And Mrs. Koufax, who lost an architect in the family, could now say she had gained a star. "My son, the world's greatest pitcher," or "My son, the hero."

Phi Bete at Plate

Deron Roger Johnson, who just may be one of the three most valuable commodities in a baseball uniform in this country, is a man who, to paraphrase one poet of the press box, has such great respect for the English language he uses it sparingly.

He also, as it happens, uses it poorly on occasion. He had a high school education, but didn't let it interfere seriously with his pass-catching or home-run hitting. Deron never believed in prying into the affairs of Julius Caesar or any one of a half-a-dozen kings of antiquity. He adhered strictly to the proposition that the Thirty Years War was their own business and he was not one to take sides.

Deron is not a "dese, dem and dose" guy, but the principal

parts of the verb "to be" get a slight kicking around from him now and then. He would split an infinitive if he knew what one was. Up until this year, the only thing he led the league in was silence. He makes Cincinnati's legendary Dummy Hoy seem loquacious by comparison. At least, Dummy used sign language.

Deron's mother was Irish which should have loosened his palate considerably. When an Irishman is quiet, they usually check his pulse or cut off his drinks. But Deron's father was Swedish, raised in the great lonely plattes of Nebraska where there was nobody to talk to but an occasional cow and the people borrowed their conversational customs from the Indians who talked only by smoke.

Another big part of the trouble was that Deron was raised on such a depressed scholastic area of San Diego that he was the only white kid whose mother should have bussed him to colored schools for a better shake in education. His high school football team had a Japanese center, a Mexican-American tackle, and eight colored players—and Deron. Deron reports there were no racial incidents. Nobody looked down on him on account of his color, and, when he caught 18 touchdown passes, no one sneered, "oh, well, you know how these white guys are—they all can run." And no one guessed out loud that his speed came from the fact that polar bears caught all the slow Swedes long ago.

There was no question of college football for Deron. Fifty colleges wanted him but 1,000 professors didn't. He signed with the New York Yankees where Latin wasn't a requirement, but the closest he got to the Yankee outfield was rooming with Mickey Mantle.

Mantle, who was rooming in the St. Moritz which is a place where the Queen of Romania also stopped, might not be presumed to want an untried rookie to share snores with. But the outstanding characteristic of Deron Johnson is that everyone likes him. With the possible exception of left-handed pitchers.

Big, good-looking, so painfully honest he could spot George Washington two answers in a lie detector test, he is 205 pounds of concrete and, if he wanted to say red was black, the chances are the guy on the next stool would quickly say "you're right, Deron. Again."

He led the three minor leagues he played with in home runs and led two in total bases. With an annual 150 hits, he always had an annual 250 to 279 total bases. He dented centerfield walls from Kearny, Nebraska, to his home town, San Diego. He was ticketed to be the Yankees' first baseman except for a bad habit of swinging at pitches that were higher than the strike zone. The fact he knocked some of them higher than the wall didn't impress the Yankees, who, in those days, were always looking for nine Babe Ruths, or at least seven Babe Ruths and two Lou Gehrigs. The fact that they came along about as often as Halley's Comet didn't occur to the Yankees until rather late in the game.

The Cincinnati Reds paid $25,000 for Deron Johnson which was $21,000 more than the Yankees paid for him in the first place. If Cincinnati had won the pennant this year—and one guy they can't blame is Deron Johnson—he might very well have been the league's Most-Valuable-Player.

Many general managers hold to the opinion the key statistic in gauging the worth of a player is the runs-batted-in total. Deron Johnson has 126 to date which puts him 16 up on Willie Mays who has 20 more home runs than Deron Johnson, which means Willie starts with a plus of 20 runs-batted-in right there.

Deron's total to the present of 126 is already seven more than Ken Boyer had all last year in leading the league. And Boyer was a landslide winner of the MVP that year.

Deron's total of 206 total bases to date puts him over the 200 mark as usual. Characteristically, he ascribes part of his success to the fact that he has three fast men usually on base in front of him—Pete Rose, Vada Pinson and Frank Robinson. But Frank Robinson is a basecleaner of note himself and frequently leaves Deron Johnson with nobody to bat in but himself.

In a team which is supposed to have as sharply divided a line as an Alabama wash room, Deron Johnson gets more batting tips from Frank Robinson than Frank would give his kid brother or any other player. If he doesn't win the Most-Valuable-Team-Player, he can count on the most-popular. There are also signs he is breaking out of his slump in vocabulary. The other night he ran through a sign from base-coach Reggie Otero. The press wanted to know why. "Otero was pointing straight up in the air," protested Deron. "I KNOW where the Big Dipper is. I wanted to know where the ball was."

The Reds know where their Big Dipper is, too. On third base, and leading in RBIs. And he'll make more money next year than the guy who won his high school Latin medal—and by 20 or more thousand dollars.

O'Malley's Mahalley

Many years ago, on the eve of war, a brilliantly-uniformed Austrian army paraded through the streets of Vienna. An onlooker came upon an old man weeping on a street corner. "What's the matter, old one?" he wanted to know. "Such a beautiful army!" sobbed the old man. "What a shame to waste it on a war!"

In some respects, I felt the same way the other day as I stood and looked up at the majesty of Walter O'Malley's new $16 million stadium in Chavez Ravine, a gorgeous triumph of high-rise architecture in living Technicolor with levels of ocher, aqua, coral and sky-blue, with umbrellas of concrete escarping a perimeter that looks on the mountains of the San Gabriel.

It will be the Taj Mahal of Sport. A weekly payroll of 242 workers at $24,000 has worked night and day to get it in place. Enough earth was moved to start a new island in the Pacific.

But, like the old Viennese, I get this lump in my throat when I think of spoiling it on, say, the Mets and Kansas City Athletics. It's like putting on a horror movie at La Scala. You get the feeling Walter should cancel the baseball, disband the franchise and schedule in the Ballet Russe or the road company of *The Marriage of Figaro* before it's too late.

The two host managers, Walter Alston of the Dodgers and Bill Rigney of the Angels, were on hand for their first look at the blushing beauty Saturday. Walter's bright blue eyes lingered only briefly on the majesty of the tier on gorgeous tier. After all, that was only the place where people sat. His gaze stopped in the area on ground level between the dugouts.

"Will there be people settin' there?" he wanted to know in some horror. Told there would be, he immediately began speculating on the distraction the movement of white-shirted spectators might cause his infield.

Rig, proud leader of the squad that made more errors than any team in either league last year, is more concerned with the distraction the movement of a baseball causes his team. "What airport is this?" Rig demanded, eyes roaming over the expanse of infield and outfield. "Are those runways or foul lines? Throw a ball wild in this ball park and you have to send the bloodhounds after it."

There will be lively activity on the part of us sweat sock historians on Opening Day, clocking the first hit, the first base-on-balls, the first passed-ball and so on in this palace of the hit-and-run. But I would like to make a few predictions of other firsts that won't show in the box scores.

The game will start at 1:00 p.m. At 1:01 p.m. the first wad of chewing gum will be stuck under a seat.

At 1:01½, the first squirt of tobacco juice will sail out of a corner of the dugout.

At 1:02, the first trickle of beer will roll down the throat of the truckdriver behind third base who will promptly yell at the pitcher "We're wit ya, Don baby!" At 2:30 p.m. the sixth can of beer will flood down this same fellow's throat just as Drysdale is touched up for four hits and he will roar, "Get a pitcher in there, and get that bum outta there, willya fer Lawd sakes!"

At 1:45, the doctor behind home plate will have overcome his awe at the new surroundings and will cup his hands to bellow, "Alston, yer a bum!"

At 1:55, Jim Brosnan will be on P. 70 of Macaulay's "Lays of Ancient Rome," and his batting practice catcher will be asking if he can read it next, when the call will come to relieve Joey Jay.

There are 48 powder rooms, equally divided between men and women, and, by the third inning, 24 of them will have verse on the walls.

If the game is one-sided, the Stadium Club will announce at 2:10 p.m. that a new 5-inning record for the consumption of

Scotch-and-sodas has been set, topping the old Candlestick mark by a single lemon twist.

At 3:00 p.m., Alston will still stick with his starting lineup, but Concessionaire Tom Arthur will have platooned his entire corps of hot dog vendors because the starting lineup was a little wild and kept hitting the customers in the ear with the mustard.

At 3:03, the first serious fight will break out in the press box, not over whether Snider should have gotten a hit or an error over a ball that went through Coleman's legs but whether women should be admitted to the press bar. The New York writers will describe the argument in a sneer as "bush!"

At 3:30, if the Dodgers lose, 20,000 people will get up in a blind rage—stalk out of their plush 22-inch opera-type seats, past the glittering snack bars, out onto the convenient, palm-fronded parking lot and growl, "I'm never coming back!"

At 4:45, O'Malley's beautiful Alley will be given over to the used Kleenex, Coke bottle caps, and lost jackets with children in 'em. The last departing guest will roar "Call that a team, do you, Alston?" O'Malley's Taj Mahal will still be beautiful. But it will finally be a ball-park.

And that's even better.

No Needle, Watson

Next to getting into a fight between husband and wife, the other dumbest thing a man can do is get in one between the tax collector and his prey. I mean, the prudent thing to do is say "Tsk! Tsk!" and go on about your business.

But the adventures of Walter Francis O'Malley in the wilds of Los Angeles have always fascinated me. In their own way, for sheer cliff-hanging melodrama, they make "The Perils of Pauline" or "Batman vs. Godzilla" seem like home movies. The latest one should be titled "The Bowery Boys in City Hall."

Walter F. O'Malley is an improbable, rumpled old party you have to pinch yourself to believe is real. You picture a kind of

200-pound elf smoking a cigar and wearing rimless glasses and you got it. He looks like he believes in leprechauns. Like most Irish, he believes he could charm a hungry puff adder down out of the trees if he wanted to. He goes everywhere trailing a rich aroma of imported Havanas and good whiskey. He is a fond father and husband and keeps the Sacraments.

But he has gone down in history as a kind of reckless pirate with a cash register for a heart and a mind as open as a bank vault. Through no particular fault of his, his name will go into slang as a transitive verb: to "O'Malley" someone means showing them a shell game in which there are no peas under any of the walnuts.

This is kind of unfair. Walter really runs more to Don Quixote or Donald Duck than Commodore Vanderbilt or Barney Baruch.

In the first place, if YOU were able to wheedle 315 acres of downtown real estate and a $16 million loan out of a community, would YOU agree to blow it on a ball team? I mean, does AT&T have to worry whether Frank Howard gets a hit or not? Does Anaconda Copper bite its nails because a lefthander's blood count disappears in one finger? Does U.S. Steel have to call in Ron Perranoski?

Walter came West with about $10 million worth of ballplayers and a license to play them in the big leagues. But part of the community reacted as if he had shown up with a basket of beads and a tab of snake oil.

To be sure, Walter first came into focus wearing a black mask and training two pearl-handled revolvers on the city. When the city first sought out the Dodgers, it hadn't seen those kinds of demands since Black Bart went to that great stagecoach-in-the-sky.

All Walter wanted was 400–600 acres of Chavez Ravine, a pile of hills that had served the city as a political football and goat refuge and not much more. It was tax-free and Walter thought it would be a dandy idea if it remained that way. He said so in his initial memorandum to the then mayor of Los Angeles.

Walter was willing to pay rent—up to $1 a year. He was also willing to turn over Wrigley Field—if he could beat condemnation proceedings in time enough.

The then mayor thought this sounded dandy. After all, Walter didn't ask for Catalina, too. "That's what you do," explained Norrie Poulson later. "You get them in a frame of mind of wanting—like an auto salesman. When you get 'em in the car, you tell them it's going to cost more than they think."

O'Malley was midway in his dreams of his second billion and wondering if perhaps he hadn't been hasty in offering a whole dollar when they might take 98¢ when the city hired a paint manufacturer, Chad McClellan, to explain to Walter there ain't no Santa Claus.

They cut his acreage in half. They told him to put it on the tax rolls just like the rest of us. They told him he could do anything he wanted with the property so long as it was something you could keep score of or eat in the bleachers. He couldn't drill oil, put in rollercoasters, sell it to the Indians or build any buildings higher than you could jump off. He could barely play baseball on it or rent it out occasionally to Jehovah's Witnesses but that's all. They even made him pay $494,000 to clear the squatters off.

He had to get a crash loan from Union Oil, win two elections and a dozen court fights. His critics freely predicted he would build a papier-mâché park which would be swiftly torn down to make way for a roller bearing plant but Walter confounded them with an edifice so imposing it seems a shame to waste it on the Dodgers.

Now, it is 1963 and O'Malley wants to convert his short-term loan into one where everyone can breathe easier—a 20-year document full of fine print in which the $16 million grows to $26 million before it's paid off and the first year alone provides payments of $1,760,000.

Now, there comes on screen another guy in a black hat, a personable young tax assessor who got himself elected by promising not to peek in people's windows to see whether they bought a new divan since last year. Phil Watson took one look at O'Malley's cement and marble palace, whistled admiringly and decided it would be a crime to carry it on the tax rolls at a lousy $20 million. "Why, it's worth $31 million if it's worth a penny!" he cried. "With the Dodgers in it?" demanded O'Malley almost swallowing his cigar.

O'Malley has 315 acres—14 for the stadium, 41 for something

loosely called "youth recreation," 51 in roads and paths, 51 in slopes, and 27 to shore up a city reservoir. He pays 52% corporate tax on income. Out of every $1 admission, he pays 10¢ to the feds, 27½¢ to the visiting team, 5¢ to the league and 4½% on net to the state.

"They are taxing it as if it were Rockefeller Center," moans Walter. "But what would Rockefeller Center be if you could only play jai alai in it?" Getting 315 acres and turning the direction over to Walter Alston is not like getting 315 acres and turning it over to IBM, he complains.

Baseball is more of a gamble than a blue chip. O'Malley has not yet lumbered off in search of a deal with Patagonia. He has not yet announced that unless his tax is stabilized at $360,000 instead of the $750,000 Phil Watson wants, he will shutter his park and sell the livestock to the Mets.

But he does point out the New York Yankees pay only $168,000 in yearly taxes, the San Francisco Giants only $102,000 and that he may not get his loan if the insurance companies feel his taxes are going to double every other year. And you don't get a carry-back in this business if you finish 10th one year and wonder where everybody went.

This is not to suggest, Mr. Watson, that you transfer O'Malley's tab to mine. I have enough trouble with that bucket of shingles and cesspools I support. But O'Mallcy feels this is one time Watson was too quick with the needle.

Hit 'Em Again!

All right, places everybody, it's time for our annual "So You Think You Know Football?" quiz. Remember, one answer and one answer only. Winner gets an all-expense one-way trip to Tijuana. By burro. Runner-up gets a bound copy of a list of places Paul Hornung can't go in any more. Ready?

Q. Now, what do we call a team that has 12 Slovenes, 2 Laplanders, a Sioux Indian, 11 Italians, a French coach and German athletic director, more Poles than the Warsaw Symphony, and hasn't won a game in two months?

A. The "Fighting Irish."

Q. It has been said "Most games are won or lost in the line." Is this true? Explain your answer.

A. Most games are won in the living room of 240-lb. high school prospects. By alumni bearing fur stoles for Mama, blank checks for Dad and keys to the convertible or a year's supply of bananas for Junior.

Q. The statement was also made that, at the University of California, "out of 20,000 students, they ought to be able to get one football team." Comment on that.

A. Anyone that thinks you can get a football team out of students must think you can get a debating team out of a backfield. A football team is not a natural resource in a college, it has to be imported. Fortunately, just as not every student can be a football player, not every football player can be a student. If a team wants a good football team, they should not hang the football coach in effigy, they should hang the dean of admissions in person. Or lower the standards to where the first-string line would have to play in muzzles.

Q. What is a "tight end"?

A. A guy who will be suspended as soon as the coach gets downwind of his breath.

Q. How do you defense a "tight end"?

A. Well, you might try with a sober one.

Q. What is the "tackle eligible" play?

A. Damn complicated.

Q. How does the "stutter play" work?

A. First, you need a quarterback with an impediment in his speech. Then, a tight end might be helpful.

Q. A coach who is semi-literate, recruits in barrooms, puts plaster-of-Paris on arms that have nothing wrong with them and teaches boys to use them like elbow-length brass knuckles, bullies his college president into admitting players that had to be treed or paroled before they could be recruited is said to be what?

A. A character-builder.

Q. What is meant by "dissension on the squad"?

A. The center found out the quarterback is getting a bigger convertible than he is.

Q. What causes most injuries in football?

A. People.

Q. When a player is thrown off the varsity squad for "disciplinary reasons," who usually makes the recommendation?

A. The police. Except, sometimes, it's the girl's father.

Q. If a 130-lb. halfback tries an end run against a Big 10 line, what should the guards do?

A. Excavate him.

Q. How would you handle a "hand-off" play?

A. Get the guy to surgery right away.

Q. When a boy is light but fast, aggressive, practices hard and charges hard at opposing linemen in a game, what can we say he has an abundance of?

A. Concussions. Also, bleeding.

Q. Conversely, when a lineman is big and hard and fails to charge first, but fights the other guy off by hand, what can we say he lacks?

A. I dunno. But I'll tell you what the other guy will lack: teeth.

Q. What do you understand "Desire" to mean?

A. A streetcar in New Orleans.

Q. No, no, in football?

A. Oh, in football, it's a guy who doesn't understand the situation at all. Or a guy who just loves transfusions.

Q. What is the most important thing for a coach to have?

A. A lot of sick relatives and a working knowledge of the school's honored dead, or a list of the terminally ill at Central Receiving Hospital. These are important for halftime exhortations. But, a word of caution: when you beg the players to "Win this one for old Uncle Claude who is in an oxygen tent," it is sometimes wise to skip the details—such as the fact that Uncle Claude is in one because of cirrhosis of the liver or from singeing his eyebrows (and the rest of the rooming house) smoking in bed. Or, if you say cousin Ned is dying, you don't HAVE to add that the warden can save his life a lot quicker than your football team can. Or that Aunt Clara is in surgery all right, but it's for a nose bob. And when you tell them of old Pudge Bottleflinger, of the class of nought-nought, and his deathbed request that the team win one for him, you don't have to say he'd be alive yet if he hadn't chased that nurse down the corridor at the age of 90 and missed the first tackle of his career at the head of the stairs. An onion in the handkerchief is as important in these cases as a passing attack.

Petrified Woody

When Woody Hayes and the Ohio State Buckeyes came into the L. A. Coliseum Saturday to play USC, they were rated No. 4 on all the better polls and there was some thought they should enroll in the NFL, not the Big 10. When they left Harvard was trying to get on their schedule.

USC, which was down in the fine print of the standings along with Catawba, Juniata and the powerhouses of the intra-mural leagues, will probably now pass several teams which have already beaten it. "Football polls," Woody Hayes pointed out solemnly, "are a joke."

So is Woody's attack. As usual, Woody showed up with a team that looked, on size, as if it had been cut out of a herd. But I have seen subway crowds move faster than this bunch. They actually clanked when they walked. They acted as if the ball had a load of bricks in it. You could climb a ladder faster than they could run.

I think USC could have beaten them with the faculty. In fact, coach John McKay did everything but suit up an English Lit class to hold down the score. And when Tom Lupo intercepted a pass and ran it into the end zone, John was eyeing the gal cheerleaders.

The tipoff on Ohio State came when the water boy beat them to the bench—carrying two pails full. He could have had a hod on his back, too, it turned out. These guys couldn't catch a standing bus. Women move faster getting ready to go to a party. You could lay sidewalks faster than they could move the ball.

Watching them, you kept hoping they could do bird imitations.

They acted as if they had a five-year contract to make a touchdown. They put 17 passes in the air. Their players caught three of them and USC caught four of them. Woody Hayes normally doesn't throw 17 passes a season and I can see why. They had this one fullback who could have moved faster in leg irons.

When Ohio State is behind 32–3, as they were Saturday, there is no way they can catch up before Christmas. You could build freeways between touchdowns the way they make them. Yet, when they were behind 22 points in the third quarter and it was obvious they had about as much chance as Landon in 1936, they chose to punt the ball to USC. "We hoped they'd fumble," Woody explained in the locker room later.

When your offense is based on hope of a fumble, I'd have to say you'd better be ready to pass out lollipops to keep morale up. But the Buckeyes never wavered. They just took the ball doggedly and ran it right up the center. I thought for a while there that USC's Larry Sagouspe was going to tell the rest of the team to take ten and he'd handle the play alone. I am sure that even if he did, Woody would run the play right at him anyway. Ohio State thinks it's chicken to run around anyone.

They kept taking the ball and scraping ahead by inches like a roadgrader machine. Then USC would take the ball, rush it quickly into the end zone. Ohio would get the ball back and start the whole painful process all over again. They reminded me of a kid who keeps building a house of cards and, before he gets to the top, a bigger kid comes along and kicks it in. Instead of getting reproachful, the first kid starts it all over again. They acted as if it wasn't a real game but an audition. If so, the answer is, "Don't call us, we'll call you."

Of course, they just might have had a thorn in their paws. If USC had stood still when Ohio charged, a lot of them wouldn't be able to eat corn-on-the-cob till their new dentures fit. But USC has now played Colorado, Oklahoma, Michigan State, Notre Dame, and Ohio State in a row and nobody has had so much as a severe nosebleed. That's a bigger upset than going through Labor Day with only a dented fender or two and they should be No. 1 on all the National Safety Council polls no matter where the AP puts them.

Meanwhile, back at Ohio State, Wayne Woodrow Hayes is going to have to do some reevaluating on the relative importance of brute strength. Unless they start handing out the Grantland Rice award for overturning street-cars, his teams ain't going to win any for a while. Woody never counted a touchdown unless you could trace the scorer's footprints over the bodies of the line-backers. Now, they got a revolutionary system where they run around or away from you. But that's modern civilization for you: Chicken.

Football and Halo

SOUTH BEND, Ind.—This is where it all began, this lovely tree-lined, leaf-strewn, crucifix-bedecked campus where they name the lakes after saints and the buildings after football coaches.

This is where they first won one for the Old Gipper. This is where Pat O'Brien found the juiciest role of an actor's history—a lop-eared, broken-nosed, bald-headed old geezer who was a high school dropout, a tramp athlete, a gambler who knew when to play the ace, a master psychologist who could fill a locker room with tears or with growls, a concert master playing on the emotions of boys and the legitimate aspirations of holy, dedicated men. Upon this Rock, they built this institution.

This is where the cynics say football ceased to be a game and became a business, but they can find proof only in their own hard hearts. Football is a joyous thing on this campus of Our Lady, a little-boy thing, a Norman Rockwell painting of an urchin tugging at the moleskins of a hero-halfback.

This is where the cynics say education comes in hip pads. "What did you learn at school today, John?" "I learned first downs." That kind of thing. Jeer, jeer, for old Notre Dame.

They joke about the statues on campus. Are the hands of the good father outstretched to heaven? Or is he calling for a fair catch? Is that painting a signal for a touchdown? Is Moses holding his right index finger to point out the law of the Lord? Or is he saying, "We're No. 1"?

But scholars have come out of the halls of Our Lady of the Lakes. Boys battered by poverty and parental indifference have succumbed to the evidence of God's handiwork in these gently-rolling meadows of northern Indiana. God is patient. And Notre Dame is patient. Render to Rockne the things that are Rockne's.

The stadium is full every Saturday afternoon. But so is the church every Sunday. There is Standing-Room-Only at Sacred Heart, too. At all the Masses.

The rules are relaxed now. You don't have to sneak down the fire escape. The girls are several miles away and in a cloister of their own. "If you want a car and a girl, go to Ohio State," the office of the president sternly warns. "If you want an education, get it before lights-out."

The ludicrous comes with the sublime. The boy choked with emotion is not showing downright piety at the pep rally when he prays, "Mary, protector of the Just, beat Southern Cal!" But the mind plays back to a stoical Red Sanders, only infrequently religious, similarly saying once of another encounter that is now just a dust-catcher on the sports pages, "Twice is he armed that hath his cause just." Mary has bigger problems than the USC game, the rest of the campus knows.

This is Notre Dame. The football factory with the halo around it, in the minds of some. "How about the football players who stole the transistor radios in Lafayette?" they want to know. Well, these have always been among us, even in the best company, the old padre tells you wisely. There were two on Calvary, if memory serves, he reminds you. Besides, he says, these boys weren't larcenous, they were bibulous. The "spirits of Notre Dame," the wags sneer. Snitching transistors off girls' windows seems like a lark when you're full of beer. It comes out worse than throwing yourself in front of two trains when it comes out on the AP wire.

Rockne started it, and Frank Leahy refined it. Rockne relied on emotions, craft—with the imagination the Celt is supposed to excel in, but in which he was badly bested by this dent-nosed Norwegian. Rockne put the team in gold pants, green jerseys and green backs. Rockne put the team on the road—"Have football, will travel." "The Ramblers," they called them. They led the nation in train trips. Also in polls. They were adored by every immigrant-descended truck driver from coast-to-coast. They made Yale-Harvard look like intramural athletics. It was the school of the poor, and the poor took vicarious thrill in its exploits. There was a bit of the Robin Hood in a coal-miner's son beating the future officers of our armed services, or the affluent sons of riches from the big Eastern universities. There would be time enough to take orders from them later. For now, "Hit 'em again! Harder! Harder!"

Leahy made it a science. The films, the charts, the logarithms of the blackboard, the criss-crossing of recruiting lines across the country. He got so good, there were Saturdays when even Notre Dame couldn't bear to look.

It's the "era of Ara" now. Notre Dame has a new gig going for it in the athletic department. An intense, handsome young Armenian-American they put in the driver's seat and leave the praying to us. Leahy is gone; it's a little unclear whether it was because he got or gave ulcers.

The legend of Gipp in a way is the story of Notre Dame or, how we went from a 62-yard drop kick to a $13 million library.

Gipp, like Rockne, was a high school dropout. Football wasn't his game, pool was. Frail, tubercular, he had an incandescent career that still has elements of mystery and romance, syllables that linger in the ear of Notre Dame to this very day.

He gambled on the gang. He lived in a hotel room so he wouldn't have to play his poker games in the dark. He knew more speakeasies than Al Capone. He quit the university as regularly as the football season ended—or it quit him. He passed exams without ever taking a lecture note.

He was a renegade, an outlaw, but when he got a football under his arm, even Rockne got goose-bumps. It was only when he was dying that he realized he never wanted to leave Notre Dame after all.

It is not known whether he ever said "Win one for the old Gipper," but he did say "Get me a priest." George Gipp did not want to bring a pat hand into heaven. In case someone called it. I like to think Notre Dame got through to him finally. So does Notre Dame.

Dan Is Dandy

Most college football coaches are a gypsy lot of characters who sleep with one ear out for the telephone, their bags packed and the motor running—because they never know at what hour the alumni will show up, hand them a ticket and point to the door.

Conversely, the alumni can't be sure at what point he will use that new Cadillac they gave him to drive out of town to a better job.

What makes Daniel Edward Jessee of Trinity College in Hartford, Conn., unique is that he has been in continuous service at one place longer than any coach active today.

When Dan arrived at Trinity, Herbert Hoover was President, coffee was a nickel, airplanes had two wings and people thought Hitler was funny.

It was 1932 and Dan had just seen a professional baseball career aborted due to a knee injury. An Oregonian, he had been an infielder with the old Seattle Indians, San Francisco Seals and Salt Lake City but his major league career was no threat at all to Babe Ruth. With Cleveland, it was exactly one game long.

It was during the Depression and the bread lines were full of football coaches—as well as doctors and lawyers—when Dan, armed with a Master's Degree from Columbia, applied for the Trinity job.

Trinity College will never be famous for it but it is where I slept through more Latin classes than Julius Caesar but at the time Dan Jessee and I were there, it was a 400-student pastoral school run by an Episcopalian minister and was distinguished for the highest percentage of non-athletes (of which I was one of the most outstanding) in the western world.

They offered Dan Jessee $3,000 a year, the likelihood of an all-time losing streak, and provided that he would have to pick up the towels, conduct classes and, if the endowment investments continued down, he might have to sharpen pencils and wash windows. Dan would have to coach baseball as well as football and take his turn in the squash court making sure all the showers were turned off and they didn't leave anybody in the bottom of the pool.

They never gave athletic scholarships at Trinity but they didn't necessarily bar a student just because his neck happened to be 18 in. thick. Dan could occasionally get a Connecticut Valley roughneck past the admissions gauntlet peopled by profs who could speak ancient Greek better than English, but even to get them he had to arm-wrestle Notre Dame or Michigan State for them or smuggle them out of their mill town homes in the dark.

Recruitment was even more difficult because Trinity played the kind of intersectional schedule where some years they went clear to New London and if they had a game over in New York State, the boys got so excited they couldn't sleep. Long trips were out because profs took the position if a boy had a Saturday class he ought to be in it and not gallivanting around the country in a football suit.

He had a succession of captains who could double for Mickey Rooney. He had more straight A's in the lineup than the English Lit class and so many Phi Beta Kappas in the backfield that they had to elevate Dan to full professor just so he could carry on a conversation with them. He was never "coach" or "sir" on campus. It was always "Dan."

Usually, straight A's are as useless as monocles in a football pileup but Dan's teams, incredibly, won. They knew who Chaucer was but they knew what a slant block was, too. You rarely had to worry about your first string line spending the afternoon in a tavern because it would interfere with tea.

Most people around the country were under the impression Trinity was a girls' school and there were times when Dan, taking a look at the kids out for football, knew why. But no one mistook them for girls when Dan got through teaching them. He regularly lumped the little Ivy League. He gives an annual lesson to Otto Graham at Coast Guard Academy and, if Otto's been paying attention, he may be ready for that Cleveland Browns job at that.

He has beaten Yale seven straight years in baseball. In 31 years, he has won 142 football games, lost 54, tied 6. Lord knows how many towels he's picked up, showers turned off and lectures in first-aid and hygienics he's given, how many phys. ed. classes he's conducted. He worked as hard to harden the skinny kid with the bottle-bottom glasses as he did his strong-side tackles.

He sent a handful of players to the pros. Roger Leclerc of the Bears placekicked the Detroit Lions right out of a chance at the championship this year and Dan is sure no one will ever have to give Roger a lie detector test.

But he has sent even more to places like Westinghouse, General Electric, Du Pont and the Stock Exchange, whose president is an ex-Trinity president. Dan's salary has moved up but he still can't afford a poker game with Bud Wilkinson or Bear Bryant.

Yale, Cornell, Lafayette and Virginia came forward with juicy offers but Dan takes the position: Where were they when he needed them, in the days when there were more people selling apples than in college?

I sat with him at the recent coaches' convention in L.A. as the USC Rose Bowl champions took the stage for an illustrated demonstration of their plays by coach Dave Levy. Dan almost got tears in his eyes as he watched those powerful young men rattle the stage. "Never mind the plays," he murmured. "Give me those players!"

If they did, Otto Graham would have to start playing him with the Cleveland Browns.

Tiptoe to Greatness

The world champion Cleveland Browns come to town today—bringing with them the most awesome human offensive machine in the history of football. Take Babe Ruth, Red Grange, Bob Cousy and Joe Louis together and they don't dominate their sports the way he does his.

He's durable. Tough. Consistent. Explosive. Shrewd. It's impossible to calculate his worth to his team. He's one of the most remarkable athletes of all time.

He's a fine physical specimen. He's still in his early 40s. The waistline can't be an inch over 48. Or maybe 50. He can see fine without glasses—unless, of course, the print is small. He can run the 100 in—oh, say, 25 to 30 seconds. He can do two or three pushups at a time.

He watches his diet—never eats more than two helpings of mashed potatoes and always turns down a third piece of pie. He likes his lasagna hot and his chocolate eclairs cold. His digestion is good. His teeth don't bother him. If they do, he sends them back to the dentist.

He has a smashing career-lifetime total of one touchdown. Up until the time he got his nose broken in a block last year, he hadn't had so much as a nosebleed in five years. He only needs his uniform laundered once a month and that's for sweat stains, not grass stains.

And yet, he has scored more points and won more games than any athlete who ever played the game. He never played a game of varsity football. All he has to do to get in shape is clip his toenails and make sure his shoes are laced.

Give up? Why, Louis Roy Groza, the well-known Hungarian, of course, the son of "Big Spot" Groza, of Martin's Ferry, O., pop., 12,000, number of football players, 9,000. "Big Spot" got his name from the hole in his head where the mule kicked him down in the coal mine one day.

Big Lou has racked up 1,444 points in pro football play, most of them without breaking a bone—in fact, most of them without breaking a sweat. Compared to him, Jim Brown is just another fullback. Lou has seen them come and go in his 19 years with the Browns.

Frank Ryan might be better at calculus but, when it comes to counting points, a reserve safety back named Bobby Franklin figures as importantly in the Browns' attack. You see, he holds the ball for Groza's place-kicks and makes sure the laces are facing the goal posts, not the toes. He may one day go down in history as "Fingers" Franklin.

They haven't missed a point-after-touchdown all year—41 for 41—and they have thrown 14 out of 21 field goal attempts, laces outward, through the uprights. One was for 47 yards. Another was for 49 yards. The rest were "gimme's" for Groza. In fact, the league may be considering conceding him anything under 40 yards to speed up play. Anything that close is within the leather for Lou.

Jim Brown is 37 points ahead of Lou Groza this year. But he had to score 20 touchdowns and tire himself all out to do it. And every time Jim gets 6, Lou gets 1. The easy way. One year, Jim scored 18 touchdowns—and just did tie Lou Groza in team scoring (108 points apiece). Brown probably got shin splints, black eyes, multiple bruises and corns doing it. The only thing Old Folks Groza, the Greatest Toe on Earth, has to be careful of is that the shower is not too hot.

Groza has led the Browns 13 times in 18 years in scoring. No one is even close to him in the history of the game, not even when you take into account that his National Football League totals are only kept since 1950, the year the Browns transferred over from the defunct All-America Conference. Groza had totalled 259 points in four seasons there and has totalled 1,185 in the NFL, well ahead of Bobby Walston's second place total of 881.

Brown will need at least seven seasons of 100-point scoring to catch up and it may be like the donkey trying to catch the carrot tied on a stick in front of his nose because Lou Groza, who will only be 42 next month, has no present intention of retiring. Brown may need all his skill just to maintain his relative position.

When you are born and brought up in Martin's Ferry, O., you have a choice of careers. Wall Street is several hundred miles away. The State Department does not habitually canvass the graduating class—the nearest set of striped pants is clear up in Columbus. But you can get a lamp and a canary and go down in the coal mines (and keep your eyes on the mule at all times). Or you can get a hammer and a set of goggles molten metal won't cut through and go to work in the steel mills.

Or you can learn to kick a football over the telephone wires with a three-step run-up. This is what Lou Groza did. He interrupted a few party-line conversations but he was also the high scorer in the boom lots and he beat Belleaire with a field goal in high school football where field goals are rarer than Statue of Liberty plays.

Lou got a scholarship to Ohio State where he played only freshmen ball before the Army whisked him on a scenic tour of Leyte, Okinawa and Mindoro—tourist-class accommodations and free ammunition. But OSU's head coach, grim, ascetic Paul Brown, was a man to forget a face but never a toe. When he became head man of the newly formed professional Cleveland Browns, one of the first things he did was send a contract to Okinawa where Lou Groza was probably the first football player in history to sign a contract by the light of the teahouse of the August moon.

He kicked field goals by tape the first few years until it was outlawed and now he kicks them by rote. He has "broken in" a succession of successors but they usually take up some other line of work after a few days of watching Groza "teach" them. What they usually learn is that they can never be as good as he is.

Lou puts on his shoulder pads and helmet as a gesture to society but he could score in a top hat and white tie. It's only on kickoffs that some eager young bull rams into his ample midriff. They don't always get up smiling because Lou was an all-league offensive tackle back in the days when Truman was President and, while the 255 pounds contains a lot of goulash and paprika, it contains a lot of muscle, too.

Nonetheless, there was the day when Lou, and the rest of the Cleveland Browns, were serving as dress extras for the Billy Wilder movie, "The Fortune Cookie," and the script called for Jack Lemmon, the star and a 150-pound Harvard jayvee scatback, to crash into Lou on the sidelines and Lou not to notice it. Several people swear they distinctly heard Lou say "Ow!"

The New Breed

You read the recently-concluded pro football draft list and you have to ask yourself whether these guys are drafting for piano movers or football players. I have never seen a spookier collection of athletes in my life. I mean, you get way down into the fine print of 20th-round draft choices before you begin to run into breakaway backs, piston-armed quarterbacks and churning fullbacks. Instead of Galloping Ghosts, these guys drafted ghosts, period.

The Rams' first draft choice was an interior lineman, whatever that is. The interior line must be where guys on the lam from the police hide out. They're as anonymous as telephone operators. The Washington Redskins' first draft choice was a guy who place-kicks sideways, to give you an idea. "We are drafting for need," an NFL owner announced loftily. "This is the age of the super-specialist."

Accordingly, we bring you today a series of interviews with the New Breed, the specialists of pro football, the high draft choices.

First, we bring on camera "Stoop" Nagel, the No. 1 draft choice of two teams and high on everybody's list. He is interviewed by announcer Triple Tongue Tannenbaum.

Triple Tongue: "Stoop, can you sign in and tell us what your specialty is?"

Stoop: "Right, Trip. I'm a place-kick holder. I have held place-kicks for many of the greats in college ball and I set a record for getting the ball on the ground 1,000 times without a miss."

Triple Tongue: "Great, Stoop! Stoop, is there a knack to place-kick holding or can anyone learn it if he's willing to sacrifice?"

Stoop: "Well, Trip. First, you have to have this long finger. I have one of the finest fingers in the game for place-kick holding. What it is, is 18 inches long. It's hard when you're trying to buy gloves, but it lets you hold the ball and keep your head out of the way. With our place-kicker, Cockeye Clancy, this was quite important. The last place-kick holder had very short fingers. He also had very short teeth by the time the season was over."

Trip: "I see. Anything else?"

Stoop: "Well, yes, Trip. You also have to learn to place one knee firmly on the ground. I have found that a good exercise for this is walking around the house on your knees. I have always thought Toulouse Lautrec would have been a great place-kick holder but he was born too soon. Then, you have to guard against injuries."

Trip: "Getting knocked on your arm, eh?"

Stoop: "Well, no, Trip. Water on the knee, actually. Sometimes, in Minnesota, it's snow on the knee."

Trip: "Thank you, Stoop. And now, we bring you 'Sideline' Schwartz, another bonus pick in both the NFL and AFL. Sideline, what's your specialty?"

Sideline: "Well, Triple Tongue, you know that play where

the quarterback throws the ball out of bounds over the sideline to stop the clock late in the game?"

Trip: "Yeh."

Sideline: "Well, I run the pattern on that play. I'm not meant to catch the ball, of course, just stand there and make believe. The quarterback is supposed to throw it into the first row of seats. Then I get down and pound the ground with my fists and make believe I'm unhappy."

Trip: "And for this, two clubs drafted you?"

Sideline: "It would have been three, Trip, but I made one mistake my senior year."

Trip: "And that was?"

Sideline: "I lost my head and caught one."

Trip: "Thank you, Sideline Schwartz. And now we bring you 'Slapper' McCoy. Slapper, will you tell our audience what your specialty is?"

Slapper: "Gladly, Trip. You know that play where we're in a goal line stand and one guy runs up and down the line slapping all the guys on the backside and saying 'O.K., you guys. Get in there and fight!' Well, that guy's me."

Trip: "And then you get in there and fight?"

Slapper: "Oh, no. Then they get someone in there who can make a tackle. This is an age of specialists, Trip, old boy. All I do is slap people, then get out of the game. You've heard of 'Mr. Inside' and 'Mr. Outside'? Well, I'm 'Mr. In-and-Out.'"

Trip: "Thank you, Slapper. Our next guest is 'Suicide' Smith. Suicide, can you tell us what your function is?"

Suicide: "Sure, Trip. You know, when we need a time out and the coach says, 'Somebody go in there and get hurt'? Well, that somebody is me. I get hurt."

Trip: "Oh, I get it. You fall down and grimace and pretend great pain or you spit out a mouthful of phony teeth or break a vial of ketchup alongside your head—like the wrestlers, eh?"

Suicide (horrified): "Oh, I don't pretend, Trip. I really DO get hurt. You see, my teeth are kind of loose anyway. And I bleed easily. You know how some people get a nosebleed at altitudes? Well, I get one fixing the TV antenna. And I don't pretend great pain when I fall down. I feel it."

Trip: "And for this you get $200,000 and a no-cut contract!?"

Suicide: "Oh, definitely. I'm invaluable to a team. One year in the Rose Bowl, I got 14 time outs in the last 39 seconds of play. Took them an hour to play it. They gave me the game ball. Also several transfusions."

Trip: "Well, thank you, Suicide, and the rest of you super stars. Ladies and gentlemen, this has been your weekly program 'Countdown to Fumble,' your pro football stars of the future on parade."

Mighty Mike

If a movie company ever makes the life story of "Mike Garrett—All-American"—which I don't make a longshot by any means—and the casting director trots out the real Mike Garrett, the real director is going to clap his hands to his head and shout, "No! No! No! Not HIM!" I want someone who LOOKS like a football player. See if Ronald Reagan is busy. Don't you ever watch 'Countdown to Kickoff' or the Knute Rockne Story? I WANT Jim Brown and he brings me Joe E."

The only time Mike Garrett looks like an All-American is when he's got the football. After a game, he always looks like the last guy out of a train wreck.

In the first place, he's got a splay-footed walk, like Charlie Chaplin. He gets places on land the same way a duck does. Red Grange might have been "The Galloping Ghost," but Mike Garrett looks more like "The Galloping Goose."

In the second place, he's too short. Some guys miss tackles on him because they can't find him. He's as elusive as a collar button.

In the third place, he comes out of a scrimmage like the loser in a main event at St. Nick's. His nose looks like a baked potato. That's because it has been lovingly massaged by a half-dozen 250-pound linemen. You can't tell where the uniform leaves off and Mike Garrett begins because they're both the color of blood—even when he wears the road-game whites. You go in the locker room and say, "Which one's Garrett?" and the attendant says, "He'll be the one bleeding the most."

Being an All-American in a football game is about as much fun as being the bull in a bullfight. The other guys say, "So you're Mike Garrett, All-American, eh? Well, when we get through with you, you won't be all-city." He eats more dirt than a gopher. Floyd Patterson wouldn't survive the kickoff if he caught the hay-makers Garrett catches. His throat has the fingerprints of every linebacker in the league on it. If he were found murdered, they'd have to try at least 40 guys for it. Every game is like going to the electric chair.

Mike Garrett loves it. And not because it feels so good when it stops but because it feels so good when it starts.

There's no explaining it. Some people like to clean chimneys. Some people like to ride sharks, hunt rattlesnakes, rassle alligators. Mike Garrett likes to run through elbows, knees, cleats, fists and helmets. I think for kicks he goes out and butts rocks. They do everything in pileups but bite him. They couldn't stop him if they ate him.

A national magazine nominated him for defensive back. That's a little like nominating Albert Schweitzer as one of the top ten ballroom dancers of all time. Somebody missed the point. Mike Garrett is good on defense, too. But nobody kept Babe Ruth on the club for his glove. The Dodgers don't pay Sandy Koufax 75 grand a year to bunt. And whatever Mike Garrett does on the playing field, he should do with a football, not a tackle.

He's the greatest running back the game has seen since Hugh McElhenny. But where Hugh was tall, long-legged and had blinding speed, Mike's legs are just long enough to keep his wallet from scraping. He's not even the fastest runner on his own team. Rod Sherman is a step or so faster. Of course, Garrett is never in any danger of being run over at an elephant walk, and if he ever gets two steps ahead of you, your only chance of catching him is a rope. Or a rifle.

But what makes Mike Garrett the greatest is what football coaches, who have a language of their own like Casey Stengel, call "desire." Now, "desire" to some people may be a street car in New Orleans, or what you feel when Brigitte Bardot walks in the room, but with Mike Garrett, it translates out to "guts," willingness to suffer for his art, contempt for pain. Lots of people can stand the sight of blood as long as it is someone else's. Mike leads the conference in nosebleeds as well as neck-twists.

But he's as indestructible as a bride's first set of biscuits. The body doesn't look as if it was born, it was chiseled. He's as easy to tackle as a safe falling out of a second-story window.

The Trojans want him to get the Heisman Trophy. The other teams would rather hit him with it. I will say this: If he doesn't get it, the guy who does better not show it to anyone who saw Mike Garrett play. Or anyone who felt him play. They might put their cigar ashes in it. Or let the dog drink out of it. Because the only way anyone else should get Mike Garrett's Heisman Trophy is in a pawn shop.

Love Him, Hated Her

It was Jack Teele, of the Rams, on the phone. "How," he asked, "would you like to come over and see some movies?"

"Oh, boy!" I said. " 'Tom Jones?' Peter Sellers? Adults Only?"

"No," he said reluctantly, "not exactly."

"Wait a minute!" I said. "Don't tell me! Doris Day with fudge on her nose? Frank Sinatra pulling a cannon across Spain? I know! A Walt Disney movie called 'Some Day My Prince Will Come!' "

"Nope," said Jack.

"Well, what?" I got sharp with him. " 'Girl of the Limberlost,' for heaven's sake?"

"I'll give you a hint," he said. "It's a horror picture."

"Ah!" I said. "Love THOSE. 'Frankenstein Meets Godzilla,' eh?"

"No," he said, " 'The Rams Meet the Cleveland Browns.' "

There was a pause.

"Now," he said. "I have another conundrum for you: who is the world's greatest movie critic and why is it Harland Svare?"

I gave up and went to the Rams office with him. Sure enough, there was coach Harland Svare and his staff in shirtsleeves with scratch paper in a darkened room. A Cinemascope image flickered on screen.

"Some critic," I whispered to Jack. "Bosley Crowther would at least wear a tie—even to an Italian film."

"Just wait," whispered Jack. "You think 'The New Yorker' critic is tough on performers? Wait till George Jean Svare gets going."

On screen, two guys bumped into each other. One of them got a nosebleed.

"That's the way to hit!" roared Svare. "Run that again!" He turned to me: "That's what we call a 'Cross 29—Give,'" he explained needlessly. I tried to look interested.

"Do you prefer The Method in your acting or are you a John Wayne Man?" I asked. Harland ignored me. "We grade as we go along," he explained. "We're using a new grading system. It used to be the 0, 1, 2, 3 system. It didn't give us the full story."

"I know," I murmured. "They had the same trouble with the '4-star,' '3-star' system." Harland looked at me funny.

"Anyway," he said, "now we use the 'Good play,' 'Bad play,' 'Average play,' 'Hustle' or 'Loaf' scoring system. Lookit, here. Here's Roosevelt Grier vs. the 'Skins—Washington. Rosie had five bad plays. Rosie kind of stunk up the joint in that game."

I demurred. "What you must say, Harland," I cautioned him, "is 'Miscast as a tackle.' Or you might say, 'This Roosevelt was an Unhappy Warrior.' That's the way a critic has to handle it. Or, you might say, 'Loved Them, Hated Him.' It's a question of delicacy, don't you see? You have, after all, your box office to consider. You might leave it ambiguous and say 'R. Grier, a promising newcomer at left tackle, is a sleeper.'"

Harland paid no attention. "On the other hand," he said, "look here. In the Cleveland game and the Green Bay game, Rosie played tremendously. He knocked the blank out of everybody."

I clucked disapprovingly. "He 'lighted the screen' is what you must say," I warned him. "Or he was 'luminous.' You could even say 'As left tackle, R. Grier gave a moving performance which brought tears to the eyes of the audience.'"

"It was the 'Skins' game where he brought tears to our eyes," corrected Svare. "By not giving a moving performance. He didn't move an inch all day. It was a terrible bore."

"There!" I told him triumphantly. "You see! There's your mistake right there! A critic must always give the producers an out. Instead of saying, 'A terrible bore,' the compassionate critic should say 'A colossal bore.' Then the company can take out ads and leave the last word out and say 'Colossal!—Time Mag.' The way you do it, Dan Reeves would have to advertise 'Terrible!—Coach Svare.' Get it?"

On the screen, Harland's quarterback was being thrown on the seat of his pants. "Can't we get a block?" he complained.

I sighed. "Harland," I admitted, "you're incorrigible. The least you can say is 'Our blocking is unbelievable.' The ad man can then say, 'See for yourself! The film they're calling "Unbelievable!"' After all, even in Sinarta's cannon film, some guys had the decency to say 'Audiences will be glad when it's over.' That enabled the ads to say 'Audiences will be glad . . . The Times.'"

"Teele," Svare said evenly, "will you get this George Bernard Shaw out of here?"

Payoff for Paul

Paul Brown, the unfrocked genius of pro football, has left the game on the end of a toe and there isn't a wet eye in the house.

A man of glacial contempt, spare and fussy, he treated his players as if he had bought them at auction with a ring in their noses and was trying not to notice they smelled bad.

His position was they were just a lot of, so to speak, tackling dummies. He turned them loose to play football like a mother putting her kid on a bus with a note pinned on him. He didn't trust them to pass the salt on their own. You had the feeling he wanted a whip and a revolver with blanks more than a blackboard.

When they came into camp, he greeted them with a three-hour lecture on the evils of liquor, women and gambling on the (sometimes-sound) theory that under each of those shoulder pads and face guards lurked a practicing sybarite.

His icy disdain was such that he experimented with the idea of putting radio receivers in their helmets so they wouldn't have to bother thinking at all. Yet he gave each candidate each year a 200-question IQ test and they had to pass this before they could pass a football. Most coaches wouldn't care if a boy had to take his shoes off to count. If he could make touchdowns they'd get someone to count them for him. Legend has it one guard was cut one year because, as he explained it, "I could tackle all right, but I didn't know the answer to the question 'If John got three apples for 10 cents, how much would three dozen cost?'"

Brown's notion was that anybody who couldn't sell apples couldn't play guard.

He even gave aptitude tests and if they showed you were more suited as a plumber, Paul suggested you become one—which earned him some press accolades as football's version of the plumber's helper.

Even his better players were treated as if they were campaigning for village idiot. George Ratterman tells in his book of the time the fans began chanting, "We want Ratterman" and Brown summoned him. "Ratterman," he said, "your fans are calling for you. So why don't you go up and sit with them for a while instead of on the bench?"

Otto Graham, one of the five best quarterbacks who ever lived—and maybe all five of them—was never given a vote of confidence to call a single play.

But Brown was all heart. When Otto got his face ripped open, Paul didn't put him in the game till it had been sewed back together again.

He beat every league he was ever in. He was coaxed into pro football by an offer that could only be topped if they threw in Lake Erie. They named the team after him. They might have named a country after him if he held out. Other squads might be named after bears or birds, but Brown's team was named for Brown and he took pains to see that no one disgraced the fine old family crest—a cake of ice rampant on a field of sneers.

When a young New York advertising type, Art Modell, bought the club and wanted to put it on the old New York Central and see if it got off at Madison Ave., Brown treated him as if he were just another football player. He waived the IQ test but told him he'd call him if he needed him, but not to wait by the phone.

For three million bucks, Art wanted something more than a seat on the 50-yard line. After talking to the players and watching them look at Brown as if they hoped he'd walk into a scrimmage by mistake some night, he decided that, while the team morals were good, its morale was not. He fired Brown. The team was too busy cheering to cry.

They haven't changed the name of the team yet, and there is some fear that when they do, the "Cleveland Playboys" will be the most appropriate substitution. But what bothers me is that Paul could have averted walking this plank if he had applied a few simple approaches out of Dale Carnegie. To illustrate, let's listen in on an imaginary dialogue between the NEW Paul Brown and his players. First, Otto Gonow, quarterback, in a crucial game:

Brown: "I think we better try that 4X counterplay here."

Otto (yawning): "Are you crazy? Think I want to block that Karras? I got a hangover. Anyway, that's a terrible play."

Brown (hastily): "That's what I mean. It's a terrible play. I just wanted to see if you were paying attention. What should we call?"

Otto: "A punt."

Brown: "On first down?! On their 20?!"

Otto (threatening): "Want me to call Art?"

Brown: "No, no. On reflection, that's a perfectly marvelous call. One thing, they won't be expecting it. That's for sure. Why don't you come in on the bench, have a Martini and relax?"

Otto: "Not now, Coach. Call time out. I gotta go call and get a date for tonight."

Or, Brown approaches his star tackle, Apeneck McGonigle, on the eve of a game.

Brown: "Hi, Ape, heh, heh, heh. How's it, old buddy? Plenty of sleep tonight? Be in shape tomorrow?"

Apeneck: "Oh, get off it, Paul. We got an all-night poker game. We're having a few boys from Chi—Frank the Enforcer, Sleep-Out Louie, Machine Gun McLurn, Frankie Carbo, King Farouk."

Brown (sighing): "Well, that's better than drinking all night."

Apeneck: "Oh, yeah, we won't have more than a quart apiece.

The game's over at my place, The After Hours. In the Anything Goes Room, if we don't get raided again."

Brown: "Well, anyway, no girls for a change, eh?"

Apeneck: "On my honor, coach, not until the Follies closes. I swear it. And that's not till 2 a.m."

Brown: "I want you to come early. I'm experimenting with some radio sets for you guys."

Apeneck (threatening): "Wait a minute, Paul, you know what Art said—no more robot football . . ."

Brown (shrieking): "No, no, this has nothing to do with football. I'm going to pipe in the race results and a little Bossa Nova. And we're having the halftime catered. Do you like your caviar chilled?"

Apeneck: "Anyway you want it is O.K. with me, Paulsy. You're the best little coachy-woachy in the world. You get my vote and, by the way, Art says we're only going to vote on the coach every other month from now on, you're doing such a swell job."

'Bama in Balkans

So Alabama is the "National Champion," is it? Hah!

"National" champion of what? The Confederacy?

This team hasn't poked its head above the Mason-Dixon line since Appomattox. They've almost NEVER played a Big Ten team. One measly game with Wisconsin back in 1928 is all I can find. They lost.

This team wins the Front-of-the-Bus championship every year —largely with Pennsylvania quarterbacks. How can you win a "national" championship playing in a closet? How can you get to be "No. 1" if you don't play anybody but your kinfolks? How do you know whether these guys are kicking over baby-carriages or slaying dragons?

They remind me of the guy who rolls the dice in a hat—HIS hat. He glances at them and says, "You lose." "Let me see," you say. "Never mind," he tells you. "It's a 7. I made a 7."

I'd like to see Alabama roll its 7 right out on the carpet where everyone can see—say, against Ohio State in Columbus. Or Michigan in Ann Arbor. Or, Notre Dame—anywhere.

"We played the hardest schedule, we're No. 1," their coach, Bear Bryant, stubbornly insisted even BEFORE Notre Dame got beheaded by USC. Maybe so. But how do you prove it by Georgia, Tulane, Vanderbilt, North Carolina St., Tennessee, Florida, Mississippi St., Georgia Tech and Auburn? THEY didn't play anybody you couldn't invite to the Cotillion either.

It's like dancing with your sister, playing cards with your mother, writing yourself a letter. It's like a pillow fight with your fraternity brothers. It won't help you a damn bit when you get down on the docks. It's not a real conference; it is, so to speak, a Gentlemen's Agreement. They don't want any you-know-what in there cluttering up the color scheme.

They let several thousand crack football players go over the wall every year to the Big Ten, Little Three, and assorted independents. These guys are Americans but not Alabamans, if you get what I mean. Alabama prefers to root for Pennsylvanians and other assorted mercenaries.

I would feel better about Alabama's claim if it found it in its heart to either play—or play against—some of these boys who have to go a thousand miles to get a football suit. Alabama competes in a league of its own, by its own choosing. Let it get a "national" championship of its own. The flag should be all white, the red and blue removed. Also the stars.

I don't, for one minute, imply the football isn't ferocious down there. I saw it two years ago, and I'm shuddering yet. But a Balkan war is ferocious, too. It doesn't mean Bulgaria could slaughter England, just because it obliterates Mesopotamia. As my grandmother used to say, "To fly with the eagles, you got to grow wings." How do we know that's not a duck fight down there?

'Bama's got a coach, Bear Bryant, a rumpled character, tree-tall, who looks as if he just got in town off the last freight. As Frank Howard (the coach, not the Munster) once quipped, "Bryant is the only coach who goes around the country toting his own president." Another associate, now with the networks, once noted, "'Bama's practices are Russian roulette with a football."

One result is, football recruiters in the South don't go out looking for Robert E. Lee types any more. "They go out and hunt till they find a boy kicking a sleeping dog," an Atlanta newsman once confided bitterly to me. "Him, they take."

Another result is, Bear Bryant wins "national" championships at the expense of traditional rivalries. 'Bama knocked Georgia Tech off its schedule by knocking the teeth off one of its half-backs who was just standing there watching a fair catch being made at the time. When they had swept up the teeth, 'Bama was in the Sugar Bowl and the halfback was in the hospital.

One "good" thing may come of this—if the adjective is not ironic. 'Bama may find the kids next door won't play with it any more. Their parents are sick of the orthodonture bills. THEN, it may have to venture up in the snow country where the field is white but the players not necessarily, to meet some tooth-loosen-ers its own size.

You can't be "Numero Uno" in the bullring slaughtering cows. They have to be certified bulls and they have to fight back. When 'Bama beats these, THEN we'll give them the ears and throw flowers in the ring. Until then, don't make me laugh.

Last of the Fancy

The world of boxing, which can ill afford it, lost a staunch friend over the weekend.

A. J. Liebling, the writer, was a contributor to highbrow magazines, a master of lace-cuff clothes, a composer of consider-able hyperacidity when dealing with the American press, which he used to criticize with skill and vigor.

Editors shuddered when he turned his brilliant pen on them. But with fighters and fighting, he was as gentle and caressing as a parent with a backward child.

He found in this cruel sport a sad sweetness, or vice versa, and a oneness with history. A beaten fighter, standing blooded, welted, jeered at, semiconscious but courageous was, to him, proof that human majesty had not died out with witless kings or bloodless aristocracy, but survived in the gray-thatched dignity of an Archie Moore toppling before a young brawler from Brockton like a great redwood sawn in two, or in the dazzling rhythmics of a Sugar Ray Robinson laughing at time and touching a match to both ends of the candle and then drowning its light in his own incandescence.

Joe Liebling loved the prize ring. He could beguile a quarter of a magazine out of an editor pressed for space, for an otherwise-meaningless encounter between two welterweight trial horses by the very magic of his description of it. A great toad of a man who would have been cast as a sinister spy in a melodrama, he moved through the fight scene like a benign, neckless snowman with rimless glasses, a felt hat on even when he didn't wear a coat. Like all great reporters, he listened a great deal and saved his speaking for his typewriter.

He dubbed his book on boxing, "The Sweet Science." His literary mentor was Pierce Egan, a nineteenth century English author and chronicler of the manly art in the days when it was illegal and thus enormously popular. And Liebling sometimes mystified pugilists and pugilism with allusions to "milling coves, traulls toss," and the other nomenclatures of old England where spectators were referred to as the "fancy" and a knockdown was known as a "floorer."

Joe treated a fight, even the least, as Toynbee might the Thirty Years War. He defended the sports as an intellectual and by his silence, condoned even its grisly aspect, its high mortality rate and even higher stockpile of live debris. Friends took this to mean Joe believed tacitly that there are many ways to die ignobly but that in the ring defending your pride was not one of them. If this was a curious defection in a lifetime of defending human rights, Joe Liebling saw no contradiction in it. Sonny Liston's prison record was of no moment to him, only his ring record.

His love of The Game shines through every adjective. He liked nothing better than to wander down to the Garden on a rainy New York night, pay for a seat and sit among sandpaper-throated rooters who, in his mind's eye, turned from a pack of Broadway losers into a bona-fide throng of the fancy sitting on an English hillside in 1814, keeping a sharp eye out for the constabulary.

He hung around a pub called "The Neutral Corner" on Eighth Avenue but saw it as Twentieth Century Castle's tavern where at any moment the door might fly open and Pierce Egan himself, escorted by his "faction," might drop elegantly in.

Yet he could spot and report with great solemnity the presence of the sign in the gym "WASH YOUR CLOTHES—BY ORDER OF THE ATHLETIC COMMISSION."

He could record uncritically the fact that the heavyweight contender, Hurricane Jackson, had acquired three managers and such a hazy grasp of arithmetic that each of the managers got exactly 33⅓% of his purses. He stood in the rain outside the Garden the night Jackson, a melancholy creature with dark recesses in the mind either put there congenitally or by gloved fists, got knocked out by the Cuban, Nino Valdes, and spent the rest of the night mournfully jogging around the block outside the arena in the rain ignoring the entreaties of girls and other friends who wanted him to break off this senseless centrifuge and join them on some other more expensive merry-go-round in the city.

He could call the Englishman Don Cockell "a fat man with a gift for public suffering." He could decry the televising of boxing, not because of what it could do to the sport, but what it could do to the Fancy. "Watching a fight on television has always seemed to me a poor substitute for being there. For one thing, you can't tell the fighters what to do. When I watch a fight I like to study one boxer's problem, solve it, and then communicate my decision vocally . . . for example, the pre-television Joe Louis. 'Let him have it, Joe' I would yell whenever I saw him fight, and sooner or later he would let the other fellow have it."

Who comes to speak for boxing now that Joe Liebling has left it? The mute, the self-serving, the opportunist, the calculating. Joe Liebling embraced boxing for reasons of the heart, not the head. And there may be a neutral corner of Paradise today filled with a rumpled man in a felt hat listening eagerly to Pierce Egan explaining in detail the "floorer" Tom Cribb landed on the Negro Molyneaux in 1811 or letting Doc Kearns explain all over again how "I" won the championship from Willard in 1919.

The Good Old Days

Well, I see where boxing's long-playing record, that master of the diplomatic quote, that tower of modesty, Cassius Clay, has announced he could knock out Jack Dempsey in two rounds. That figures. Dempsey is 69 years old. Jack Johnson probably wouldn't last that long. Johnson is dead.

Archie Moore went four rounds with the Larruping Larynx. But Arch couldn't have been a day over 55 at the time. I'd make old Mickey Mouth 3–1 to put Albert Schweitzer away early, too. And he'd be even money against any ranked hemophiliac.

It's bootless to compare fighters of one age with another—athletically, at any rate. But it's perfectly possible to yearn for the good old days when, as happened the other day, James Joseph Tunney and William Harrison Dempsey passed through our town.

You were reminded again that Tunney, when he was champion, read Shakespeare. Liston couldn't handle McGuffey's First Reader. In fact, if you can believe the Denver police, he has trouble with speedometers.

Dempsey was a hobo. But he never got caught rolling drunks in St. Louis or chasing strange ladies through the park in Philadelphia after nidnight. He went to jails for a night's rest, not a 5–10 sentence. Tunney was never modest. But he never tried to form his own country or even his own camel corps.

These guys had long counts, and slippery rings, and $2 million gates. But you never needed X-rays to see if the bout was on the up-and-up. Dempsey didn't quit in his corner. They had to drag him off Tunney when the final bell rang. He couldn't see too well, his legs ached. So did his head. If Tunney stopped breathing Dempsey wouldn't have been able to find him. But he fought till somebody held him.

Tunney didn't bring all the natal skills in the world to the ring. Tunney made Tunney a fighter, not nature. He engineered a prizefight the way Ben Hogan engineered a round of golf. He didn't go out there and swing wildly. He couldn't. He was a guerrilla fighter against an army. He had to take every advantage of terrain and surprise.

And he lost only one fight in his life. Harry Greb cut him up so bad, he swallowed more blood than Dracula—some doctors estimated two quarts. He looked as if he had just lost a razor fight, not a fist fight. They almost needed a sewing machine to put his face back together. But he never hit the deck in 15 rounds. And he fought Harry Greb four times after that and never even got a nose bleed. He outpointed him so cleverly that Greb, exasperated, even missed him once with spit.

It has been 37 years since the great Dempsey-Tunney fight. They still meet occasionally, as they did the other day, a couple of toothless old lions remembering the hot sun of their youth—the bright glow of the ring lights, the clatter of the ringside typewriters, the hysterical babble of the radio announcer.

The fight game has been in a slowly gathering eclipse ever since, but they have a semi-vested interest in seeing it doesn't dim out all together, vilified, abused, and scarred with history's summation as a useless, barbaric, if incandescent, interval in the story of man. No man likes to see the industry that gave him his start equated in time with slave-trading, narcotics-peddling or witch-burning.

"There is a place for boxing," Tunney insisted at an airport interview the other day. "It's not the sport that's lacking, it's the sportsmen. The rematch controversy is foreign to the way we did business. In those days, you couldn't expect to get a licking and then get another chance without licking someone else."

Gene never was a dese-dem-and-dose guy even in boot camp, and the words seem to get longer as he gets older. He spoke in a cultured semi-whisper—"A legacy of my second fight with Dempsey, the left hook to the Adam's apple," he explains softly. "It has raised hell with my singing career"—and he is on the board of so many corporations he tends to like to talk like an annual report.

He is in California to aid a son running for Congress. John V. Tunney, an ex-Ted Kennedy roommate, a Yaley, Air Force captain, is, you might say, a credit to boxing. So, it happens, is his father. The politics are a little more vague. "I have been a Democrat," Tunney admits bewilderedly, "off and on."

Tunney has not kept too abreast of the developments in

boxing, of late, probably because they don't appear in the *Saturday Review of Literature* or *Standard & Poor's*. When he gets a night out on the town, he goes to the opera. "I have been a Metropolitan Opera club member since 1927," he murmurs, "an associate member."

"I met Caruso once in a barbershop," Dempsey observed brightly. "He was a nice fella." Tunney nodded. "I should have liked to have made his acquaintance," he acknowledged regretfully.

As it was, he made do with George Bernard Shaw, William Lyon Phelps, Hemingway and H. G. Wells—and Dempsey.

Like the nation, both Dempsey and Tunney think boxing needs a czar before it finds it needs a keeper—or a curator. The way it's going, 20 years hence the only gloves and trunks in the world may be in glass cases.

But both are baffled by the Liston-Clay proceedings. "The last fight was, er, ah, um, curious," opines Tunney. "Rather, say, even, mysterious. I shall be interested to see what, er, ah, um—'arrangements' they have made for the forthcoming one. Very intriguing. Rather like those Saturday afternoon serials."

Gene is not likely to see the Boston fight unless they make it into an opera. Meanwhile, he thinks the Federal authority, the Department of Health, Welfare and Education, is the logical one for boxing. Personally, I know some who would lean more to the Department of Sanitation—or the Bureau of Wildlife.

Dracula of Sport?

Will the defendant please rise and face the court? Professional boxing, you are charged with being an accessory before the fact of murder. Do you have anything to say for yourself?

A. You bet I do! You can't do this to me! It's a bum rap. What have I done?

Q. Well, there are three counts outstanding: People vs. Boxing in the case of Benny (Kid) Paret, a clear case of homicide in the third degree, aided and abetted by you. People vs. Boxing in the case of Alejandro Lavorante, a former member of the human race, exiled by you. And People vs. Boxing in the case of the late Davey Moore. You're not a sport, you're a Dracula.

A. Wait a minute! Who comes to accuse me, just ask yourself that. A lot of politicians looking for a headline, that's who. A couple of emotional slobs of sportswriters. A little old lady from Pasadena who faints at the sight of a guy getting hit by a ping pong ball. What kind of evidence is that?

Q. (softly). Would you care to have me call Mrs. Benny Paret? Mr. and Mrs. Lavorante? The five fatherless Moore children?

A. (hastily). Never mind.

Q. Would you prefer the ghost of Ernie Schaaf? The substance of any one of dozens of blind or half-blind persons who have suffered crippling injury at your hands? If you want us to turn this courtroom into a base hospital we can do it. You will have to submit transportation money for most of these people, though. They are broke. Most of them have only their white canes.

A. I tell you I'm just a victim of a lot of lousy, stinking coincidences.

Q. Yes, I know. About 10 coincidences a year. Tell me, what do you do about these coincidences? After you bury them, that is.

A. (desperately). We have done everything possible. We have brain wave machines, Pulmotors, doctors at ringside, stretchers, ambulances.

Q. (quizzically). Caskets? Pallbearers? You make ringside sound like a prop shop for Shock Theater.

A. Listen. You guys are all alike. Squeamish. I bet you never had a fight in your life. What can you know about it unless you're a fighter yourself?

Q. You don't have to be a chicken to know when an egg's rotten. You don't have to be a fighter to count the dead.

A. Why single out boxing? What about auto racing? Football? Do you know there were eight people killed in golf last year?

Q. How many brain-wave machines have you seen around a locker room? Do you put a collodion in a golf bag? Do you know that there are 22 men at a time in a football game and, on a given Friday night or Saturday afternoon in season, there are more young men playing football at one city than there will be boxing professionally in a whole year in the country? Boxing deaths per capita, that is for the number of participants, are far out of proportion to any contest short of a world war. There aren't 100 top-flight fighters in the world today and two of them have been killed in a year and a third might better have died.

A. But what do the fighters themselves say? Why don't you ask the fighters, not the governor?

Q. I heard what poor little Davey said: "Don't worry about it, fellows. Everything is going to be all right." He was dying at the time. A Puerto Rican fighter, dying, once told my friend, Doc Greene, the writer, the only guy he could recognize in a Chicago room full of doctors and interns, "Dauk, quiero volverme a mi casa." ("Doc, I want to go home.") Would you like these entered into the record?

A. How else can a boy from an underprivileged background get into the big money?

Q. What big money? Beau Jack grossed $1,578,069 for 21 fights in the Garden and he was shining shoes in a Georgia locker room two years later. Ezzard Charles grossed $2,378,078 for title defenses alone from which his take-home pay was $778,607, but he has announced he is broke. Joe Louis earned $4,626,721.69 in his ring career and if the government didn't suspend his tax interest he wouldn't even have the 69 cents. Most big boxers are just complicated paupers.

A. But boxing can help President Kennedy's Fitness Program.

Q. Sitting in a seat and yelling "Kill 'im!" helps fitness? You have now killed in one year two of the most physically fit specimens it has ever been my pleasure to look at in Paret and Davey. Somehow I don't think this is what the President has in mind. Yours is the kingdom of the blind, the maimed, the dead. Not the fit. The live half of boxing is pot-bellied, cigar-smoking, card-playing and whiskey-drinking. You got the thing all turned around.

A. (resentfully). You should be praying for Moore like I'm doing, not looking for a cheap headline.

Q. You should be praying for the numberless Davey Moores who will be coming along. And the headlines aren't cheap for the Moore family.

A. I tell you it wasn't my fault. It was the ropes done it.

Q. I tell you it was boxing done it. Again.

Brown Bombee

The trouble with Floyd Patterson as champion of human dignity and the American Dream is that he keeps coming home on his shield.

Send him out for the Holy Grail and he comes home with an empty Coke bottle. Put him in charge of a ship in a storm and he runs it aground. If he was a bloodhound you put on the track of an escaped convict, he'd lead you straight to the warden. And bite him. He's the kind of guy who goes through life spilling soup on the boss' wife. He saves his strikeouts for the ninth inning with the bases loaded. He only fumbles in his own end zone. If he tried to hypnotize you, he'd be the one to fall asleep.

He's gone from comparison to Joe Louis to Jerry Lewis in four easy steps. From the Brown Bomber to the Brown Bombee. The Brown Thud. If they did his life story, they'd cast Buster Keaton. Floyd's been floored so often, ringsiders can only recognize him by the top of his head or the soles of his feet. His opponent refers to him as "The Rabbit" and there are those who think he's overestimating him.

Patterson is one of the best gym fighters you will ever see. His punching bag hasn't laid a glove on him in a thousand rounds of boxing. He is a heavy favorite over his shadow, and if there was a heavyweight championship rope skip, he'd retire undefeated. But he's not a fighter, he's a situation comedy. Don Quixote in six-ounce gloves.

He's a lovely man with all the right instincts—except when you throw a right hand at him. If they collected his pre-fights speeches in one volume, he'd make Albert Schweitzer look self-centered. He's shy but articulate, believes in all the verities, Motherhood, the Flag, the Ten Commandments, the Salvation Army, Apple Pie and Doris Day movies. He's a capitalist, a Catholic, and could probably run for President tomorrow and win, as long as it didn't entail a fist fight. He believes in everything Joe Kennedy does.

The guy he's fighting, the Arabian Knight, comes on as the

heavy in the piece. Cassius Marcellus Clay, whose family has been American for several generations, but who apparently got shish-ka-bab poisoning and the next thing you knew he was tour director for a camel caravan, hasn't even got a good word to say for hotdogs any more, or cheese on pie. I think he's trying to lead his people back to the Garden of Eden. By way of the Garden of Madison Square. He's bucking a trend, of course, but then, he never was too good at geography. I mean, Louisville can't be THAT bad. Personally, if I wanted to go back to the burning sands, Palm Springs would be more my idea than Port Said, but Cassius is headstrong. If he has a weakness as a fighter, the Brown Bombee is probably no man to exploit it.

I bounced the whole problem off that other eminent seer of the occult East, Louis I. Nova, the well-known headstand artist.

Louis you will remember as the best of a poor lot of title contenders in the reign of Joe the First (Louis, that is). Like Floyd Patterson, Louis (Nova, that is) could lick all but three or four heavyweights in the world in his day. Like Floyd, he was always getting the wrong three at the right time.

Lou came on stage like Cassius, with a gimmick that was right out of Fu Manchu. He was a disciple of Yoga. This was a spiritual exercise which called for a lot of standing on the head—which was fortunate in Lou's case because that's what he did in a lot of his fights.

The trick was to get the blood rushing to the brain, and, when Lou fought Joe Louis, he got a lot of much-needed therapy. In fact, his face looked like a tomato when they finally stopped the fight.

Lou had been a fine athlete in California high schools and at the university agricultural campus at Davis where he was Northern California javelin record-holder, a football fullback, and a basketball corner man. Somewhere in his travels, Lou picked up Yogaism, probably from some guy with a cobra in a basket and a self-starching rope and a piccolo. Lou reported he was unbeatable because he had a new "cosmic" punch and a dynamic stance.

The beetle-browed mystic made one serious miscalculation. He accepted a fight with a human beer keg named Tony Galento, an unstaved barrel of a man from whom, when you hit him, you drew suds. Galento was very possibly the least Marquis of

Queensberry fighter ever to step in a ring. The only thing he didn't do to you in the ring was kick you. He thumbed, battered, butted and generally systematically destroyed Lou Nova one September night in Philadelphia in 1939 while the referee was busy doing his nails or something, and Nova actually hovered between life and death for days afterward.

Nova took the fight with a strep infection and left it in a coma. "I was," confides Lou, "the worst beaten man you ever saw. I entered the ring with a temperature, and left the ring almost cold." He set a Philadelphia knockdown record. As the knockee.

It took him 13 months to heal and he whipped an overweight, overplayed Max Baer and drew 56,549 people and $583,711 to the Polo Grounds one night to see him "fight" Joe Louis. Even Louis had been beguiled by the mysterious releases on the "cosmic" punch, but, as Dan Parker disgustedly noted after Nova got carried out of the ring after the fight, the "S" didn't belong in the word.

Nova now sells Dodge cars in Hollywood and has an invention called "Isometric Yogi" which is supposed to cure "dropped muscles," a condition not to be confused with dropped prize fighters, but Lou has what he considers—and drawing on his vast experience in the matter—the only sensible solution to the Floyd Patterson problem, a simple equalizer he found in some ancient ruins. "You handicap race horses, runners, pool players and golfers—why not fighters?" demands Lou. "Why not make Cassius Clay wear 25-pound weights?"

The idea has merit. There are those who think it's a capital idea and even recommend that Cassius wear them around his neck—in the middle of the Red Sea.

Baffle of the Century

O.K., sports fans, the subject for today is "So You Think You Know Boxing?" or "The Manly Art of Self-Delusion" which will be released in Arabia as "What Time's The Next Camel?" or "Is There Really A Muhammad Ali And Why?"

We have brought with us a qualified expert, "Comma" Cohen, the well-known heavyweight from the mid-30s who led all active fighters in nosebleeds, towel throw-ins and unconsciousness. He made more trips to the canvas than Rembrandt. He earned his unusual nickname from his manager, Yussel the Mussel, who said one night, "Cohen could of been a great fighter except he was always getting knocked into a comma."

All right, Comma, take your time and explain any of your answers:

Q. Now, we have two fighters. One of them, Fighter A, had a horrible childhood. He was brought up in a rough section of a rough town, Brooklyn. His family was disadvantaged, his father left them and he had to steal coal just to keep warm. He kept getting picked up by the police, finally was sent off to a correctional school where he became so shy he used to run away and hide in the woods. He became a fighter hanging around in the gyms where he had to wear trunks so many sizes too large for him he had to hold them together with a safety pin. He saved his own money to go compete on the Olympic team and rode the subway to his first important professional fights.

Now, Fighter B came of a good home in a border state where he passed a not-unpleasant childhood, was his mother's pet and learned to fight only because a neighbor kid stole his bicycle. When he started to fight, a committee of the town's richest citizens bankrolled him, got him a Cadillac, put him on salary and took the worry out of life for him. The only time he had to work was a few rounds in the ring once a month. He got rich, handsome, successful, the toast of two continents.

Now, Comma, one of these fighters became deeply religious, patriotic and figured he owed society a living. The other one rejected society, scorned it, mocked it, joined a group which recommended its obliteration and which helped him travel around the world putting the knock on his country and his countrymen. Now you guess which was which?

A. Fighter B is grateful. He's on the President's fitness committee, regularly turns back half his salary to the Olympic movement and is a goodwill ambassador for the United States of America, the land of opportunity. Fighter A wants to blow it up.

Q. What if I told you it was the other way around? Fighter B is the guy who hates. What would you say?

A. I'd say, does he go around in a Napoleon hat the rest of the time when he's not fighting?

Q. Now, Comma, what do you think of a fighter who changes his name?

A. Oh, it's done alla time. I mean, here's a guy named "Schapiro" in a Irish neighborhood, he comes on as "Paddy Shaw" or "K. O. Kelly," y'know what I mean? And a guy whose real handle is "Clancy," he wants the Jewish crowd, he goes in as "Ruby Goldfarb," the Hammerin' Hebrew.

Q. What if a guy changes his name to "Muhammad Ali"?

A. I'd say he's not gonna get much of the Jewish crowd that way. Come to think of it he's not gonna get much of the Irish crowd, neither. In fact, what the hell crowd would he get? The only Egyptians in this town are belly-dancers. What did he have against "Benedict Arnold"?

Q. Now, there's a kid heavyweight champion who's had 21 fights. He won the title when the champ quit in his corner because his shoulder hurt or his teeth ached or his corns throbbed or something. He's been dropped by Henry Cooper, an Englishman with so many stitches on his face it looks as if it was put together with a sewing machine. He was dropped by a guy who was so unknown his own dog used to bite him. Now, how would you compare this champ with the greats of the past?

A. I would say he could of held his own with Otto Von Porat. He mighta made Johnny Risko extend himself. I wouldn't rate him with a really great fighter like Jack Sharkey or Ted Sandwina or Yale Okun, THAT caliber of fighter. Mickey Walker might of carried him a few rounds. Phil Scott might of had to fall down and yell "Foul!" but he coulda handled this bum.

Q. How would you rate him with Jack Dempsey or Gene Tunney?

A. Oh, he might decision them. Dempsey is over 70 now, you know. And I think Tunney got the gout.

Q. No, no. I mean IN THEIR PRIME. For instance, how would he compare against Joe Louis? Could he beat Joe?

A. Bite your tongue. He couldn't even fight Joe Louis in places where they outlaw capital punishment.

Q. But this kid has SPEED!

A. He'd need it to catch up to his head where Joe Louis would knock it. What's speed got to do with it? They gonna race or fight? As far as speed goes, this guy wouldn't of known which way Billy Conn went. He woulda had to go see the movies to get a square look at Billy.

Q. What's your understanding about a "white hope"?

A. Well, usually, when they got some non-white champion who gets caught kicking dogs or feeding canaries to cats or letting the brakes off baby-carriages, they usually go out and find some guy to teach him a lesson.

Q. What kind of guy do they usually get?

A. Usually, some old has-been who quit boxing 10 years before, is overweight, has gas on his stomach and can't get any insurance. Some guy they not only have to carry out of the ring but, also, in.

Q. Can a non-white be a "white hope"?

A. Oh, sure. If he's inept enough.

Q. What would you say of a guy who got knocked down by Pete Rademacher, Tom McNeeley, Roy Harris, about 14 times in three title fights and twice in one round by his sparring partners?

A. Sounds like a "white hope" to me. In fact, I'd say he's perfect.

Q. Who would you say was going to win such a fight as I outline?

A. I dunno who's gonna win it but I'm beginning to get an idea who's gonna lose. All of us.

The Nose of Luis

The face is old, yet young. The eyes are merry, yet sad. It is not a fighter's face, it is a clown's face. Fernandel in burnt cork. Grimaldi without bells. Durante in boxing trunks.

The nose is most fascinating of all. It is not a nose, it is a monument. It spills over the cheeks like a relief map of a mountain over a prairie. It would take an ant a week to scale it.

It is an expressive nose. It wrinkles with merriment, curls with disdain. It is an instrument wasted on mere smelling. It has a magnificence all its own, as if the person belonged to the nose rather than the opposite.

Someone has said a big nose indicates nobility of soul and I believe it. A man whose mind is small rarely has a nose that's big. And Luis Rodriguez, the boxfighter, wears his nose as a badge of grandeur, not an object of scorn.

Miscast as a prizefighter, not by virtue of skills but of personality and inclination, Luis is as natural and uncomplicated a being as a child playing on a riverbank. He approaches life with humor, not rancor. His spidery fingers and pipe-stem wrists do not seem to equip him to be welterweight boxing champion of the world and neither does his outlook. A happy man should not be turned by society on his fellow man. The prize ring is a place for the man with a score to settle, a man whose enemy is mankind and who sticks his opponent the way a voodooist sticks dolls.

Luis Rodriguez should be dancing, which he does exceptionally well. He should be making people laugh instead of bleed.

Born in the canebreaks of Cuba, raised in the teeming streets of Havana, the adored brother of four sisters, Luis has a gentleness and considerateness about him seldom seen in a warrior. The false pride is totally absent. The shoulders seem constantly hunched as if they were trying to suppress the laughter which is always close to the surface. The eyes, dwarfed by the nose, sometimes look like two brown berries a-dance with amusement. But when the nose is swollen with punches and tears course down its mighty slopes, it must be a very melancholy sight indeed.

Luis meets the welterweight champion of the world next week, Emile Griffith, a peevish young man whose eyes glitter more than they twinkle, a fighter who has killed, a champion whose pride is fierce.

To Luis, the fight is a simple business proposition, nothing more. They tell you to unload that sack, you unload the sack. They tell you to knock the man out, you knock him out. "I know Emile a good fighter and a good person. I think I am good fighter and good person. Is all right. We have to fight. After fight, we continue. I, good person, he, good person. Fight has nothing to do with this."

Luis has a habit of reducing complexities that simply. For example he finds one part of training irksome: roadwork. It's not the mileage, it's the hours. Roadwork historically is done at the crack of dawn. So, in the mind of Luis, is sleeping. Ergo, Luis does his roadwork the night before. The crack of dawn (and sometimes the crack of noon) finds him sleeping—as befits a man of quality.

Roadwork at night has its pitfalls. In the public parks where Luis does it, there are first the police and second the lovers. Both of them are now used to him. The lovers look up from their necking at the sound of running feet. They see a nose glinting in the moonlight, followed by the rest of Rodriguez. "It's only Luis," they reassure each other. And go back to their embraces. In Miami the police merely accompany him a mile or so and chat.

Luis has lost only two fights, one to Griffith, and one to a nobody from Texas he fought after spending a night under Castro's machineguns in a hijacked plane. He cannot conceive of harm coming to him in the ring. "The matter of Paret was an accident. It was the destiny of Paret," he shrugs.

He disdains an interpreter even though he has been in this country a short time. But sometimes the idiom of his homeland trips him. What, he was asked, would he do when he quit the ring? The shoulders hunched and shook, the eyes brightened with merriment. "I do not plan to work. I will live off my reputation such as it is. I will play out the farce." He laughed happily. "My destiny," he added, "is like my nose. It is something I got from my grandfather. I must protect it. But I can't change it."

The Sheik of Araby

Well, I see where Muhammad Ali, formerly known as Cassius Clay, has come up with his first challenge for the heavyweight championship of the world.

It has come from Floyd Patterson. You remember Patterson? The unlisted heavyweight champion of the world? His reign was listed "Top Secret," the phantom of sports. He just bobbed up in odd corners of the world fighting people nobody ever heard of and, once you saw their fighting style, you found out why.

Now that Muhammad is the champion, guys are jumping off trucks all over the country to get in on this good thing. When Liston was champ, everybody suddenly remembered he had promised his mother not to fight. Nowadays, you'd think Elsa Lanchester had won the title, the line is getting so long. Patterson hasn't been that warlike since the Rademacher fight. He even offered to fight for nothing which leads you to think he thinks it's a pillow fight.

Patterson is upset because the new champ belongs to a rather, shall we say, racy set that doesn't believe in helping old ladies across the street or taking up the collection in church or canvassing for the Red Cross.

The "Muslims," as a group, think white folks are all right in their place, but how would you like your sister married to one? They kind of wish Abraham Lincoln had minded his own damn business, only the next time around they mean to have the whip. This time, the girl crossing the ice floes in the movie will be Doris Day and the guy shooting at her will have a capital X in his name.

But you talk to the heavyweight champion of the world and the "Muslims" come out hopelessly confused in your mind (and, you're sure, his) as "Moslems," sons of Allah, and lovers of peace. To hear Cassius tell it, they come on like "Amos 'n Andy in Saudi Arabia," or the Mystic-Knights-of-the-Sea-on-Caravan. Cassius is like the guy in the movie who has wandered into the haunted house to use the phone and hasn't noticed the butler is a werewolf, that's blood on the floor, and he thinks the suit of armor in the corner is empty and that it's just an optical illusion the eyes in the wall painting are following him.

I think Cassius sees himself as Lawrence of Arabia or the Red Shadow rather than a guy licking stamps for hate literature. Cassius has always had a lively imagination and it was only a question of time before he'd wrap a towel around his head and begin to play Saladin, the Saracen. I expect him to trade in his Cadillac for a camel any day now.

You may recall that when he went to England, he turned into

a combination of Disraeli and Dizzy Dean for the occasion. If he went to see "Indian Love Call," he'd come out as an Indian—or Nelson Eddy. Cassius needs two things: a big role and a big audience. The heavyweight championship of the world will do for a start but nothing short of Armageddon will do for a sock finish.

Which is why I think Floyd Patterson went about it all wrong. Floyd never was much of a showboat. Instead of dashing off a curt, formal challenge—an offer to fight for nothing—he should have modeled his defy after 1001 Arabian Nights or an old Turhan Bey-Maria Montez movie and ridden up in a rented tarboosh on a shaggy horse and shouted at Cassius:

"O, Mighty Muhammad, Shah of Louisville, it is I, Abou Ben Ali Patterson, of the Scarsdale Bedouins, who comes to challenge thee to mortal combat. Come, test my scimitar, oh mighty despot, conqueror of the Sonny and hunter by the moon!"

And Cassius, delighted, could roar:

"Infidel! Pig dog of a Christian! Who comes to rail in idle boast at the tent of Mighty Muhammad?! By the beard of the prophet, thou shalt fall in eight, thy shoulder shall become separated, thy cheek shall bleed and on thy bones shall the beasts of the desert feed and the dogs carry thee away. Know thee not, I am the Greatest, thou miserable rug merchant and glass-chinned heathen? Go, tell thy king, Cus D'Amato, that we will send thy head home on a pike, thou great-grandson of a goat and parent of a camel!"

If Floyd can keep a straight face, and not notice the tarboosh has "Property of the Istanbul Hilton" written on it, and that the camel has a zipper and two guys from Central Casting in it, he might get his fight. He better hurry, though. Next year, Cassius might be playing Pepe Le Moko.

Sad Song for Sonny

There seems to be some misunderstanding what my position is in the Sonny Liston matter, although why anybody should care beats me.

Sonny Liston, you will note, is the ham-handed, strong-backed heavyweight contender whom admirers have already awarded the championship of the world because he stopped such ferocious tigers as Zora Folley and Mike De John and carried Eddie Machen to a decision in 12.

Sonny can't read or write, which isn't his fault, but he has a prison record, which may be his fault, and he is alleged to be managed under-cover by Blinky Palermo which is sure as hell somebody's fault, not mine.

Harry Sanford, a flack at a TV studio, is Sonny's self-appointed drum-beater in this area and he has fired off missives to every sportswriter within air-mail distance and to the National Boxing Assn.

His story would bring tears to your eyes. Liston, one of 25 or so children in his family, is a victim of our society and what has happened to him is all our fault. Personally, I would finger Sonny's father who took his responsibilities a lot less seriously than Harry Sanford and shoved off on his growing family before Sonny got old enough to swing on him, which shows there is a strong strain of common sense somewhere in the line.

The big point about Sonny is that he got in trouble with the law a second time while he was still on parole from prison. An armed St. Louis cop accosted him one night and Sonny not only disarmed him, he broke his leg in the process.

But, the story goes, it was the cop who asked for it, went out of his way to make trouble for Sonny and called him names. All I can say is, if you ever got a good look at Sonny Liston, you would have to conclude this cop is one of the all-time brave men.

To pick an argument with Sonny Liston on a St. Louis street corner at night with anything less than a Gatling gun is a new form of suicide. Sonny even had a friend—and two girls—with him. The cop is lucky he only lost a leg. In fact, I'm glad Sonny can't read this.

I have to admit I'm fresh out of tears for the Sonny Listons. For one thing, I have just finished reading the saga of Jake La Motta, the slum kid who parlayed a jail record into the middleweight championship of the world. Jake, by his own admission in *True* magazine, began stealing at the age of 10—little things like hub caps, copper wiring and typewriters. Once, it was a violin. He got caught, but he always had such a heart-rending story that he was released immediately with a lollipop and given a ride home.

Caught in a burglary, he threw a hatchet at a cop. While awaiting sentence for that, he waylaid a shop owner and hit him over the head so hard with an iron pipe that he didn't find out till he got out of jail that the man had lived. "He was paler . . . grayer and weak-looking, but alive," writes Jake.

When he became a famous fighter, Jake repaid his loyal fans by throwing a fight to a Blinky Palermo fighter named Billy Fox. When he quit fighting, he left his faithful wife and three kids, opened a saloon in Miami and ran it until he got picked up and sentenced for contributing to the delinquency of a 14-year-old girl.

Jake still doesn't understand why they didn't give him a lollipop and send him home, if you read his piece.

When he got out, his old buddy, Rocky Graziano, got him a job as a TV actor. You know Rocky. He wrote his tragic story, too, "Somebody Up There Likes Me." He did most of the things La Motta did only he ended up punching an Army captain in the jaw in wartime and went to Leavenworth for 10 months. I'm always glad to see someone saved for society but Graziano sold his life story for $250,000. You can't help wondering what happened to the poor kids who did what the captain told them.

Anyway, the moral of the story is Jack the Ripper would be forgiven if he had a good left hook.

I wouldn't worry about poor Sonny, Harry. As you can see from the La Motta, and Graziano tear-jerkers, class will out. Liston will get his title shot and his fortune. Then you can write his life story and sell it for a half-million or so. Title it, "I Never Had a Chance." But don't bother to send a copy. I've read it.

A Job for Joe

In the kitchen of his home, the greatest heavyweight champion of his time, perhaps of all time, sat staring at the television screen flickering before him.

It was too early for television. The sun was not yet up high enough to shine in the lifeless eyes of the two stone lions guarding the massive front door. But it was too wet for golf. And Joe Louis didn't have anything better to do.

"I get up at 7:30 to watch it," he admitted, indicating the screen which was alive with deafening action. "Tomorrow I got to fly to Kentucky. Got to cut a ribbon for a new supermarket."

He paused for a moment, studied the picture critically, then turned to a companion. "Turn it off," he instructed. "I seen it before."

He directed his attention to a newcomer. "What can I tell you?" he wanted to know.

The newcomer studied him. The hair was graying at the sides of the temples. The face was puffy from sleep. But the eyes had the same impassive steadiness that used to reduce ring opponents to masses of gibbering fear. The gaze was level and honest. The Brown Bomber had a gray casing but it was possible in the mind's eye to still see the sleek, destructive outline of fury that had made this man the most celebrated athlete of his decade.

Joe Louis is a man who looks without surprise on life. And sometimes, without much interest. He has seen it all before. His youth was spent in such a pitch of constant excitement and swirl that it is possible now to be bored enough to start watching TV at dawn.

I have always thought Joe Louis the most honest athlete in the history of any sport. His phrases had the simple uncomplicated sincerity of the child who sees no need to lie or the adult who sees no fear to make him want to. In a chorus of politicians' patriotic fervor, it was Joe Louis' simple declaration "There's a lot wrong with our country, but nothin' Hitler could fix" that bolstered the resolve of a whole generation of his people.

"We are on God's side" was more eloquent than a coast-to-coast line of posters. When he was old and awkward and knocked out by the young bull from Brockton and his dressing room was awash with the tears of his friends, Joe shrugged. "I knocked out lots of guys." He had a simple dignity about him a king might envy. He hit with the explosive detonation of a dynamite cap but even in losing fights, he stepped back when an opponent lost his footing.

He left his cruelty in the ring. He ripped Carnera's mouth into a Niagara of blood, knocked Paolino Uzcudun's gold teeth into the press row but helped them to their feet and ever had a generous word for the courage of any foe. "Another lucky night," became his post-fight interview trademark.

It is a wrench to see this great champion scuffling for something to do—not so much for money because the government, bad advice, and bad friends have made money as meaningless a part of life as a gold belt. As an economic entity, Joe Louis disappeared into a hole years ago and pulled it in after him. He cannot tunnel out in his lifetime. He owes the United States more than some European allies.

"It all began with that first $98,000," he told me the other morning, with that crooked grin that seems to light the whole Louis face with merriment. "They got that 50% penalty and it's not hard to double and triple what you owe as the years go by. I could have paid that first $98,000 but my accountant advised me to let it go by. 'The bigger it gets, the quicker they'll settle,' is what he told me. Pretty soon it got so big there was nothing to settle.

"If I were to live another thousand years and have 250 oil wells, I couldn't catch up to it now. It was over a million dollars when the government finally stopped the penalty. With the penalty, it was growing like a weed. But they didn't stop the principal. You know how long it would take you and how much you'd have to make to clear a million dollars?"

Louis was victimized by more than tax accountants. Sport should have hidden its head when it found Joe Louis forced to referee the comedy of wrestling or to appear in court for Jimmy Hoffa to pay off a favor to people he shouldn't have had to go to in the first place.

Joe wants to promote boxing in L.A. now. His right to do so is under attack by resident promoters Aileen Eaton and George Parnassus. As usual, Joe can see their side of it. "You know how it is: people have something so long, they hate to give it up. I don't blame them."

But if Joe Louis had been a different kind of person, there might not be any boxing today. The game owes him something. The country owes him something. It's time sports stopped dumping its great champions into a pile of boredom, stopped sweeping its heroes under a corner of the rug. It's time somebody showed concern when Babe Ruth dies a lonely, bitter, bored man; when Ezzard Charles winds up broke and neglected two years after he quits the ring.

It's time Joe Louis was too busy to be watching television at seven o'clock in the morning and too hard at work to be cutting ribbons in Kentucky. There should be room for two boxing promoters in L.A. If there's room for any. If there's no room for Joe Louis in boxing, there should be no room for boxing period.

LITTLE SPORTS

Introduction

When talking of "Little Sports," it's well to remember that, not too many years ago, golf was unqualifiedly a "little sport." It's like the cute little puppy you took into the house who turned out to be a tiger—and now has the rest of the family cowering in the closet hoping he'll eat himself to death, or get a bone in his throat.

Soccer, in America, is a "little sport." Never mind that it's the biggest sport in the world on every other continent and on one half of this one. But it got its foot in the door in America in 1967 and made baseball so nervous that 9/10ths of every executive office in baseball bought in. Television began to empty its pockets of loose change on the off-chance this latest "little sport" would some day become (like golf) the new "Man Who Came to Dinner."

Waiting in the wings are lacrosse, horseshoe-pitching, dry-fly-tying and ice-fishing.

There used to be a song titled "There's No One with Endurance like the Man Who Sells Insurance" but the insurance huckster was short-winded compared to the evangelist selling The Columnist a new "little sport." "Don't you realize," he will snarl, "that more people pitch horseshoes than play major league baseball?"

You try to tell him that's precisely the trouble—but he's not listening. He's sure that, once the bulk of the American public is exposed to the nuances and graces of throwing a leaner and what the difference is between throwing the ex-footwear of a horse end-over-end or in a whirling circle like a boomerang, every ballpark in America will be empty and long queues will line up outside the world horseshoe-pitching championship pitch-off.

The trouble with most "little sports" is they are more fun to play than to watch. They are not of the stuff of which controversy is made. The charm of baseball is that, dull as it may be on the field, it is endlessly fascinating as a rehash. Conversationally it is *really* America's National Pastime.

All winter long, the season is probed, examined, gone over. "Should he have bunted?" "Shouldn't Alston have taken Drysdale out?" "Why don't they hit-and-run more?" "Do you think Wills was *really* safe on that throw to the plate? I mean, didn't you *see* the pictures in the paper next day? I say he was out!"

And so on well into the winter.

Football is another case in point. "He should have thrown a pass on fourth down, the dummy!" yells a man, waving his fourth martini at the office Christmas party. "Why didn't they trade for linemen—we've got enough quarterbacks!" the resident Knute Rockne of the Truckdrivers' Bar & Grill growls. "They should of run the ball more—that Allie Sherman's pass-happy," mutters the cabdriver.

The artisans of professional sport were artful enough to make their games complicated—full of subplots. Soccer, if it ever catches on, will have to introduce something in addition to the swift movement up and down the field, a sport for the swivel-headed like tennis.

No one likes to watch a man fish. No one roots for the fish. About once a year, the "Wide World of Sport" will endure a fishing trip—If the fisherman is Bing Crosby, or the King of Saudi Arabia, or SOMEONE who would be interesting to watch even if he was only cleaning his fingernails. "We are now going to watch Peter J. Nobody of 1457 East Poinsettia Place, Question Mark, Kansas, fish for bullhead in a pond near his home" would attract about as many viewers as test patterns.

Chess as a sport can be shown in a series of still pictures. But so can baseball. The difference, of course, is that chess is a "sport" that can be played sitting down. Or lying down, for that matter. Baseball requires a high degree of muscular coordination.

But so does soccer. The difference here seems to be that the

American sportsman requires a modicum of cerebration to go along with coordination. You can *think* your way out of a jam in a ball game, just as you can muscle your way. Ditto with football.

We have arrived, then, at a definition of a "little sport." It is any sport in which either pure muscle or pure brain is decisive. You don't have to *think* to win the horseshoe pitch. And you can be as bloodless as a Ptolemy to win a chess match.

Golf is an almost perfect example of a balance between the two. You first must be able to strike the ball athletically. Now come the decisions, decisions, decisions! A 1-iron? Or a 3-wood? Draw the ball around those trees? Or hit it safe up the left side? Does the putt break right? Or is it straight in?

How do I *engineer* myself around these 18 holes? Not, how do I muscle my way around!

Wherever the athletic and the cerebral share equally in the prize, there the American sportsman is willing to shell out good money to sit in on the contest. A boxer versus a slugger—a mongoose versus the cobra—is the meatiest attraction in pugilism.

It is also the stuff of which those nice, *safe* midwinter colloquies are made. (I say "safe" because a conversation based on athletics is a middleground of dialogue whereby neither of the participants has to *reveal* much of himself except inferentially. I mean, ask a man his religion, his politics, what he thinks of Vietnam, and you have explosiveness, divisiveness, even enmity. But a man can *safely* disagree on the World Series, the decision in a prize fight, the National Open. "He should have—" the conversation starts. You can insert the words "bunted," "used a 7-iron," "not tried to slug with him," "run through the middle" and you have a pleasant, casual conversation going.)

I think this is why "little sports" present special challenge to the historian. They require extra effort on his part. Hunting wild bear can be wildly boring unless you take the time and trouble to do it. A writer needs imagination but it must be tethered some place to truth.

I do not want you to take up a collection for me, or put a statue in Pershing Square, but I have crewed to Ensenada on a 30-foot sloop even though the promise of seasickness (in my case) was 100 per cent. You can't write about sailing unless you sail (witness Richard H. Dana, Herman Melville). You cannot have any idea of the challenge of fishing till you try to catch one. A fisherman will read the dullest tract publishable about his favorite recreation. A sports page reader will only read one where his eye is caught by wit and imagination. The information therein is secondary.

But today's "little sports" are tomorrow's runaway best sellers. The first sportswriter who tentatively picked up a golf club and said to himself "Hey! this is fun!" was like the first prospector who yelled down the creek "Hey, you guys, I think this is gold!"

Professional football was a sport as esoteric as court tennis 40 years ago, known and admired only by an "in" group. It behooves the prudent sportswriter to watch the formation of such "in" groups. He may have opened up a whole pipeline of columns, controversies and comedies for himself for the days when baseball finally arrives in its anecdotage.

Where golf is now a "big sport" where once it was a "little sport," tennis is now a "little sport" where once it was a "big sport." (Incidentally, I've included golf in this section because, even though it has graduated from the ranks of "little sports," it is still more a "little sport" than it is "rough stuff." But it's a little out of place, like a pro athlete who returns to his old high school to do a little strutting.) The vanes of human taste can change like a rooftop cock with a 180-degree wind shift. If soccer today seems still a "little sport" in citadels where more sophisticated and complex sports have whetted the appetite for more on-field intrigue than soccer seems to offer, this is not to say a spectacularly exciting player or a revolutionarily imaginative coach may not make it so popular we have to put moats around *our* fields, too.

I hope history, then, will deal kindly with me if the offered "little sports" in this book turn out, as golf and pro football suddenly did, to be very big sports indeed by the time somebody blows dust off this volume as he finds it in a long-unused attic along with a ladies' dress form, a gramophone and perfumed letters tied in a bundle and delivered by an archaic public service known as a "post office" and not piped in by facsimile the way *his* missives are.

Scots, Wha Hae?

Once upon a time there was a game called "Golf" and it was a right interesting little game. They played it in Scotland and they played it in places where the rain fell and the wind blew and the gorse grew thick and barbed-wire-like. They set a standard called "par" and very few people broke it.

Then they moved the game to America and the Americans set to tinkering with it—naturally. Americans didn't care for the ball. So they made one bigger. So you could see it better. They didn't like the wooden shafts. So they made steel ones. So you could hit the ball farther.

The Scots had this stymie rule which said that if a ball was in your line on the green you had to go around it. The Americans threw that out. I mean, supposing a fellow had a chance to make a 65 and looked up and saw the other fellow had thrown the ball up on the green right in front of him? The Scots said "That's the idea, laddie!" But the Americans would rather have a 65 than a lot of Old World trickery like that.

They used to have a thing called "match play" in which you contested an opponent instead of a standard. In other words, you might shoot an 8 on one hole and your opponent a 3 and all you would lose would be the hole, not 5 shots. Americans were dismayed. "A fellow might shoot a 65 and get beaten by a guy who shoots 76!" they protested. "So what?" said the Scots.

So the Americans went along for a while. In the meantime, they moved most of their games from the rock-ribbed, tree-lined North and Northeast down to the flat, sunny places of the hemisphere where, if a tree grew, people came from miles around to look at it. But they scattered a few potted palms around, piped in two or three rivers and everybody shot 62. "See!" they told the Scots. "You guys just didn't have the hang of this game."

Then, television—which the Scots never took into consideration, either—came along and television (which is a lot of guys in sun glasses and Italian shoes who play at La Gorce and Palm Springs and can all break 70 and answer the phone in their golf cart at the same time) noticed that one of the year's top three tournaments, the PGA, was match play. And some years the finals had Walter Burkemo versus Felice Torza and Chandler Harper versus Henry Williams. And television said: "It'll never play, baby. Everybody'll switch over to watch the Jalopy Derby."

So the Americans did away with the match play, and the finals of the PGA saw Palmer and Nicklaus on camera just like every other tournament. Since they were on camera five or six other times in the week everybody recognized them and knew they were the guys in the white hats and everybody felt good.

Except the Scots. "The way we look at it," they said, "we like to see Felice Torza win once in a while. That's why we have two kinds of play."

But the Americans invented golf carts so you didn't even have to walk. Fortunately, no stretcher cases ever won major tournaments, but a lot of guys who would puff climbing a flight of stairs did.

The National Amateur was usually contested by a lot of rich guys who didn't need television and were better at match play than medal or stroke play because they had to spend all week in the office and were likely to be erratic on one or two holes. You can't shoot 65 and be erratic. But you can win a match 1-up.

Then, amateurs got just like everyone else. They played every day and they made almost as much money betting as the old-fashioned type of amateur made on the stock exchange. And someone said, "Look. In this match play, a guy's liable to have a 62 going for him, only he shuts the other guy out 9-up and 8 to play. And, besides, if we get to televise the National Amateur and one guy ends up at noon being dormie, which is 9-up with 9 to play, for instance, we will have to go to him and tell him to throw a couple of holes or all the television will get is a couple of club members fitting in a late nine holes."

So the Americans said "Well, we threw out 'stymie,' why not 'dormie?'" And there went that match play.

The only thing they had left was the National Open in which they play 36 holes in one day—the last day. And they said, "My goodness! A fellow could get mighty tired." And someone said "Not only that, but television has nothing left for Sunday."

So they threw that out and now the National Open—like the Tucson Open—is just 18 holes a day. And the Scots said "Why don't you just play 9 holes a day, medal play, of course?" And someone said "Why do you say 'only 9'?" And the Scots said, "So your carts won't get tired, of course."

Golf Is a Bogey

It has long been a pet theory of mine that one of the things every columnist should do is set his sights on some public service. You know, cancer, heart disease, mononucleosis. So what I think I'll do is warn you against golf books.

I get them by the bagful this time of the year. Every golfer who ever broke 80—and plenty who didn't—writes a golf book. "Power Golf," "Jockey Golf," "How to Break Par in 8,341 Steps," "How to Break Your Clubs," "How to Play Your Best Golf and Not Get Caught at It" are all part of the library. And, of course, the most recent winner of the National Open always rushes into print with something usually titled "Three-Putt McGillicuddy's Golf Secret." I've read them all. His secret is invariably, "Hit the ball straight."

The nice thing about these books is that they usually cancel each other out. One book tells you to keep your eye on the ball; the next says not to bother. Personally, in the crowd I play with, a better idea is to keep your eye on your partner.

"Let the clubhead do the work," says another and I strongly urge this chapter on friends of mine who are apt to let their feet do the work, particularly when they're in the rough and no one can see them.

They spend a great deal of time in these books telling you how to get out of close lies with an iron but never a word about how to get out of them with unclose lies. A close lie, to me, is one in which you take a chance the other fellow wasn't looking—or wasn't counting.

Walter Hagen once weighed in with a brilliant bit of psychological advice: "Every golfer can expect to have four bad shots a round. When you do, just put them out of your mind." This, of course, is hard to do when you're not even off the first tee after you've had them.

Instructional books are downbeat. They're always telling you how to get out of a sand trap or out from behind a tree or out of the rough. I like Sam Snead's advice on how to handle the rough best. "Don't get in it," he said.

The tipoff on golf books is you never see a pro in the Open walk up to a shot, then open a book to see how to play it. They devote whole chapters on how to judge distances on the fairway, then ask their caddy, and if he can't tell them, they're sunk.

They make the game unnecessarily complicated. You'd think there was something magic about the way the "V" between your thumb and finger points on the shaft. Follow their instructions to the letter and you'll have to call a plumber to get loose.

What prompts my outburst of public weal at this time is no desire to see you cut golf books off your Christmas list. Some of my best friends are publishers. Some are even golf pros.

Which brings me to Joe Novak. Joe has been the pro at Bel-Air since the days when W. C. Fields drank 18 holes a day there. He's one of the sweetest guys I know and a fine golf teacher. But when it comes to titling books, he should be arrested. Or register the copyright with the Burlington Liars Club.

Know what the title to Joe's book is? "Golf Can Be an Easy Game." Well, you could fool me, Joe. Also Ben Hogan.

Joe's book is full of fascinating instructions. But if they can transform golf into an easy game they should make Steinbeck give back that Nobel prize. "When and How Do You Use Your Hands in a Golf Shot?" is one of the chapters. I already know that one, Joe. In a sand trap. "The Most Common Fault in Golf" is another. That's easy, too. Teeing up and lying about your handicap.

But I'll read Joe's book. I only hope he doesn't mind if I also pick up a copy of "How to Play Golf in the Low 120's," by

Stephen Baker. The flyleaf fascinates me. "In his book," it says, "Stephen Baker offers welcome words of hope to golfers everywhere. His researchers have convinced him that almost anyone with an exceptional sense of co-ordination, powerful muscular development and a natural 'feel' for a flawless golf swing can, at one time or another, break 120."

That sounds to me like a man who really understands the game as we play it. Most players, he says, lose confidence much too soon—after only 10 or 15 years of daily play. That might be my trouble. I give up too soon. You might be right, Joe. Golf CAN be an easy game—if you live long enough.

Helpful Hints

It was in the middle of the PGA that I caught Arnold Palmer looking at me as if I were a four-foot putt he needed to win the tournament.

"What," he asked menacingly, "do you mean by knocking my golf book?"

"Mr. Palmer," I told him, hoping somebody would mark where I was on the green in case he knocked me into a sand trap, "I didn't knock your golf book, I knocked all golf books." He looked unconvinced.

"See," I told him. "Your book, 'My Game and Yours,' has a lot to do with your game but very little to do with mine."

"What," he asked, hitching up his pants and selecting the right club to split the fairway with me, "would you write?"

It was a good question. And I am herewith offering the Old Pro's handy hints to better golf, to be titled "My Game and the Hell with Palmer's."

In the first place, all the pros can teach you how to hit the "intentional slice." It's the unintentional slice we have to work on. There are several things you have to look for to tell you when you are going to hit the unintentional slice. It is often the result of too much right hand—at the bar before the match.

Other tell-tale signs include sweating in the palms just before the shot and a slight tremor in the knees. If you just bet five dollars on the hole, it is a sure sign the unintentional slice is coming up. You don't have to check the wind condition, the distance to the hole, the curvature of the earth or the time of day. Just stand at right angles to the hole. Pray, if you want. And let fly. With a little luck, the ball will banana right into center fairway and leave you with only seven easy shots to the green.

Now, I am the world's foremost master at the topped shot. Not everyone can learn to play this delicate little line drive around the green with finesse. The important thing to remember on this shot is not to keep your head down. You louse up the shot if you do. The preferred position for the head at the finish of the swing is looking right up into the sun. This way you'll not only not hit the ball square, you'll not even know where it went. The shot calls for you to inquire anxiously, "Did you see it?" the minute the ball leaves the blade. Never have any more conversation with your caddy than that. Never let him tell you anything more than how deep the hole is and what time it is.

The sand trap shot is the easiest shot in golf in my game. Remember, you do not hit the ball, just the sand. Right? Okay, so hit the sand. What's so tough about that?

There is entirely too much emphasis on par in golf. Forget par. I have a friend, Myron Cope, who once took four fans—complete misses—on a par 3 tee. He bogeyed the hole before he left the tee. This is the right mental attitude to have. Having gone one over par before he even struck the ball, he could now settle down and play up to his capabilities—an 11. The secret of golf is relaxation, but does Arnold Palmer's book tell you to relax any better than that?

On the 40-yard chip to the green I can shave five strokes off your game if you will remember one important thing: don't concentrate. Think of the mortgage, the fight you had with your wife last night, the fact the boss thinks you're in the office. Try to remember if you shut off the bathtub water before you left home.

It is imperative you bend your elbow on this shot. And, at impact, look up. The only fun in the game, Jackie Burke says, is watching the ball fly through the air. Yours, of course, will only fly through the grass, but remember, nobody's perfect. Even the pros miss one now and again. Your shot will come off beautifully if you remember those five checkpoints: no concentration, head up, elbow bent, teeth chattering and tongue out.

The pros tell you to keep your weight on the right foot going back and the left foot coming down. Hogwash. Don't keep your weight on either foot. On the 39-foot topped chip shot, it's even better if you fall down. Miss just one of these handy Murray reminders and the first thing you know you will hit a perfect 9-iron shot and it will fly over the green, over the trees and out into the parking lot and you will have to drop another ball. The beauty of the Murray system is you never have a lost ball. If your glasses are clean and you can see 30 feet in any direction, your ball will never leave your sight.

If your caddy coaches you on the tee, "Hit it down the left side with a little draw," ignore him. All you do on the tee is try not to hit the caddy.

The fairway wood shot is fairly simple. The object here is to move the ball 11 feet, hopefully forward. Again, you begin by collapsing your left arm. If you can't collapse your left arm, you can't play the shot. Just remember, Nicklaus would be sure to louse up this shot. But not you.

Ball-marking for fun and profit would be another important chapter in the Murray book. Say you have a 40-foot putt. You can eliminate at least the first two feet of this by artful ball-marking. The preferred method is to have a pocket full of coins which fall out in a shower as you bend over to mark your spot. Pick all of them up except the one nearest the hole. You can cut off the last six feet of the putt by inquiring innocently after your third putt, "Gimme that?" Argue that it's inside the leather even if it's barely inside the green. You've got to be tough in this game.

If you're three-and-a-half feet from the hole and playing with dopes who don't consider that a tap-in, remember to hit it firm. Never up, never in. You will end up 20 feet from the hole on the other side but it will help to keep you from crying if you yell "Bite!" or "Sit!" or "Hit something!" as it slithers past. On the way back, try to stub the putter in the grass and you can keep your poise by shouting "Legs. Get Legs." Try not to take more than four putts.

There are any number of artificial aids you can buy but remember that liquor is the best. It can't help your game but if you play the way I am telling you, it can't hurt it either. Also you won't give a damn. I would never recommend gloves, unless, of course, it's cold.

Okay. Now that you've read this, go out and get "Your Game and Mine" and ask yourself who's giving the best advice on how to master this stinking game, me or Palmer.

Keep It Low

It has been said a golf professional is a fellow who never knows what town he's in till he calls downstairs to the desk clerk in the morning to see what language he's speaking—but he can read you the left-to-right break on every green in the town from memory.

He can't fix a light bulb but he can tell you two fairways away what is wrong with your grip. He sees more of the world than the Secretary of State but the only way he would notice a scenic wonder like Mt. Fuji is if he had to pitch over it for a birdie.

He and his whole whacky, wonderful fraternity come to our town this week for the traditional kickoff tournament on the golf trail. Chances are he has a new set of clubs, an extra putter he's going to try out, a lockerful of alligator shoes—and high hopes that a new stance will solve all the problems that made him break less than even last year.

But, wherever he is, he still has the same old problem: he has to get a 1.68 in. diameter ball in a 4¼ in. diameter hole without touching it, kicking it or blowing on it. It is a problem that sounds simple only if you have never tried it.

This is to say, Welcome, fellow sufferers, to my town. This is Los Angeles. You'll recognize it by the dog-leg left of Hollywood Freeway. That lateral water hazard off Wilshire Boulevard is La Brea Pits. The wind generally blows from the West and if it comes up smoggy just club yourself down one notch and put some Murine in the bag.

You'll recognize Rancho, where the tournament is held, because of the 9th hole, which gets so narrow on the approaches to the green there's barely room for a ball to get through, and Arnold Palmer had no trouble at all taking a 12 there last year although I must say if he played it a little smarter he could have made a 9.

You'll recognize it by the shivering starlets on the 1st tee in net stockings and plumed hats, and otherwise dressed in goose bumps. They are part of the natural terrain in this part of the country, but if you happen to hit one of them with a tee shot, you get a free drop. The girls don't know a 5-iron from a steam iron or a chip shot from a chipmunk, but you won't want to talk golf to them anyway.

You will recognize Los Angeles, too, by the gallery, which is like no other in sports. It will range from the truant-playing bank president to the arrogant movie hero, blindingly decked out in checked coat, smoked glasses and trailing billowing fumes of cologne as he sashays down the fairway followed by a chattering band of sycophants in collars that look like sails in a good wind.

It is a gallery that revels in disaster. "Palmer just took an 8!" will ring through it from time to time, and the town criers who hurry from fairway to fairway with the bad news are as happy as an old maid reporting a new divorce.

But it is a gallery that is never downbeat or derisive. The guy who is scornfully nasty in the anonymity of the baseball bleachers is as polite as a relative at the will-reading when he is standing so close to the athlete he has to pretend to be glad of a birdie even if he bet against the guy.

Occasionally, a galleryite will be heard to complain "Should have used a 9-iron there" when a golfer comes up short on his approach. But it is never the teeth-bared snarl of the two-dollar bettor whose nag just cantered. It is always with regret. Once, a few years ago, as Mike Souchak pulled a 2-iron out of his bag on the back-breaking uphill 5th hole, a spectator shook his head: "Never make it with that," he warned. Souchak never changed expression, swung—and didn't make it. The crowd turned on his adviser as though it were his fault.

No one would think of showing up for the L. A. Open in simple slacks and sweater. It is the duffers' one chance to trot out their 4-handicap finery without having to live up to it on the greens, and there will be more vermilion alpacas in the gallery than in the tournament and more alligator skin than there is in the Everglades. For you, it's a living. For them, it's a picnic. YOU well know that one-quarter of a stroke a round can mean the difference between red ink and black. But they never think about it. The concentration and the pressure can be such that George Bayer once, when he logged seven putts on one green on the tournament trail, pocketed the ball and stalked off the course.

"Where you going?" someone asked. "I've had enough of this burg," growled George. "I'm going on to Oklahoma City." The guy gave him a funny look. "This is Oklahoma City," he said.

This is Los Angeles, George. Play everything to the left. The greens break toward the ocean, and better keep it on the ground with your second shot to the 9th.

Anyone for Golf?

For those of you who have never been there—and you probably haven't unless you owned a bank or an oil company—the Los Angeles Country Club is a 300-acre plot of the plushest real estate in the world. It's so lush, it seems a shame to waste it on golf. You could retire on the proceeds of the sale of one green if they subdivided it.

It's as hard to get into as Windsor Castle, so exclusive you can get the bends just driving by it. The 800 members comprise the elite of California and legend has it that when one member proposed a movie star for membership once, they not only turned the star down, they threw out the guy who proposed him.

You don't have to have a Hoover button to get in but you may have to take off a Kennedy one. I won't say the average age of the membership is high but unless you show up with gray hair or none they'll know you don't belong. Most of the fellows are rich enough to buy a country on their signature alone and when they drilled for oil there recently and came up with two dry holes hardly anybody even noticed. They didn't need the pin money anyway.

It has two golf courses. The north one is a brute, a deep canyoned horror that only a Hogan or Snead can bring to its knees. The south one is just slightly harder than dominoes. The result is, traffic is heavy to the south while the north one could have pumas ranging over it for all most members know.

You can imagine my consternation when I was invited to play at this place on my return from Canada this week. Usually, I play golf with the kind of people who rob banks, not own them. All the same, a hustler would starve to death at L.A. What I mean is, these fellows didn't get rich throwing their money around to strangers.

The first thing I had to do to get ready was rummage around in my desk for some old literature from the Republican Assembly or my letter from Dick Nixon. Then I got the car washed and the "I Like Ike" sticker dusted off and everything was Go. That's when the tire went flat.

"You'll have to take the Chevy," my wife told me. "The Chevy!" I almost wept. "I can't! They impound anything that's sub-Cadillac. You have to get a special meeting of the committee to even allow Pontiacs in. I doubt if they even let Chevys make left hand turns off the highway. Besides, the Chevy has all those damn orange peels and bubble gum cards in the back seat. How can I drive up in that to play golf with architects like Welton Becket and bakers like Paul Helms and so on?"

"Tell Mr. Helms to leave two loaves of white in the morning and find out when they're going to have hot cross buns," she instructed. She looked at me. "Don't you have a better shirt than that?" she asked me. "You sound as if they played golf in tuxedos there. Why don't you take yours along?" "I can't," I told her. "It's double breasted and they're out." "Oh, well, just don't tell any of those awful jokes of yours," she advised.

When I got there, they looked at me strangely. "You're young," they accused. "I'm over 40," I said defensively. "Around here," they sniffed, "that makes you an adolescent."

They paired me with Norman Chandler who only owns this paper along with a few other things but that was all right because I have just the kind of a game for playing with your boss. I got a natural "customer golf" swing only with me I'm leveling. I could go around quicker using a putter and a rake if people just wouldn't stare. In fact, I'm the inspiration for the old gag about the fellow who staggered around 18 holes and just broke 200 and when he asked his partner what he should give the caddy, they looked at him for a minute and then said "Why don't you just give him your clubs?"

But I got through the day in great shape. I shot 110 if you don't count the holes I picked up on. I was afraid to ask what the stakes were, mentally figuring I could always sell the Chevy, but it turned out it was a lousy dollar Nassau. I know truck drivers who lose that much on the way to the first tee. Perhaps that's why they're truck drivers.

But the wealth is not ostentatious at L.A. There aren't any Renoirs and Vermeers in the locker room, the showers are just ordinary marble and the fixtures are not solid gold, just plate. Of course, it was the first time in a long time I played cards in a Chippendale chair with chips that were genuine antiques. And I have seen roughs that weren't as deep as the carpet.

But it's nice to know that I finally arrived. And if worse comes to worse and the West Virginia militia comes looking for me, I can always hide out at L.A. It's the last place anyone would expect to find a Murray.

Call Him "Lucky"

Even if he were not the only non-Caucasian in the field, you could recognize Charlie Sifford in a golf tournament by the cigar clenched in his teeth. You could almost keep score by the trail of butts. He chain-smokes them but, on the days when he's on his stick and the birdies fall, he barely gets time to light more than three or four.

Charlie Sifford has won only one tournament—a three-round affair at Long Beach in 1957. His swing is nothing to go home and press in the leaves of the family Bible. There are days when he could putt better with a rake.

Yet, he is as big a cinch to go into golfing's Hall of Fame as Sam Snead. This is because Charlie is the only Negro ever to win a PGA tour tournament and in one month will become only the second of his race to become an official paid-up member of the Professional Golfers Assn. The only other one is 74 years old.

Golf did a better job for years than the government of Alabama in pretending the Negro wasn't there. A colored man on a golf course was either handing you a stick or picking up paper cups with one.

To become a member of the PGA you had to play for five years, show up with a shave, and not throw clubs or drink out of your bag where the public could see you. People with jail records made it. Kids who didn't need to shave regularly made it. But not even if you brought a letter from your chaplain could you make it if you weren't white.

Sifford was raised in North Carolina where he caddied by day and practiced by moonlight. It wasn't the golfers who were prejudiced, it was golf. The game is too tough for anyone who plays it regularly to fear someone is going to come along and surround it. A man who has just missed a 4-ft. putt would gladly hand the club to a Martian and burst into wild applause if he could make it.

Charlie played with the likes of Skip Alexander and Clayton Heafner, a massive man who once kept his PGA standing intact by not dropping his clubs in a lake but dropping Charlie instead. Charlie didn't complain. He was slow in coming up with a $5 Nassau. To tell the truth, he didn't have the money. But a study of the fast backswing of one of his partners encouraged him to think he would in a few holes. Heafner couldn't wait. He had a pigeon of his own whose feathers were showing.

Charlie took his methodical backswing and box of cigars to Philadelphia where his artistry in arranging first-tee bets earned him the nom du course of "Philadelphia Shorty." A chunk of a man who looks more as if he were quarried than born, Charlie runs 5-7 and 180 lbs. He once dropped a donkey with a single punch in the Philippines to win a bet from Willie Hunter Jr. "It was $10 'Do or Don't,'" explains Charlie. The donkey went down, shortly followed by Willie and Charlie as half of Manila set upon them. "There were several jackasses on the floor before the evening was over," Charlie recalls.

Charlie didn't start out on the tour under prodding of the

NAACP but under the prodding of money. He won respect with his sticks, not a court order. He still thinks it's the best way although his independence has earned him an occasional sneer as an "Uncle Tom." But, like the original, his methods pricked the conscience of the white community, in this case golf. And it stirred the attorney general of California into action on at least one important occasion when he ran the PGA tournament right out of Los Angeles and the "Caucasians Only" clause right out of the PGA because of Sifford. There was no way golf could contend Charlie didn't belong. The scoreboard contradicted them.

Charlie didn't get an "approved player" status until he was almost at the bi-focal stage. The best way to describe Charlie's age is "somewhere between 40 and 45, mostly the latter."

But he began showing up at tournaments, cigar and all. He had to qualify for every tournament. PGA-ers and "approved players" get a rash of exemptions but Charlie could even finish second (which he did once in the Canadian Open) and have to hustle to the next town to qualify.

He used to drive Mike Souchak's or Bo Wininger's or Frank Stranahan's car from tourney to tourney whenever they made a good score and wanted to fly to the next stop.

For Charlie, the tour stopped at the Mason-Dixon line on the South and the Mississippi River on the East. "When the tour left the United States, I left the tour," he used to explain. But he was the first Negro ever to tee up in an open in North Carolina. He led it after the opening round.

He has since played in other Southern tourneys. He dast not drink, chew, swear, cuss out the customers or bury his putter in the skull of a green or a caddy. He has to have a haircut and a shave. His clothes must not be loud even when his buddy, Joe Campbell, shows up in gold shoes and orchid pants. The difference is Joe also shows up in blond hair.

He has to keep his counsel even when, as has happened, someone kicks his ball out of bounds. He has to pretend he thinks it hit a rock. "I think," said Jay Hebert carefully once, "that Charlie's the greatest player out here. If we had his problems not one of us would shoot the way he does."

Putting is just as tough for a colored man as any other man. Charlie gets the yips the same way Sam Snead does. He has left a ball in a sand trap occasionally, has hit a tree, and the ocean. For years, he couldn't play in enough tourneys to get on the complicated ladder of golf that means Ryder and Cup trips, mass exemptions, the Masters, the big money.

But now he has signed on as public relations counselor with a beer company whose slogan is "It's Lucky When You Live in America." Charlie has seen the day when there was more poetry than truth in that but now he drives his own car which Buck gives him. He occasionally bunks in with his good friend, Mike Souchak, and Charlie is looking forward to the day when HE can turn to Mike and ask HIM if he'd mind driving the convertible to the next town while he, Charlie, takes the plane.

My Fair Ladies

Quick now, who is the world's greatest golfer? You have ten seconds. I'll give you a hint:

The world's greatest golfer is a husky blond who hits the ball out of sight, has a figure that could do without a girdle and squints down the fairway with big blue eyes with just a shade of eye-shadow on them.

Jack Nicklaus? Who said anything about Jack Nicklaus? And what would he be doing with eye-shadow? Or nail polish, for that matter? And does Jack Nicklaus keep curlers in his glove compartment?

No, I have reference to Mary Catherine Wright, who just the other day won her 51st tournament, more than any woman golfer has ever won before and almost more than Arnold Palmer and Jack Nicklaus have won between them. Sam Snead won over 100 tournaments but it took him nearly 30 years. Mickey Wright has won 51 in just eight. Mickey has won 12 tournaments already this year. Even if you're only playing your brother-in-law and two guys who need your business, that's a remarkable record.

No athlete in the whole canvas of sport so dominates his or her field. Mickey Wright hits a ball farther, harder, straighter than any woman who ever lived and quite a few men.

To be sure, the competition is limited. The biggest field ever in women's golf was 43. In an ordinary men's tournament that many tee off before the dew dries off.

But just ask yourself how good Nicklaus would be if he had to do his nails and put up his hair every night before a tournament? What if he had to rinse out a few things in the motel sink before he could even tee off in the morning? How about if he had to stop and pull out a compact and re-do his lipstick after a drive out of the rough? Could he shoot 68 if he was trying to make up his mind which dress to wear to the party that night?

Mickey Wright does all of those thing. She travels from town to town in a Starfire Oldsmobile with a rack full of dresses in the back seat. She tries to keep her nails up, her weight down and her mind on her game all at the same time.

Time was, not so long ago, when a woman golfer was a kind of leathery old harpie with a face that looked like an old shag bag, a voice that came out of a bottle, and a swagger that made you think she chewed tobacco—or at least smoked cigars. She was about as feminine as the Smith Bros. On "What's My Line?" they'd guess her for a mule-skinner.

But Mickey Wright is a girl you wouldn't be ashamed to take to the Cotillion. A beautiful blond with soft skin and a quiet voice, you might guess her for a small-town librarian. Tall and leggy, she wears glasses for near-sightedness and she either has a golf club or a great book in her hands. When she hits town, she lights out for the art museum and the beauty parlor in that order. She has a swing so effortless she makes strong men want to sob as she outdrives them 25 yards per crack.

The school of thought that holds that women should be in aprons, not alpacas, and making fudge, instead of par, dies hard. But any long-suffering male, who spends half his time on a golf course murmuring, "Mind if we play through?" behind a quartet of mother hens in Bermudas bunting the ball along 12 ft. at a time, knows that golf nowadays is co-ed. The touring women pros contest for a mere $300,000 a year vs. $2 million the men shoot at. But there are fewer of them. Mickey Wright does Right Well, thank you, and, while she couldn't get in a poker game with Arnold Palmer, she could probably scare a Dow Finsterwald out of three of four pots.

Mickey, in a sense, exemplifies the new-style ladies' pro. The Professor 'Iggins who turned the pro circuit from "Tugboat Annie" to a "My Fair Lady" is a tough little tour director named Leonard Wirtz who got the gals to doing each other's hair instead of pulling it, pressing their clothes instead of their bets, and putting a convent school approach on the game instead of reform school.

The Ladies National PGA tournament will be held soon and the final round will be televised. The prize money is $15,000 or about $6,000 more than the girls usually get. That will buy a lot of eye-makeup and a closetful of those adorable little Italian pumps, but if you see one of the girls squirt a putt off to the side, that wouldn't be nerves—it'll just be that she suddenly realized the camera was catching her bad side, or her pancake was running. And the winner, just before she goes on the air, is sure to burst out wailing "Just my luck when I haven't got a thing to wear!"

Lizard or Bogeyman

Did you ever go to a movie theater with signs on the outside, "Warning! Don't Go In If You Have a Bad Heart!" and "No Fainting in the Aisles, Please!" The marquee advertises something like "Bride of Frankenstein Meets Reptilicus," and "All-Shock Show!" And then you go in, and they have some damn lizard photographed through a shot-glass or Victor Mature photographed at 1/10th scale? And the only shock is they had the nerve to charge for it?

That's the way I felt when I sat down to watch the final round of the Crosby golf open Sunday. Every year I wait for this, my favorite TV show. It's kind of like going to a movie where you know the guys in the white hats are going to get theirs for a change.

I clicked on the set and said confidently to my father-in-law, "Watch this. Remember how easy these guys toured around Rancho L. A. Open? Warm sun? Greasy fairways? Marshy greens? Wait until you see Pebble Beach. Quail-high clouds. Icy blasts.

Rain-in-the-sand traps. Balls in the ocean. This'll do your heart good."

Then I turned it on: Know what we saw? Warm sun. Greasy fairways. Guys in shirt sleeves knocking in birdies. Amateurs putting for net eagles on holes that normally make strong men consider tossing their clubs in the fireplace.

I could have bawled. Ordinarily, this tournament has more shock thrills than those old movies where the ingénues kept opening closet doors and stiffs fell out of them.

Most years, the telecast is featured by Bing Crosby walking on camera bundled to the ears like a Russian soldier about to take off on maneuvers. He has to keep his pipe in his teeth to keep them from chattering.

It's not really a golf tournament, it's a survival test. When they say they have a "Sudden Death Play-Off," it's not always just a figure of speech. You need penicillin in your bag more than a 1-iron. It's known to some of the pros as "The VapoRub Open."

Most tournaments, when a pro can't find his tee shot, it's in the cup. Here, it's in the ocean. But not this day. I didn't hear a single "A-Choo!" the whole time I listened. "I have never seen 17 playing so easy," marveled Bing Crosby. Only a handful of scramblers took double-bogeys on this par-3 horror bordered on three sides by the Pacific and on the fourth by a fairway that is half sand.

They even had a guy with a putter that looked as if it had been caught in a pipe or found wrapped around a tree limb. He looked like he came to fix the plumbing with it. He putts with it like a croquet mallet, and if he had won the tournament, I'll guarantee you the manufacturer wouldn't be able to keep up with orders for the rest of the year. I was just about to snap the show off. "It's just a walk in the park this year," I said disgustedly to my wife. "Crosby doesn't even have any hot water bottles in his overcoat pockets." The screen even showed a kid in surf-boarding.

It was then the voice of the commentator put a new light on the tournament. It took a turn for the better. "Arnold Palmer," he said, "just took a 9 on No. 18 but it doesn't matter because he has been disqualified for striking an unauthorized provisional on No. 17."

As far as I'm concerned, "an unathorized provisional" is having one more drink when your wife says to get right home. But my ears perked up when the announcer then said, "Somebody walked right in back of Bill Casper as he was lining up his tee shot on No. 18."

"I think I know that guy," I told my wife. "Only with me, he throws a club on the ground on my back swing. This course must be getting to these guys, after all."

A moment later, I knew it was. Jack Nicklaus came up to 18 needing a par to tie. Since it was a par-5, you had to think Nicklaus would have a putter in his hand by the third shot. Indeed, he boomed a good tee shot. Then, he pulled out an iron for his approach and people couldn't have been more surprised if he had pulled out a tire iron.

"He's afraid of the ocean and trouble on the left," the announcer explained. "There's no wind," I found myself contradicting, "therefore no trouble. The course has got him jittery." Nicklaus pushed his iron shot behind a tree. He found more trouble there than on the seawall. He took four to get down.

Suddenly I was proud of the course again. It had just reached up and clutched Palmer, Gary Player and Nicklaus in a row by the throat.

"You know something?" I asked my wife. "These guys don't know it's just a lizard and trick photography. They still think it's a real dinosaur. It scares them to death." "Talk sense," she told me crossly. "I think it's terrible when nice players have to take bogeymen." "The word is bogey," I told her. "And, I think it served them right. Some courses have to make up for all those 62's."

Your Shot, Honey!

Throughout history, there have been certain tribes among which it was the custom to let women do all the work. I don't just mean drive the kids in the station wagon to the bus but the plowing, planting, building the teepee and clearing the trees. I think the Piute Indians and certain nomadic bands of Asians, who lived on yak milk, held to this theory of living.

To them, we can now add professional golfers. The pioneer, who handed the rifle to his wife in the middle of the Indian raid and said, "Hold them off as long as you can and say goodbye to the kids for me—I'm going to try to sneak out through the back woods" has nothing on his modern counterpart in an alpaca sweater, reptile shoes and a soul to match.

Take the Haig & Haig mixed Scotch tournament this weekend at La Costa Country Club. Here is togetherness on the links—a man and woman golfer as playing partners. Here is the way it works: Each partner hits a tee shot off every tee. Then they go out and pick the best one.

In the six years of this tournament, chivalry has taken a bigger pasting than par. It is customary for the male pro to check the tee shots carefully. If he finds them buried in a divot, lying under a twig, sitting in a foot of water, all of his gallantry comes to the fore. He hands the club to the lady. "Here, honey, you have a better angle to the green from here. Try to keep it under those tree branches and don't let that water bother you. The green can't be more than 240 but don't hit it too firm. There's a bunker on the other side."

If both shots alight in water, the male of the species is apt to murmur, "You better play it. My shoes leak." If they are buried in a trap, guess who gets sand in her shoes? If the tee shots land on the green, she gets all the downhill putts.

I suppose it's no worse than handing your wife the plumber's helper when the kitchen floods, or holding the light for her while she nails the roof back on in a high windstorm. But if you noticed the second-day story on the leaders in this tournament, one twosome drove into a trap. I quote from the dispatch: "Miss Stone blasted out 3½ feet from the cup, and HE sank it for a par." Farther down in the same story was the tell-tale note: "Miss Mann made two of the day's most spectacular shots, chipping in from 70 feet out for a birdie 3 on the 14th and blasting a 30-yard shot out of the water 14 feet from the cup on the 563-yard 8th hole."

You can see knighthood is hardly in flower on long par-5's,

lateral water hazards and deep sand traps. None of those old-fashioned notions for our heroes. These are the kind of guys who would get in the lifeboats first or take advantage of their reach at a boarding house dinner to spear the last piece of meat right out from under the nose of a little old lady.

I don't disapprove, mind you. When woman invades man's world, she gives up certain alienable rights. I mean, the right to vote doesn't mean the right to birdies, also. If she can wear pants, run for President, drive trucks, sue for alimony, she has to play them as they lie. Right?

It is the view of some misogynists that a woman should take a golf club in her hands only to beat a carpet. She should think a "Scotch foursome" is four guys around an open pinch bottle.

Ladies on a golf course have certain natural advantages, too. The same ones they had in the Garden of Eden. Shorts and a tight sweater have caused more guys to bogey a hole than a bad slice. I bogeyed a tee once just because I was playing with Barbara Romack who looked a little like Brigitte Bardot in cleats.

There was a time when women's golf was full of types with leather lungs and faces to match. They were built along the svelte lines of Tony Galento and you found yourself checking the field for cauliflower ears or tobacco-chewers.

They're prettier now and softer—even though they have names like "Clifford Ann Creed" which sounds like something that should be in a harness. I expect the male pros will still give them all the shots off the backs of alligators, all the underwater lies, or the over-water shots, buried lies, hanging lies and little white lies. Anything, in short, that you have to swim out to or climb up to.

But some day, some young thing with big round eyes and a haircut that doesn't look like she got it in the German army, is going to come up to a ball which you can only get at by tunneling and she is going to begin to dab at her eyes, knowing the pro is going to make her hit it. Whereupon, the pro will say, "Here, I never could stand to see a woman cry. I'll go up on the top of the hill and give you the line."

Women regularly beat men at par-3 golf. They're neater. Men play par-3's like they clean up the kitchen. But the girls say the men never leave them the simple little flips to the green.

"They leave us the wood shot or the long iron to the green," complains Carol Mann. "When they come up and find a long shot which they're supposed to be better at, they say, 'Well, you better play your ball. I'll play the wedge shot.' When they have a short iron to the green, a good lie and good position, they say, 'Here, I'll handle this one. You make the putt.'"

Kathy Whitworth agrees but contends women are better with the 3 and 4 woods. "We're more accurate. We have to play these clubs more often than men do. In fact, they take their motto from that commercial and even leave the driving to us."

In short, the girls are surrounded by cads as well as caddies.

The Man in the Hat

PALM SPRINGS—If you had a letter from God with permission to build yourself the perfect golf player, you would begin with a palmetto hat to put on top of its bald head.

Underneath, you would have 5 ft. 11 in. of bone and muscle, with forearms like Popeye the Sailor's, a long, supple back, a distance-runner's legs, hands as sensitive as a safecracker's and he'd be so loose-jointed he could scratch his ear with his elbow.

His eyesight would be perfect, he'd be a little tight with a buck. He'd have an accent that came from learning to speak English through a mouthful of hominy grits.

And his name would be Sam Snead.

Sam Snead is to golf what Paul Bunyan is to the North Woods, John Henry to railroading, and Black Bart to highwaymen—larger than life. With Sam, it's hard to tell where the facts leave off and the legend begins. Because the facts are legend enough.

Sam has won 114 tournaments, more than anyone has won before him or will after him. Even his goofs are monument-sized. He has shot a 59 in tournament play and missed putts on that round that were inside the leather. He had a total of 112 shots for two rounds. In the Texas open one year, Jimmy Demaret put together last rounds of 67 and 65 but saw a 5-stroke lead over

Snead melt to a one-stroke loss because Snead had two final rounds of 63. And he missed 5 putts under 10 ft. on the last day.

He has three-putted more greens than any golf pro in history but he has also sunk more 70-ft. putts than any pro in history. He has a swing so perfect he will be able to get on a green in two until rigor mortis sets in.

Only a few athletes are identified by their nicknames alone: "The Man," "The Bambino," "The Manassa Mauler." In golf, only two made it. "The Slammer" can only mean Snead. "The Hawk" means Hogan. Golf is a game which fights anonymity. You go below Arnold Palmer and Jack Nicklaus and the field becomes a faceless army of sun-tanned kids in alpaca sweaters. Twenty tournaments can turn up 20 different winners. The public is bored. The public demands heroes, not whozits.

Snead is older than Archie Moore, balder than Y. A. Tittle and his feet should creak when he walks. But he is a threat in every tournament he enters. His swing is so perfect he shot a 76 with a maple twig and a putter once. It wasn't as difficult as it sounds because when he learned to play the game in the hills of Virginia, he didn't even have the putter. He learned it with a maple twig and a round rock.

He was a ridge-running barefoot kid who never had store-bought food till he was old enough to vote. His dinner, he caught, trapped or shot. He didn't know shoes came without spikes in them until he hitchhiked to Greenbrier in 1936 to take a job cleaning clubs at night and suckers in daylight. He hit a ball so far he didn't know what a 9-iron was for until he started to lose his hair. He thought a spoon was just something to eat with because as a young man he wouldn't have had to use a fair-way wood to cross Rhode Island.

Sam Snead is most famous for the one that got away—the National Open. He missed a 30-in. putt in an 18-hole playoff in 1947, largely because his opponent, Lew Worsham, interrupted him on the backswing of his putt to demand a measurement. He was sitting in the clubhouse and had all but cashed the check in 1937 when Ralph Guldahl caught and passed him.

But the explosion of 1939 at Spring Mill was so violent that there were pieces of Snead still to be found lying in sand traps for miles around there. He came up to the 72nd and final hole of that Open so far ahead of the field he could have won it with a rake and salad fork. As it turned out, he should have used them. He was in more sand, longer, than Gen. Rommel's Afrika Korps. He invented new ways to leave a ball in a sand trap.

Snead could have won the tournament with a 6 but when he got through that hole, not one but three golfers had passed him. He went out that night looking for a guy with a gun so he could pay him to shoot him.

Golfers, normally, are about as athletic as operatic tenors but Sam Snead, whose mother was 47 when he was born, comes of such hardy turkey-shooting, coon-treeing stock that he was his high school champ in high jumping, sprinting and anything else that didn't interfere too much with his hunting and fishing. He could catch a fox barefoot. He was a lodge-smoker prizefighter, a semi-pro football player in a coal mine league, and a pitcher in baseball good enough to get a look from major league scouts. He mastered tennis in one easy lesson and can out-fish Ted Williams, a quondam tackle-making partner for whom he once relegated baseball to the minor sports by observing in a famous colloquy, "In golf, when we hit a foul ball, we got to go out and play it."

His parsimony is as legendary as the rest of his reputation. His idea of charity is that it begins—and ends—at home. He kept his money in tin cans until there was too much of it to carry. Stories run to the kind about the guy who wanted a lesson one day and Snead said "Now, take an 8-iron out of the bag," and the man said, "Wait a minute, how much is this going to cost me?" and Snead said, "How much were you willing to pay?" and the man said "two dollars" and Snead said, "put that club back in the bag, you've already had $2 worth."

Snead plays so infrequently in tournaments now that rumor has it he will only come if you send a Brink's truck. A FULL one.

He won't take tobacco, hard liquor or a doubtful check. He has made the coconut straw hat as famous a trade-mark as Coca-Cola but he could play in a stovepipe hat—or a stovepipe—and still break 70.

He is lending a dash of class and a large splash of color to the Frank Sinatra Invitational here this weekend and it may be your last chance to see him play without challenging him to a $1,000 Nassau and a stroke a side and any guy who would pass up a chance to see Sam Snead play golf would pull the shades driving past the Taj Mahal.

Palms and Springers

Palm Springs is an inland sandbar man has wrested from the rodents and the Indians to provide a day camp for over-privileged adults.

It is a place where every palm tree has its own spotlight, swimming pools come marked "His" and "Hers," and anyone caught riding two to a Cadillac gets a ticket.

Even the rattlesnakes have live-in maids and when a kid wants to run away from home he has the chauffeur bring the car around. A mere millionaire is considered under-privileged here and the Community Chest regularly calls on them with baskets of money to keep the wolf from the door.

It's the only place in the world where the bank didn't get top heavy when Bing Crosby moved in with his money and where the Crosby boys, when they felt the pangs of hunger, used to say, "Dad, write me a check for a thousand, will you? I'm going downtown for a malt and a burger."

It's a land completely surrounded by slag heaps in the shape of mountains and the sun sets so early that most of the adult delinquents who sleep past noon, haven't seen it in years. It doesn't matter too much because you could play night baseball in the glare of the diamonds, but Palm Springs is California's answer as a tourist attraction to "The Land of the Midnight Sun." It's "The Land of the Noon Moon." You have to get up at 5 in the morning and drive 20 miles to the east to get a tan.

They have so many swimming pools here you could go home at night by canoe. I won't say it's ostentatious but when people use mink stoles to dry themselves off coming out of the pool you have to wonder what they dry the dishes with.

The town used to be crawling with movie moguls. You could

always tell them. They were the ones with the fat cigars and the girls too young to be their daughters. But lately it has been overrun with Midwesterners who've either got a lot of money or careless bosses.

The Indians used to own it but they thought it was just a place to hold a Rain Dance. In those days, the place was so dry if you spit, a hundred animals would consider it a water hole and run out of the rocks to surround it. Today, they got so much swimming pool water they have to go on a diet and have developed a taste for chlorine.

The government made the newcomers give some of the land back to the Indians—but they had to wake the Indians up to tell them and after they did, they went right back to sleep again. They think the whole thing is just a round-the-clock rain dance the palefaces are staging.

The Indians didn't know what to do with the place because they didn't know about golf. When an Indian picked up a club it was to hit a head, not a ball. But the white man has used golf as the biggest real estate come-on since they abolished down payments. Palm Springs has so many golf courses that when an architect starts a new house he finds out first where the owner wants the first tee. You look out of place down here without a putter in your hands. Even the poodles wear alpaca sweaters—with matching pearls.

The women even go swimming in their jewelry and lose so many that when the bus boys say pearl diving, they don't mean doing the dishes.

Some people come down here for the 100-deg. heat but most come down for the 100-proof whiskey. The only part of them that gets tan is the end of their nose. You tell time by the color of the drinks around the swimming pool—Bloody Mary red at breakfast and Scotch-and-water plaid at dinner. When they say you hold your liquor well they mean you can tread water without spilling a drop. They import so much they should run a pipeline to Scotland.

Some of the motels are so incredibly lavish—like Desi Arnaz' Indian Wells, around whose pool I'm typing these lines and holding my liquor well, on the typewriter space bar—that if the

Queen of England ever came here she would go home and set fire to Windsor Castle.

I won't say this luxury encourages decadence but I will point out that Ben Hogan, a man of monumental strength of character, was the world's greatest golfer when he came down here and six months later, just before he fled, he had to ask his caddy what club to use for a putt.

The mountains are gorgeous in the setting sun. They are the favorite hangouts of rattlesnakes and golfers with slices but are otherwise as empty as a Russian promise. There is wild life down here but most of it is the platinum-haired variety and always in season. Some of it's the overflow from Las Vegas, others the overflow from the House of the Good Shepherd.

I came down here for the usual reason—golf and the mineral water. I'll say one thing for them: they don't cut the drinks. Two more days and I'd be a candidate for a liver transplant. It's all right if you can hire somebody to be sick for you the next morning. Otherwise you leave the palms sprung.

The golf is the Indian Wells Baseball Celebrity tournament. Over 40 prominent ballplayers were imported by Desi and cohorts at an expense only slightly under the Point Four program.

I had the foolish idea I might walk around 18 holes with Mickey Mantle and have a long chat. I say foolish because with Mickey a grunt is a long conversation. He did speak to me once. "You're in my way," he told me evenly on the 13th. He also asked me what club to use on his approach to the 10th, then said, "Oh, excuse me. I thought you were the caddy."

Mickey plays golf about as you would imagine. He hits a 310-yd. drive, then follows it up with a 310-yd. putt. About like that gorilla they matched Sam Snead with in the story.

Whitey Ford, who played with Mickey, golfs like he pitches. He puts the ball where he wants it—low and away. Whitey is different from Mickey. He's garrulous, gregarious, not suspicious of strangers. He's not at all impressed with the fact he's Whitey Ford and he and his pretty wife, who share a home on the ninth fairway with the Mantles, given them for the tournament, had a ball. He didn't even get mad when some idiot (me) surveyed his buried trap shot on No. 11 and shouted "Hey, Whitey, you want Arroyo to play this out for ya?"

The Fords rhumba'd and cha-cha'd enthusiastically at the tournament party and Whitey looked as cool as though he had an 0-and-2 count on Gene Freese (who by the way hits a golf ball as though Whitey Ford were pitching it).

All in all, it sure beats haircuts in Cincinnati and I hate to go home because I want to hear how that joke came out Phil Harris started two nights ago. Phil is listed as a natural resource by national distillers and I won't say he was living up to it—but when you forget the words to a song YOU wrote somebody's spiking the coffee.

If you haven't got anything better to do—in fact, even if you do—you might run down to Palm Springs this weekend and watch Mantle keep his mouth shut and Whitey and Mrs. Ford having more fun than the rest of the rich people. But if your car's more than three years old, please, have a little consideration. Park it outside of town and rent a limousine from there on in. Otherwise, people will stare.

Bessie's Burgers

As everyone who reads the papers knows, we are in an era of headlong athletic morality.

Shucks, it has been 45 years since they fixed a World Series. I think.

Primo Carnera has quit fighting. The clockers give you an honest count on the morning workouts. Most of the big stables seem to be trying.

Pro football hasn't seen fit to ban anybody for a year and a half, and I was gratified to note that, of the 100 Air Cadets caught cheating on exams, only 30 of them were football players.

It's a Victorian Age of sport. The district attorney has even quit going to basketball games in New York.

There is only one serpent in this Eden. The Royal and Ancient game of Golf, it has come to the attention of authorities, is subject to the sinister and corrupting influences of wagering. Keep this from the kids, if you will, but the PGA has discovered to its horror that golfers bet on themselves.

Now, to me, this is not as horrifying as a discovery that they were betting on the other guy. But the PGA probably knows its business better than I do.

Exhibit A in this devastating exposure is a lanky, loose-jointed veteran of the pro tour with a head of such curly golden locks that they look out of place without a sunbonnet around them. Al Besselink is the only guy I know of whose hair gets blonder as he gets older. He may not be the best player in the world but he's the blondest.

At the San Diego Open, Al got a proposition that was too good to pass up. He got 10-to-1 he couldn't break 66. Now, ordinarily, this is no bet to leap at. But the Stardust course down there is so free of interesting trouble, your main problem is not to fall asleep.

The details of the wager get a little murky here. Besselink recalls the bet as 10 hamburgers to 1. The party of the second part, never identified, maintains a discreet silence, but it will be recalled that a simple bet of cigarettes was enough to put Alex Karras out of football for a year. Once you have established a man is a gambler, the degree of his vice is not the main issue. The Puritan code dies hard in this country and a San Diego writer, Howard Hagen, suggested darkly that, while the bet may have STARTED out as a simple hamburger-to-hamburger bet, who's to say they didn't press it into a steak dinner by the third hole? By the 18th, squab under glass may have been up for the winner and THIS, you have to say, calls for sterner enforcement.

The Besselink reprimand was so slight that when he heard about it in the steam room, he was insulted. He was, in effect, put on probation for a year. One more instance of this kind and he would not only be put off the tour for six months but the American Meat Institute would be notified. "You mean you're not even going to fine me?" roared Besselink. "What do you take me for, a tinhorn?"

Besselink is actually a highly patriotic citizen, fighting poverty in his own way—with a 9-iron. History does not record whether he needed a stomach pump after the round, but it does record he shot his 65. A simple solution might have been to weigh him after the event, but there are other computations involved which might have thrown all the figures right out the window—like how much cornflakes the concessionaire wove into the ground beef, the density of the pickles, whether mustard or ketchup is higher in calories and whether Bessie took all his winnings at one sitting or spread them over a 2-year period for tax purposes.

Besselink had also taken the precaution of declaring bankruptcy a few months back, probably in anticipation of this windfall.

But the imputation that he's a hustler is as false as a first-tee bet. If Bessie had been Titanic Thompson or The Fat Man or some other phantom of the fairways, he would have carefully shot a 67 that first day and saved his 65 until he had very carefully doubled and re-doubled the bet until his hamburgers came in herds and on hoofs—and with oil under them. A man that can shoot 65 deserves at least meat loaf.

But the PGA announced it not only takes a dim view of hamburger-matching, but that it was also looking into the problem of love. They would prefer that the PGA become an order of monks and that anyone caught squiring an unattached lady around town during a tournament be given a two-stroke penalty.

It's a novel idea, substituting birdies for dollies, and leads to the interesting speculation that the next czar of golf will be Cotton Mather, the tournament marshals will be Salvation Army sisters and anyone making a hole-in-one will be tried for witchcraft. And if you know anyone who wants a good deal in ready-to-go hamburgers, contact A. Besselink's receiver.

Fairy Tale

On Feb. 15, 1961, in the little town of Berg, Belgium, a Boeing 707 jetliner crashed into a field, killing all 72 aboard and one farmer on the ground. Searchers, reaching the scene in a matter of minutes, were struck by the number of ice skates strewn through the wreckage. Soon, the word went out to an aghast world. Included in the manifest of death had been the entire 18-member U.S. figure skating team.

In the spangled little world of ice skating, it was a catastrophe comparable to a plane carrying a World Series team plunging into one carrying the Green Bay Packers. Gone was the leggy, graceful Laurence (pronounced "Lo Rance") Owen, the heiress-apparent to the vacated title of Carol Heiss. Gone were her mother and teacher, Laurence Owen Sr., and her sister, Maribel.

The tragedy wiped out more than a team. It wiped out a decade of careful programming which had seen American skaters virtually take over this sport art form. It left anarchy on the ice.

Figure skating is almost the most beautiful form of athletic competition I know. It has none of the sweat of the landlocked summer sports, none of the violence of the water or snow-slope events. It is as graceful as a music box figurine, as full of intrigue as an Italian opera. The stakes are higher—for women anyway—than in any other amateur sport. A chunky, spunky Norwegian fjord skater translated 10 world and three Olympic championships into half the real estate of New York and Hollywood, bigger grossing motion pictures than Jean Harlow and a whole new industry—the ice show. Ever since, figure skating has been given over to quite a few hair-pullings, center-ice temper tantrums and outraged shrieks of women scorned. Not by beaux, by judges.

The competition—except for the gold and silver dances which are just kind of 40-mile-an-hour tangos and the "pairs" which are more athletic, but not much—is divided into two phases. The "school figures," a series of complicated arabesques, all derivations of the ever-lovin' Figure 8, find the skaters writhing in semicircles—now on one edge of the blade, now on the other.

Judges come solemnly on ice, peer at these tracings like a hock-shop proprietor testing a ring for glass content, and then score the performance—six for perfect, zero for lousy. They require six judges because nobody trusts anybody in figure skating.

A judge who can spot a marking made by an inner blade versus one made by an outer edge qualifies to determine the sex of a gnat two blocks away and the discrepancies in scoring are sometimes as remarkable as if three umpires converged on the same play at second base and one waved "out," the other "safe" and the third ruled "interference." Contestants do not hesitate to yell "We wuz robbed" and Carol Heiss and her mama got so shrill in Europe one year that the judges never dared vote against her again.

The real charm of a figure on skates comes with the freestyle. This is kind of an amateur Ice Capades where contestants don their most fetching costumes, put the Peer Gynt Suite or Rachmaninoff's Prelude or Sibelius on the phonograph and take off on the most breakneck but breathtakingly beautiful ballet you have ever seen. It makes Swan Lake look like an elephant parade. It only counts for 40 per cent in the scoring but it is sports' most beauteous moment, where choreography counts more than charging and aesthetics more than athletics. It's truly a fairy tale come to life.

The spins and turns are known as "Axel Paulsens" or "Salchows" and are so difficult and moving that spectators in Europe have been known to sob when a girl—or a boy—falls.

They take to the ice as soon as they can walk, these girls and boys of figure skating. Every day they spend 4–6 hours on ice or enough to go from Sioux Falls to St. Louis if the river is solid enough.

The national championships are at Long Beach Arena Feb. 7–10. Contestants come from all over the country and—after 364 days of the most gruelling preparation—they have exactly five minutes and a few Figure 8's to get their name up in lights—or Papa and Mama have wasted all that ill-afforded money for travel and lessons.

I traveled over to the Polar Palace the other day to watch my own best bet for future stardom on steel runners—a saucy, brown-eyed honey blonde named Jennie Walsh. Jennie can do everything Sonja Henie could do at that age except speak Norwegian. She is a better skater at 12 than most people ever are and you could see it as she and Billy Chapel whirled through a demonstration of "pairs" skating.

There was a hole in the ice and Billy hit it and flew through the air. So did Jennie. Her wrist broke her fall. But the fall broke her wrist. She'll be the one skating at Long Beach with a cast. I don't think it can stop her any. Not even if it were on her foot.

By the Old Seaside

The scene is a rampart above the Pacific Coast Highway, the time, the first Sunday in July. Two sentinels hidden in the brush tensely scan the horizon. One of them lowers his binoculars. His face is ashen.

"Here they come!" he whispers hoarsely.

He scrambles down to a courier. "Pass the word," he says brokenly. "They're on their way. Put Plan B into effect. Scatter out or the first wave will get us all. Chainlock your driveways; get the kids in the house. Give Mother a tranquilizer and put Uncle Soak to bed. Put away the 'No Trespassing' signs or they'll scrawl obscenities on them. And remember! Passive Resistance! Don't give them any excuse to get violent! Turn the other cheek or they'll break both of them. Help them out when they get stuck in sand or they'll stick you in it. Love Thy Neighbor or he'll break your damn neck!"

The most devastating army since Attila the Hun or the Visigoths is on the way: the American public.

It is an invasion in force. They are girded for battle as their motorized units pour over the defiles of the Santa Monica Mountains in search of the sea, a sunburn, sand in the sandwiches.

They have left their previous despoilments behind—their sheared-off mountains, bill-boarded-up highways, polluted air, their neon nights. Now, it's the beaches' turn.

The roads leading to the shore are a long hydra-headed serpent of moving vehicles populated with grim-faced, battle-hardened veterans. They are pulling boats or tents or trailers. The top of the sedan is a forest of aluminum chairs, surfboards, food hampers.

They are armed to the teeth. Junior has his rubber duck. Sis has the record player and the transistor. Grandma has the egg salad. Dad has the beer but forgot the opener, which means he'll need the Band-Aids which he also forgot. Mom has the pickles and the baby already has diarrhea and the playpen has a broken slat in it. There is a dog in every other car.

They are READY, man!

Only the sharks are happy to see them come. The jellyfish will bite them. The waves will knock them down. The oceanside home-owners will pray for a tidal wave. The lifeguards will call up reserves. The highway patrol will make sure its guns and red lights are working. Ambulances will keep the motor running. The sheriffs will use the buddy system because beachcombers are not the soft touches bank-robbers are and they travel in schools like barracuda.

The world's greatest practical joker, the highway traffic engineer, has done his best to frustrate them with traffic mazes at the mouths of canyons that would give a compass a nervous breakdown and are navigable only by celestial tracking.

The refugees from Muscle Beach, closed as a public nuisance, will take their pects and lutes elsewhere and match muscles and swap wheat germ with other bicep-worshippers, but ignore girls who are bad for muscle tone.

By nightfall, the seaside will be a mass of half-masticated pickles, greasy potato salad, broken bottles of sun-tan lotion, rusting cans, smoldering fires, lost children and long lines at the emergency hospital of people pressing for lockjaw with slashed toes and dirty handkerchiefs wrapped around them. The reefs will be a mass of splintered surfboards, some with blood on them. A few optimists who put to sea in boats in surf too rough for anything less than a destroyer will be on their way to Japan—or the bottom. The Coast Guard will be trying to intercept them at a cost to the taxpayer of enough to support a family of two for a year.

It will look like Atlanta the day after Sherman left. But the Visigoths will finally be in retreat. The coast highway will be a-clog with flame-faced motorists with tempers to match. Five thousand yards of Noxzema later they have finally been turned back. But like MacArthur, they shall return.

Not everyone can succeed at the sport of being a noisome sunbather—without really trying, that is. Accordingly, I should like to reprint a few of Murray's handy guides of obnoxiousness to take with you on your next trip to the seashore, a service I perform free-of-charge once a year at this time. When you go to the beach, be sure to:

1. Bring your inner tubes and put the kids in them, particularly

if they're too worn out for your car. They sink easily in surf. This prevents lifeguards from getting flabby or can provide a cure for over-population if they already are. Flabby, that is.

2. Take your trash along. If you can't dump it on the beaches, you can dump it on the nearest front lawn. The residents there will take care of it. They have to. Otherwise they will get fined.

3. Bring the dogs. They liven things up considerably—paw up sand, help themselves to your lunch or your leg, fight with each other, snap at the baby and treat the umbrella pole with the most shocking indignity.

4. Bring a surfboard and shoot the surf where the most small kids are. They cut easier than adults and can't get out of the way as fast. Don't slow down. The lifeguards are expert at tourniquets.

5. Stand up for your rights when the guard yells, "Everybody out of the water! Sharks!" Statistics prove only 2 out of 5 sharks are man-eaters and 5 out of 5 sharks are cowards and men aren't. That's why sharks eat men.

6. Bring the children and turn them loose. If you keep track of them you will deprive the lifeguards of hours of enjoyable searching up and down the beach for lost parents with a crying child.

7. Pay no attention to those stories of riptides. Next thing you know they'll be telling you there's octopus out there.

8. Forget the under-tow. Even if it sucks you out, you got one chance in 1,000 of washing up on Catalina.

9. Dump your leftovers on the highway. With a little luck you can cause an epidemic of flat tires in traffic which has the added beauty of making a bad situation impossible.

10. Check your Blue Cross, Red Cross and insurance program generally. If you don't have double indemnity, don't go.

Down to the Sea

You won't read about it in the next edition of Jane's Fighting Ships, but the S.S. *Nervous Wreck*, registered out of Malibu, hit the waves with appropriate ceremony last week. We had intended to break a bottle of 7-Up over her bow. But one of the kids drank the 7-Up.

The *Nervous Wreck* is not exactly the kind of vessel the Cubans might hijack—although my wife kind of wishes they would. What it is, is a dinghy. A dinghy is a rowboat with a swelled head—and a round bottom. Actually, it's a kind of surfboard with seats.

My son thinks it will be the scourge of the Pacific. He thinks a red alert went on with every fish east of Hawaii the day we bought it.

Teddy comes by his nautical heritage naturally. His father held the record for round trips on the Hoboken ferry in the middle 30s. As far as fishing goes, he's on his own. I even hate to change the water in a goldfish bowl. I don't even know how to get tuna out of a can.

Until Teddy took up fishing, I used to think that a jig was an Irish dance. Now I know it's a hunk of wood painted like a sardine to fool albacore. I'm not sure I want to be a party to this kind of deception but that's the way kids are nowadays. I don't know why they can't just get their kicks stealing hubcaps the way we used to. Anyway, I think fish are entitled to an even break. If you've ever bitten into a bowl of phony fruit, you have an idea how the fish feel when they swallow a varnished sardine. Except, wax pears don't have hooks in them. Not unless your hosts have a funny sense of humor.

Teddy is an exceptional fisherman in that he likes to eat fish. I don't know whether you know it or not but most fishermen would rather eat their bait than the fish they catch. It's kind of ironical when you consider how much the fish would enjoy people.

Teddy usually just surf-fishes with an old man of the sea named Frank Craig who is so good the fish off Point Dume would just as soon see a hungry shark coming as Frank. Frank could cast a line into the Hollywood Freeway and come up with his limit in an hour.

My son has always been disappointed in me as a sports columnist (all I can say is he'll have to take his place in line). His beef is I don't give enough scoop on fishing. He's got more poles than a tuna fleet and his idea of stop-the-presses stuff is a yellow-tail run. He thinks Gillette ought to drop the World Series and televise the next one. A TV program called "Fishing Flashes" has it all over "The Untouchables" in his book.

I got Teddy his dinghy to get him out there where he could get a real shot at the fish and they would think World War III started so many of their friends would be missing. A dinghy, in its native state, is just a hunk of plywood which looks at first glance like one of those English dogs with hair in their eyes. You can't tell whether it's coming or going. It has no front end.

We pushed the thing off the sand and out through the breakers the first time. Cheers went up. Triumphantly, Teddy brought it back. I turned to my wife who was silently praying on the beach. "You see," I said, "a real chip off the old quarterdeck. A regular Captain Kidd." I welcomed him back like a Russian astronaut.

Our dinghy is new but it looks as if it had been sick for a long time. With smallpox. This is because we got too much advice on how to put fiber-glass on the bottom. Take it from me, there are more ways to fiber-glass a boat than skin a cat which is easier. I have so much glass under my fingernails I could start a fire holding them under the sun. Fiber-glass bubbles if you put the resin on sloppily which it is impossible not to do.

Anyway, we put this pock-marked 8-footer back in the water and this time put a fishing pole in it. That's when the ocean got mad. Before we got it out through the surf, it turned sideways. This is a condition called "broaching." It's the nautical equivalent of getting a flat tire in heavy traffic. The ocean dumped the boat, my son, the fishing pole, the oars and me. It swept my eyeglasses out to sea.

Teddy was in a fury of frustration. But I was like the College All Stars. I knew when I was overmatched. My wife was white. "What are you trying to do?" she screamed. I groped my way toward the beach. Without my glasses, I was lucky it wasn't Catalina.

"Listen," I said bravely, "the Navy piled up four destroyers on this coast. Somebody ran the Missouri aground. It's no disgrace. YOU even bump into the back of the garage on a clear day with no swells to compete with. What do you expect?"

She didn't answer me. But later I heard her on the phone. "It's called a dinghy," she was saying icily. "I think they named it after my husband."

Sun and Sixpence

Great athletes, the sport sheets of our great dailies to the contrary notwithstanding, do not always occur in nature in centerfield at Yankee Stadium, getting $100,000 a year and their pictures on bubble-gum cards. Neither do they always show up on the Ed Sullivan show swinging a golf club and explaining how they fought off a case of nerves to sink a putt for $20,000 and all the golf balls, clubs, alpaca sweaters and cigarettes they can carry.

Sometimes, they show up in little places like Lahaina, the once-kingly city of the Island of Maui in the State of Hawaii. It was in Lahaina that the last kings of Hawaii ruled and it was in the watery roadsteads off Lahaina that the great whaling fleets used to put in during the last century. It was probably here under the uncertain light of a swaying ship's lantern that Herman Melville made the notes whence came "Moby Dick," and it was here that the first New England missionaries landed, bringing to the islands the word of God and the blessings of the common cold.

The roads of Lahaina are one of the world's last reservoirs of unspoiled beauty. I almost hate to tell you about it. At sunset the sea dances like a giant tub of tumbling sapphires. Off in the distance the spires of Molokai spear the rays of the sinking sun. Across the roads rear the gentle slopes of the Island of Lanai. In the backdrop loom the cloud-caressed mountains of Maui. They usually have a rainbow over them. The rains drift down as gently as a kiss on the brow of a sleeping child.

Jack Ackerman lives in Lahaina—in a one-room shack on stilts with barely room for one bed, a refrigerator, a wife, a hi-fi and a place for your air tanks. In Lahaina, it's all you need. The population is probably 5,000, but nobody bothers to count.

Jack Ackerman, the son of an army officer, is above ground about as often as the great sperm whale and, before his marriage to the lovely Jane a year ago, his friends confidently expected him to be the first mammal to put to sea permanently since the

Silurian Age. There was a time when Ackerman surfaced only to see the sunset. He and a partner were 200 ft. below sea level so often they were thinking of having an extension phone put in.

As athletes, they were known only to the little Japanese grocer to whom they owed each month's bill until they paid off in fish. But it takes a great athlete to plumb 225 ft. to the ocean floor, to wrestle great 400-lb. sea turtles (they brought a nice price in the soup pots of Waikiki), to circulate freely among the omnipresent great sharks, the Mafia of the Pacific deeps.

The enemy is the coral, the eel, the long-toothed predators and the sea itself. At 200 ft., a man cannot even trust himself. A rapture seizes him, a euphoria known as "nitrogen narcosis" which makes him giddily devil-may-care. The tanks on his back give him just a few minutes to get aloft because it has to be done in stages to let the nitrogen bubbles simmer down and the pressures equalize. He must come up on a mental elevator with the stops marked only in his head as the ocean is far from the source of light at those depths.

Ackerman dove just because he couldn't help himself when he first came to Lahaina in 1958 and his friends jokingly checked him for gills at each ascent. But he went so much deeper than man ever had before—without a submarine around him—that he pried loose a strange-looking piece of coral tree one day and sent it to a museum where it was identified as a rare species of black coral, an almost diamond-hard piece of underwater horticulture. When polished, it makes gems of rare beauty and value. Jack has not exactly driven De Beers out of business since but he has been able to meet his grocery bill since the day the first piece was tied to a rope and sent up.

One day, though, Jack lingered too long, prying off a particularly stubborn bush. He surfaced too fast and, when he hit the boat, his teeth began to chatter, his feet doubled up, and his eyes rolled back in his head. The bends. The curse of the depths.

He would have been dead-on-arrival at the decompression chamber at the sub base in Pearl Harbor if his partner had not begun mouth-to-mouth breathing. Jack recovered, but even today he seems, at times, to be listening to a sound no one else can hear. He did not quit diving, he just quit going to 200 ft.

It is a rare sports story and the rewards are not cereal endorsements or royalties from autograph slacks. But right now, Jack is lying on his window bed listening to the water of the Lahaina roads sloshing against the breakwater under his shack, and looking out at the gentle sea where the whalers once caroused and the kings of Hawaii ruled, and he doesn't envy Mickey Mantle or Willie Mays one bit.

Menace, Anyone?

Gussie Moran was on the phone. That meant anything could happen.

You've heard of Gussie. To tennis, the menace. To mankind, gorgeous. Gussie walked out on the tennis court in Wimbledon in 1949 wearing lace pants, and the British Empire has never been the same since. I don't think Gussie made the quarter-finals but the flap she caused hasn't died down yet. Only the other day, the British Lawn Tennis Assn. ruled that only basic white could be worn on its hallowed courts and that the covering had to be wall-to-wall—no part of the girl should be showing through.

Gussie is the only dame I know of who was a baseball broadcaster. She used to do the Dodger games back in the days when they were funny on purpose. Gussie didn't know very much about baseball but only a churl would complain. Anyway, neither did the Dodgers.

Gussie was all business. "I don't want to talk about sports," she warned. "I am doing a magazine piece on you—the real you."

I groaned. "The real me," I told her, "is astigmatic, gouty, cranky, chronic gas-on-the-stomach and nobody ever calls me 'Mr. Murray.' Can't we just talk about your tennis fashions?"

Gussie was cross. "They're not tennis fashions. They are pool fashions."

I was astonished. "Woman are playing pool now?!"

"Silly!" said Gussie. "Swimming pool fashions."

"What are you pet peeves?" she demanded.

"Do-it-yourself instruction sheets," I told her. "You know. The ones that tell you to put the fram-a-fram in the brackus. I swear I think they're practical jokes, double-talk. Tell me, do you really believe there's such a thing as a clevis pin?"

"Who's your favorite athlete?"

"Ben Hogan. But for a long time it was Frenchy Bordagaray."

"Do you think Hitler's dead or in a dungeon in Siberia?"

"Either way it's all right with me."

"What do you think of Cuba?"

"It's a nice place to visit but I wouldn't want to live there."

"Be serious. Do you think we did right there?"

"Well, when you see the kid next door assembling a machine-gun, the minute he starts putting bullets in it, you better go take it away from him. Particularly if you have reason to believe he's not quite all there."

"What's wrong with the Rams?"

"Let's put it this way: how should I know?"

"George Wilson of the Lions says if they hadn't lost their first game to the Colts, they wouldn't be 1–7 now."

"That's true. They'd be 2–6. In 1941, the Chicago Bears beat the Washington Redskins 73–0 and after the game some sports-writer said to Sammy Baugh 'If you had made that touchdown in the first few minutes of the game, would that have changed the outcome?' 'Sure,' said Baugh. 'The score would have been 73–7.'"

"What do you think of outlawing prayer in schools?"

"Some people think separation of church and state means a divorce between God and man. As with all divorces, the children suffer but, on the other hand, it's been my experience the best prayers are silent prayers. So are the best people. The guy who has to shout his religion is usually afraid God doesn't believe him. Or vice versa. And not even the Russians have figured a way to stop you from praying silently."

"Do you have any political convictions?"

"Yeah. I'm against daylight-saving time."

"Don't you think everyone should vote?"

"Only if they're alive. Back where I come from the cemeteries sometimes swung more elections than free beer. Sometimes you weren't too sure about the people you put in office, either."

"Do you have any stand on the issues?"

"Well, yes. I think that everyone who likes the company of morons should vote against Proposition 1-A because if that fails we're going to get a whole generation of them. Of course, we'll save $270 million and probably won't lose anything more than the country. It'll probably be one way to learn Russian at no expense."

"What do you think about Nixon and Brown?"

"Where were they when we needed them? The third game of the play-offs? The Rose Bowl? The Alston-Durocher dispute? The water rights in Candlestick Park? I have to say the campaign has been a keen disappointment to me on these key issues."

There was a silence at the other end. "One more thing, Gussie," I told her. "Put in there that my favorite actor is Richard Barthelmess . . ."

The Last Roar?

Well (Sob!) it looks as if I won't be going back to the Indianapolis 500 this year, after all. Too bad. I'll miss those 33 kooks in the flame-proof suits climbing into those coffin-shaped, 4-wheeled banshees for America's only sanctioned 33-man suicide pact.

They won't miss me back there. I was voted the only man they'd like to see as a pedestrian in this thing last year because I pointed out it was the only sporting event in the country where there were more ambulances than athletes and, in spite of enough equipment to stop a forest fire, there were still some accidents where all they needed was a whisk broom and an ashtray.

They start this race with Taps and sometimes they finish it the same way. A guy goes 170 m.p.h. in the straightaway only so he can go 15 m.p.h. in a hearse. Your margin for error, you could pick your teeth with. "Your car," thoughtfully pointed out Eddie Sachs, who admits he spends the parade lap weeping, "moves faster than you can think."

Since art can always duplicate nature, I thought what I might do this year is lock myself in a room with the heat turned on, a sun lamp on my neck, get somebody to keep a tin of castor oil burning in the corner, hire somebody to blow a cornet with a piece of torn rubber over the end of it in my ear for 3½ hours, and arrange for a driver who had to quit when he suffered third degree burns over 40% of his body and now has parts of his hips for fingers to shake them under my nose and say, "You can't talk that way about racing! How dare you say it's dangerous? What are you, a Communist?"

Or, I might do what the Hoosiers do—take a picnic lunch or a bag of fried chicken and a case of hooch to the divider in the middle of the freeway and, like them, pay no attention to the racing traffic unless or until an occasional wheel with or without car accompanying, came cartwheeling through the potato salad.

But I find Fox West Coast and the Sports Arena are televising this thing in theaters; so I think I'll put on my black arm-band, get my hymnal and take up a seat at one of them. It'll just be another movie matinee. This year, when a car flips or does a few Immelmanns through the infield, the driver can pick the bricks and sparkplugs out of his teeth and honestly shrug, "Well, that's show biz."

I will be sad this year for another reason. If you're in the seats, listen carefully for that monstrous roar of the Offenhausers winding up in the back stretch because it may be the last time you hear it. Like the bellow of the Great Plains bison, the trumpeting of the woolly mammoth in a tar pit, or the clashing of the great Brontosaurus Rex in the prehistoric underbrush, it may be the melancholy last sound of a terrestrial animal about to become extinct. A few years from now, the only Offenhausers to be found will be in an assembly of their skeletons in the better museums.

There have been two kinds of cars and two kinds of race drivers in the world. There were the cigar-chomping, whiskey-drinking roughnecks from the dirt tracks and asphalt ovals of the American circuit—graduate garage mechanics with several generations of grease under their fingernails—and there were the effete, symphony-playing, hand-kissing, champagne-sipping international company of Grand Prix drivers whose ranks ran heavily to marquises,

South American playboys, English earls and German barons. They read poetry, not *Playboy*. If they smoked, they used holders.

The American drivers ran cars as loud, muscular and assertive as they were. They bullied their way around a track. Privately, they considered the Grand Prix set dilettantes or, more coarsely, "sissies"—guys with white scarves who drank wine in their races.

A few years ago, when Juan Manuel Fangio came to Indy, took a few practice spins, and promptly disappeared, the Offy crowd looked at each other and nodded. Indy was not some Sunday afternoon on a tree-lined French pasture. It was a 33-brute fight in a phone booth. No place for a heel-clicker.

But two years ago, the Aussie Grand-Prixer, Jack Brabham, showed up at Indy in a rear-engine car with just enough power to climb a cherry pit. His crews were inexperienced, and he stayed in the pits so long on fuel stops the crowd thought he was waiting for Green Stamps. Still, he finished an insolent 9th.

Last year, the Grand Prix invasion included the mighty Scot, Jimmy Clark, and the elegant son of a concert pianist, Dan Gurney. Their cars, rear-engined, cigar-shaped, Ford-powered and —horrors!—painted green, flouting one of Indy's hallowed superstitions, wheeled around the track like a flight of pesky wasps in a Congress of wallowing turkeys. They didn't even make much noise. They didn't have "Joe Clancy's Rear-Axle Big Bore Special" plastered all over the side, just the name of the car tastefully stenciled on.

Clark probably should have won. Winner Parnelli Jones' Offy was just a 4-wheeled oil slick at the finish. A race on ice would be less dangerous for Clark.

This year, Clark coolly flew in for a weekend, for qualifying. "I can only give you a few hours, boys, I'm due at Monaco for a really important race," he said in effect—and then went out and plucked off the pole position, the first time it has been won by a non-Offy since the days when they had running boards. The entire front row and over one-third of the field is rear-engined Fords. The silk scarf set proved a lot tougher drivers than they look despite their drawing room manners and bench-made shoes.

So, shed a tear for those automotive buffaloes, the Offies. A part of Americana dies Saturday at Indianapolis. I only hope that's all that does.

Fireball Fires Up

The greatest stock car races in the world take place every afternoon about 5 on the Hollywood Freeway. The ground rules are simple: you have to have an unmodified family sedan with radio, heater, ashtray, heavy monthly payments and, preferably, a worn tire or two. If you have kids in the back seat, you get bonus points.

First prize is an early dinner. Second prize is an early grave. The trick is to get into the lane farthest from your off-ramp until you're right on top of it and then dash across the top of traffic to get to it. If there are two or more women drivers between you and it, you get extra credit.

You don't stay in your class, you try to move up a notch. For instance, if you're driving a medium-priced four-door, you only take on a Cadillac or a Lincoln. At all costs, avoid the rust-ribboned jalopy driven by the pimply faced kid who looks as if he's two payments behind and way under-insured. You get penalized if you get wiped out by a guy who will go to jail or on the lam before he'll pay damages.

Not since the days of iron men in wooden ships has there been any competition as exciting as this between wooden heads and wheeling steel.

But these are amateurs and the competition involuntary. On Saturday, at Riverside, 44 professionally reckless drivers will volunteer for an auto wreck in a four-wheeled rodeo that may break the one-day plasma record set by the United Nations against unarmed civilians in the Congo last week.

From the outside, these stock cars rolling on the track will just look like a lot of guys going to work. But Honest John or any used-car David Harum wouldn't take a second look at these heaps. All they have is an overpowered engine. No radio, no heater, no ashtrays. In fact, no back seats. A stick shift, for heaven's sakes.

And not even the worst crook in Auto Row could claim these things were driven by two little old ladies from Pasadena.

The only reason the little old lady would get in one of these things is for a getaway from a bank robbery.

They will do 175 m.p.h. but they sound as if they have asthma at anything under 100. They use first gear only to get out of the pits. They have no mufflers and you would be sure to wake the front office—not to say the whole neighborhood—if you tried to sneak home late in one. What's more, the doors are bolted and the only way to get in is to crawl through the window—which might make the cops uneasy if they saw you doing it at 2 in the morning. The shock absorbers feel as if they have been stolen from a blacksmith.

There is room for just 44 of them on the track at a time at Riverside, a course constructed for sports cars you could park in an overcoat pocket, not 4,000 lb. Pontiacs. Since over 60 drivers will be trying for those 44 spots, the din in the orange groves should be deafening this week.

On Sunday, the spot they'll be running for will be first prize and the largest share of $66,245. All they have to do is last 500 miles, preferably in one piece and first place.

In a way, these guys have all the best of it: they have only one seat and a roll-bar. They don't have the little lady complaining, "I don't remember any of these streets at all. You're lost." They have no credit cards to worry about, no left turn blinkers, no golf clubs rattling around in the trunk—just a fire extinguisher. They don't have to call the Auto Club if they get a flat. Of course, they may have to call an ambulance.

They only get five miles to a gallon but they don't have to hide it from the guy next door who brags he gets 30. Matter of fact, they don't have to put up with any of the hazards of driving. All the other drivers are men.

There are two kinds of drivers in stock car competition—"strokers" and "chargers." A "stroker" is a guy who just tries to stay alive and in the race. A "charger" is a guy who tries to win and doesn't pay too much attention to the side issues, like life and health. It's either winners' circle or the boneyard.

The best of the "chargers" is a hell-bent young Floridian, Glenn (Fireball) Roberts, who drives as if the Feds were after him with tommy-guns. When they strap Fireball into a harness they don't worry so much about the engine standing up as the roll-bar. He won $56,000 last year in only 18 races.

He had the board of life underwriters reaching for the smelling salts at Charlotte when his brakes, steering and right front-end suspension couldn't keep up with him. He began to cross the track in rudderless figure-8's at 125 m.p.h. like a Buster Keaton serial until one of the other cars sheared his in half. Fortunately, Fireball was in the other half.

Lakers in Nowhere

FT. WAYNE—It is 4 o'clock in the morning and the temperature is a balmy zero when we bounce into Ft. Wayne.

There is no traffic pattern to get in over the Ft. Wayne international airport. There is no traffic. The Paris jets by-pass Northern Indiana. This country isn't for the jet set. It's for the Greyhound group. From Ft. Wayne, you can get to Churubusco, Harlan, Monroeville and Leo-Grabill real easy. Any place with lights in it takes a bit more doing.

The flight from Boston is a droning 6-hour journey into boredom. The card game in the back is more noisy than scientific. The cheating is lively and it's not considered cricket to notice it unless you're the victim.

The coach has laid the law down: no more high-limit poker games. So the game is Hearts and the action is considerably lower. Higher than he thinks, of course, but still lower than 2-dollar, three-raise lo-ball.

The in-flight "meal" is a saran-wrapped cardboard horror my dog Duffy would slink away from. But at 9,000-ft. with frost on the windows and the reading matter the vintage of the Spectator Papers you let your stomach take chances. There's nothing else to do. "We should have taken a plane," groans Rudy LaRusso.

"I hope they park a few cars around the airfield with their lights on," nervously murmurs Jerry West. "Tell me, can he find Ft. Wayne in the dark?"

The ground is covered with snow, the locks on the rental

cars are frozen stuck, and you can't shut the door. But the worst has yet to come: the motel has fouled up the reservations and every motel north of the town is sold out, too. At 4:30 on a zero morning, the alternative seems to be to sleep in the park. "Ft. Wayne. Nowhere, U.S.A." groans Rod Hundley.

The candy stand in the lobby is swept as clean as if a plague of locusts passed through. But, since the room clerk isn't looking, the snack is on the house. Dandy Dick Barnett clanks a nickel down but when he looks around and sees he's the only one, he hastily rebounds it.

Reservations are finally secured at a second-rate downtown hotel. It's clean enough and comfortable enough. But that's no fun. So the uninhibited Lakers strike up a pre-dawn banter. "Wall-to-wall rodents," sniffs Elgin Baylor. "I was in the other league," opines Ron Horn "and if you spread enough bread crumbs on the floor, the rats won't bother you."

A character in overalls and a work shirt sits sleepily in the corner. He has obviously come to check the plumbing which is temperamental, to say the least. "Check the manager," suggests Dick Barnett. The Lakers break up. But soon they scatter. They are on the scent of food.

The games, fortunately, on this trip include the canvasbacks of the league, the New York Knicks and the Detroit Pistons twice. But the Knicks, urged on by hostile Boston fans, push the Lakers to a 1-pt. victory. Gene Conley, a pitcher in the off-season, and Dave Budd, a career basketball player and glad enough to be that, have their best nights of the season. But the Lakers are not fooled. Their enemy is always and officially, the officiating. "Call the fouls, Rudolph," bellows Fred Schaus, shaking the Boston Garden with a size-13 foot stomp. The Lakers get 8 free throws more than the poor Knicks but this is considered off the subject.

The one veteran Laker who is never a part of the banter but a good-natured spectator (rookies, of course, are expected to stay in the background, be seen and not heard) is Franklin Delano Selvy. At 31, he is hardly a graybeard but to the Lakers, he is "Pops." "The grand old man of basketball," observes Hundley affectionately, which prompts Elgin Baylor to dub Jimmy Krebs, who has just slipped him the queen of spades "the grand old lady of basketball." "I can beat you one-on-one anytime," sunnily opines Krebs. "You're nothing."

Selvy was the Quiet Man of the Lakers till the rookie Gene Wiley came along. No one has even heard him breathe. The erstwhile Laker, "Count" Ray Felix, a western movie fan, loved Selvy as he watched him walk warily through a hotel lobby with the rolling walk of a well-armed stranger in town. "Ol' Frank, he looks just like a two-gun man, don't he?" Ray used to cackle. "Looks like the bad guy better not never mess with him."

Pops was brought up in the dark and bloody ground of Kentucky where his father raised a family of 7 by going so deep in the mine shafts a man needed a canary more than a dog. When the bird keeled over, you pushed the up-button in a hurry before you joined him.

Frank was the best basketball player ever raised in Corbin, Ky. Seventeen colleges waved offers under his nose before he chose Furman, a dot on the educational map which he turned into a red star one night when he poured 100 points through the hoop, a feat it even took Wilt Chamberlain several years to break.

"Fabulous Frank," the gushing sportswriters called Selvy, a nickname which turned to the ironic "Fab" when Pops joined the St. Louis Hawks and the coach took one look at his 6'3" 140-lb. frame, as spare as a birch rod, and told him whenever he got the ball to pass it off to one of those big guys quick. In this league, coaches like their baskets made from the top down.

The army took him to Germany for two years and gave him a gun instead of a basketball and when he came back to the league he was passed around like a basketball in an all-court stall.

He found a home with the Lakers where his peculiar gliding stride, as soft as an Indian trailing a deer, and his delicate, arched shot are as important in their way as Baylor's bulls to the basket.

He has more tape than an Egyptian king and both ankles are so calcified that returning to earth from a jump some nights seems like a leap from a roof to a sidewalk.

He married "Miss Arkansas" who was glad enough to become "Mrs. Selvy" and the road trips are a melancholy of apartness for Frank who ranks his wife and two little girls far above basketball or whatever else is second.

"He never gets mad. He bleeds inside," the coach explains. The

Lakers are sentimental about few things but to a man they were almost tearful that it was Selvy who missed the rim shot that would have given them the title last year. "Why couldn't it have been Elg—or me?" gnashed Hot Rod Hundley. "We can take it. Pops is too nice a guy to have to live with a rap like that." It is the way the Lakers feel about their grand old man of 31.

Operation Frostbite

"Good morning. It's 8:30 and 9 degrees," the hotel operator in St. Louis sings out. She sounds so cheerful you have to resist asking "How would you like to drop dead?" Instead, you ask bitingly. "Can you find out what it is in Palm Springs?"

In the lobby the Lakers gather in yawning knots and Operation Frostbite moves on to Boston. The airport is locked in snow as we board Interstate Airmotive's DC-3, a bucket of rivets and propellers, unpressurized and, as we enter, unheated.

Jimmy Krebs groans. "Lindbergh," he observes, "crossed the Atlantic in better equipment than this. Tell me, do you have to get a push to get it started?"

The trip is a hedge-hop under barely allowable ceilings. The plane pitches and yaws and the cardboard bag "For your convenience in event of motion discomfort" looks better and better. "Breakfast" is a soggy roll and instant coffee with instant cream which sits on top of the liquid like insoluble Parmesan. "Save that stuff for the lasagna," Hot Rod Hundley suggests.

"It'd be different," muses Rudy LaRusso, "if anybody really wanted to go to Boston." "A DC-3," notes Krebs. "The plane that won the Civil War." He pauses. "We will get to Boston by July," he predicts. "Our next charter," adds Hundley, "will be a balloon."

The layover in St. Louis for most is 24 hours of sack time punctuated by a few brief dollar-limit poker games. There are movies but the players favor three-color, wide-screen turkeys like "Sodom and Gomorrah" and "Taras Bulba" ("There's this chick in this dress that's all slit and not much dress and, man, is this tough.") and studiously avoid the Cannes Festival winners where you have to read sub-titles and there are no horses on screen.

The card games are loud. "Play some tonk?" challenges Elgin Baylor, riffling a deck and an invitation to a basketball form of knock poker. Dick Barnett, hat on head, flashes a gold-toothed grin "You're on, darling. Get your wallet."

The cabin is heated but the lavatory should have a crescent cut in it. It is, like the rest of the East, in the grip of a cold wave. The stewardess is shapely but she is married to the pilot. And no one wants to make HIM mad.

There is a baseball dinner in St. Louis which cuts the monotony somewhat, but not much. Among others, a Stone Age relief pitcher named Heine Meine is honored. Someone suggests it is for the most games won by a pitcher whose name rhymes.

Maury Wills is an honoree and he describes his 97th base steal which broke Ty Cobb's record. "I had this warm feeling and when I got ready to steal I was a witness to God. But Larry Jackson was pitching and he has this real good balk move and I only stole one base on him in my life and got four hits. And he threw over to first base five times and maybe he got me once, only the umpire missed it."

So Maury went down and the ball was late at the bag. And Ty Cobb was just another good .400 hitter.

And Ralph Terry, the pitcher who gave up over 40 home runs last year and would have logged a few more if the wind hadn't been blowing in at Candlestick in Game 7 of the World Series tells the crowd:

"I owe a lot to Ralph Houk but he owes a lot to me. If I don't throw a home run ball to Bill Mazeroski in the 1960 World Series, Casey Stengel is still the manager and Ralph is waving runners around at third base.

"I have put more .250 hitters in the record book than any other country boy I know. I can still see Yogi Berra trying to climb the wall after Maz's homer but I just put my glove in my pocket and said 'Forget it, Yog. Wait'll next year.'

"Johnny Blanchard, my catcher, came out just before the pitch and said 'get it down, Ralphie, this guy murders high balls.' So I got it down. Right around his belt. I never was much of a drinker but on the plane that night I threw down six Martinis and by the time we got home I couldn't even remember the score. Maz turned Stengel into a National Leaguer and me into a lush.

"But last year I sure outsmarted old Stretch McCovey. Held him to a 400-ft. triple into the wind and a line drive that Bobby Richardson didn't have to jump much for."

Stan Musial is honored but in St. Louis he is so used to it that he makes a speech if someone gives him a streetcar transfer. Archie Moore is serenaded with a parody of "Battle Hymn of the Republic" but the crowd is more involved with a bottle hymn by then—and finally the evening is over and the sport is basketball again.

The plane drones on. The typewriter tips off a lap from time to time. Across the aisle, Jim Krebs is biting a pen point and concentrating on an epic he's been writing for the *Reader's Digest* since the days before the center jump. There is no evidence the *Digest* is holding the presses in anticipation but Jimmy is hard at work. "Can't they keep this damn plane still?" he complains. "How can us authors work?"

Soon Boston is on the horizon. "Boston," sighs Hundley, shuffling the cards. "Now if you really want to see a town that's out to lunch, this is it."

You blow on your fingers and traipse drearily through one more terminal and one more day, a chain of 7-ft. zombies, 3,000 miles from Palm Springs and palm trees. "What if you don't want to be in Boston?" Rudy echoes querulously.

A helluva question.

And Baby Makes 3

Elsewhere, it may be celebrated for other things, but so far as the world of sport is concerned, this week in the Year of Our Lord has to be known as the week Togetherness Struck Back.

I mean, the *Ladies' Home Journal* would be proud of the Boston Celtics.

Hark back in your mind's eye to Sunday. The Los Angeles

Lakers had just won their third game of the world championship basketball playoffs and had the perennial champs, Celtics, teetering on the edge of the plank, three games to two.

There was only one trouble: the Lakers had to come home. It wasn't the freeway traffic coach Fred Schaus was worried about. It was the home fires.

Every traveling man knows what happens when you come home from a trip. You plunk down the bags in the living room, cup your hands and shout: "Hi, Honey. I'm home!" There's a stir in the other part of the house and pretty soon your little helpmate appears with a broom in her hand and a cloth wrapped around her head. She surveys you calculatingly, taking in the red eyes, the rumpled clothes, the soiled shirts sticking out the ends of the suitcase.

"Kids! Your father's here!" she shouts. "Young man," she says as the first one comes into view, "you get right out here and tell him how you broke the plate glass window in the dining room after I told you to stop playing with that hard ball. Buddy, show him that terrible report card! Sis, you ask your father if HE thinks it's all right for you to come home that late at night through all that traffic."

The kids file in. The home-comer struggles to look stern. This isn't at all how he planned it on the plane flying in. But his wife is busy with more welcoming speech. "I've been down on my hands and knees scurbbing out your study all day," she says accusingly, leaving out the implied "while you were having all that fun in the fleshpots of Dayton, O."

"How on earth do you track all that mud in? And the phone company made another mistake on our bill. I've called them about it three times but they keep insisting it's our fault. The insurance company says we'll have to pay for the car. The office has been calling, wondering where you were. Bobby needs his tonsils out. Your mother called just as I was getting ready for church and she upset me so much I scraped the side off the Chev and we're overdrawn at the bank again. You're to call the Internal Revenue Bureau . . ."

She pauses, then dabs at her hair.

"Did you have a nice trip, dear?" she asks sweetly.

Well, you know how it goes. So does Fred Schaus. That's why

"Beef" hired a suite of rooms for his verging world champions Sunday night. "All the guys got little kids, and they cry at night and keep the guys awake and disturbed," he explained lamely.

There was an instant sucking in of breath from one end of the city to the other. I expect there'll be an emergency meeting of a thousand neighborhood Mothers' Clubs any minute. One thing is for sure: Fred Schaus may not blow the playoff, but he has already blown the Husband-of-the-Year award.

Of course, to beat the Celtics, a coach would happily bivouac the team in the middle of the Santa Ana Freeway and lock the wife in a closet, if it would help.

The point is, it didn't. The Celtics probably kissed their wives goodbye with tears in their eyes, lied manfully about the hardships of leaving all those nice Boston icicles and all that pneumonia blowing off the Charles River for the pitfalls of Los Angeles where a fellow might sit in a draught at the Pink Pussy Cat or stub his toe on a diving board.

It was the Lakers who showed up tense and hollow-eyed. Probably couldn't sleep a wink without the noise of a squalling baby in the other room—tossed and turned all night because they didn't have to get up and boil a 2 o'clock bottle—woke up at 6 a.m. and couldn't go back to sleep because they kept thinking they had to burp the baby and there wasn't any baby. Just Rod Hundley snoring on the next pillow or hogging all the blankets.

Of course, while these little things mean a lot, it also helps in a game if you can shoot over Bill Russell. The last time this happened they were still using peach baskets.

The game was a duel between the two greatest basketball players, inch-for-inch, of the age—Elgin Baylor and Bill Russell. This night, Russell won.

History will probably say it was because the Celts could play Baylor tight—send Jim Loscutoff and Tom Sanders out to meet him in mid-court and wrap their arms around him like a cop making a pinch without worrying about his whirling around them and driving in for one of his specialized lay-ups. You don't make specialized lay-ups with B. Russell sitting under the basket like a rattler sunning himself on a big rock.

On the other hand, I suspect the Celtics won on plain old-fashioned verities. I have a feeling they stayed up late, making fudge or canning chili and after midnight, called home to ask "Honey, put the baby on the phone and pinch him, will you? I can't sleep till I hear him yowl."

Travel Is Boredom

For an athlete, a road trip is a blank interval in life, a 24-hour sleep-walk in which you hear the roar of the crowd or the roar of the engine. Everything in between is spinach.

You live like a monk 9 days out of 11. And the other two aren't much better. You can't drink. When the horn sounds and you're a basketball player, you have 24 seconds to go from one end of the court to the other. Between you and the basket are five pair of the finest elbows ever honed. Go through them with a hangover and the National Safety Council will use you as a horrible example.

You can't go to a movie. Afternoons are for sleeping. So are mornings and evenings. You sleep whenever you can. Whenever you can't, you eat. The enemy is never really the Celts, the Hawks or the Royals. It's the boredom.

If you're with the Lakers, you leave home on a night so balmy that the ocean you wheel and turn over had people in it that day. When you wake up, you're in the zero Fahrenheit belt and even the birds don't fly in it. Sometimes, neither do airplanes. You hang around more airports than a wind-sock.

You tote your own baggage because the tips would eat up your $8 per diem. So you either have a basketball, a knife and fork—or your duffel and hand luggage in your hand. Porters hate you. People stare. You go from coast to coast struggling through terminals, ducking under low ceilings. Basketball is a sport for everyone but you. For you, it's ditch-digging. Before a cheering crowd, of course.

You arrive in the nation's capital but it may as well be Long Beach. You have no time for sight-seeing. The hand of history writes all around you but history to you is your rebound average and your points-per-minute. So you scrape the ice off the windshield of your rental car and get to the dressing room. On the way, you get lost. Also, when there, you lose. You blame the officials, curse the weather. When you get home, you eat. It's 1 o'clock in the morning but the coach is on the phone the next morning at 7. He's hurting because you lost a game you had no chance to win. "Fred's in a mood, we better get down," your roommate tells you.

One more airport. One more takeoff. "Just one more week and we'll be home," says the hopeful Tommy Hawkins. "I hate basketball," says Rod Hundley.

But basketball players are not tired men. They're mischievous boys and they attack boredom the way all boys do—with pranks.

Jim Krebs is sitting in a diner in Washington, filling a thermos with coffee. He studies the sleet outside and the Celtic lineup inside. "I can't play tonight. I got 38 things wrong with me," he tells the coach. Fred Schaus grins wickedly. "Yeah. And 37 of them are Bill Russell," he diagnoses.

Hot Rod Hundley groans as he hits the dressing room. "I can't dress tonight to play," he moans. "I just can't handle it. Can I find a doctor in this place with a thermometer? I know I got a fever." And he sets off in the happy hopes he may have an infection instead of a basketball game. "Even if he did, Fred would tell him to go out and give it to Russell," predicts Hawkins.

Lost in a skidding car on the treacherous hillsides of Maryland, towering center Ray Felix suddenly chuckles. "Don't rush," he advises the driver. "They got five other men to suit up. Against the Celtics, we'll get there in plenty of time."

They turn their attention to the trainer, Frank O'Neill. He has shown a delightful tendency to react unfavorably to ribbing. The Lakers promptly dub him "J. Wimbledon Hogg." He is paged constantly over airport loudspeakers. Sometimes, he is just "Dr. A. Hogg." Whenever the dispatcher doubts the authenticity of such a real-life character, the Lakers are outraged. They produce a dignified Hot Rod Hundley, wearing gloves, phony eyeglasses and carrying a trainer's bag and quite insulted there should seem to be anything unusual about his name.

Everyone has a nickname. Frank Selvy is "Ish" or "Fab." "Fab" is short for the standard "Fabulous Frank" Selvy, which was the nickname some adoring newsman hung on him in the days when he scored 100 points in a single game. It is faintly derisive but affectionate today when 100 points a season against Boston's Jones boys would be welcome.

Jim Krebs is "Boomer" and he is the prime mischief maker. In an airport when things get too dull to be borne he leads a squad of a half-dozen of the tree-toppers of the team. They single out the shortest man in the terminal, usually some fellow buried in the *Wall Street Journal*, surround him and begin to carry on a conversation with each other over his head as if he weren't there. The fellow usually tries to pay no attention but pretty soon his air supply is all but cut off. One night in Syracuse, a man panicked and sent for the police. The Lakers pretended to be horrified they hadn't noticed him standing down there.

They burst into song—off-key song. The lyrics all revolve around "J. Wimbledon Hogg." Krebs and Rudy LaRusso promise a musical entitled "My Fair Hogg." They improvise lyrics on the back of airsickness bags and pass them out in airplane aisles. "Sing Along With Boomer," is the name of the program. The listeners usually need the bags worse than the singers do by the second chorus.

Krebs, who was dubbed by Elgin Baylor "Mrs. Basketball"—and Krebs misses his debating adversary Baylor off-the-court as much as the Lakers do on—is a collector of early American antiques. Once, in New England, he bought an old-fashioned wall phone complete with box and paneling. He carried it resolutely all over a tour, stoutly fighting off sky-caps.

The only trouble was, when a car turned a corner, Krebs' phone rang. The Lakers busily stuffed it with paper, cotton and other mufflers. The overweight charge ran up so high, the coach finally balked at paying for its further transportation. It would have been cheaper to fly another person. Krebs reluctantly left it in Boston for later pickup. LaRusso spotted him in the lobby in St. Louis a few days later. "Hey, Boomer," he said. "Your phone called today and wanted to know when you were going to come and pick it up."

You're on the road and a laugh is worth as much as a basket. The chances are good 20 years from now you'll remember the laughs better than the baskets. You got a 10½-game lead in a tough league and the Army lifted your clean-up hitter. But you're on a ball club where there are no cliques and you play it loose and maybe that's why you win even with a stripped-down deck.

And then someday you look back on it and suddenly realize it WAS fun and that it was that way only once and never will be the same again.

Thar She Blows!

An old editor of mine—who knew there would be days like this—once told me "Son, the best stories in the world are floating right by your front door if you'll only look out there."

So I did. And he was right. Of course, these days, my front door is the Pacific Ocean and at this time of the year the things floating by are the great Pacific gray whales steaming down to their breeding grounds in the lagoons around Magdalena Bay in Mexico.

The water is deep off Pt. Dume, my home, and the whales cruise in pretty close to shore. They are happy and playful on the way down. Scientists say they don't even stop to eat all the way from their home in the Bering Sea to their ancestral spawning spot. They can't wait to get there. They roll in the water, leap out and slap the surf playfully with their giant flukes, blow towering spouts of steam and ham it up. They remind me of a stream of taxicabs on their way to the Darktown Strutters' Ball.

The species was thought to be extinct as recently as 15 years ago but when they put in a law forbidding the killing of Pacific grays, their herd has now grown to 6,000. At one time, it may have been as large as 70,000.

A whale is the largest of God's creatures. A dinosaur was a pigmy by comparison. A whale tongue weighs as much as a grown elephant.

The Pacific gray is not the largest of the whales, however. It is a toothless pacifist (it has hair for teeth) and it is no

Jonah-eater, it could not swallow a man if it wanted to, its throat is too small. It is an hors d'oeuvre nibbler. It dines daintily but constantly on plankton, a sub-visual but plentiful form of ocean life, on sardines and smaller fish.

No one knows how long a whale lives. It is an air-breathing mammal, the same as you and I. It has the same body temperature and it may even run a fever. Its characteristic spout is really exhaled air, jetted out of a nostril atop its back so fast that it cools rapidly and condenses into a mist that may rise 20 to 30 ft. in the air like a geyser. The Pacific gray can run to 55 ft. in length and it can dive hundreds of fathoms between breaths of fresh air. It cannot live on land because its muscles cannot lift its tons of weight to inhale and it will first wheeze like Jackie Gleason climbing stairs and finally suffocate.

It would live longer were it not for its natural enemy, the fiercest predator in all of nature—the killer whale. This racy, deadly torpedo of the deep is the dread of everything at sea. The shark is an easy-going slob compared to the killer whale.

In the first place, it is not a fish, it is a cunning mammal. It pursues whales like coyotes do a wounded deer—in packs. Its back is black, its stomach white. Its vision 20/20 and its teeth would be the envy of every dentist in the country. It is smarter than an ape and it gets all the best of the going because the environment is all its own. There are people who swear it growls.

It catches penguins in the Antarctic by surfacing under the ice, cracking it and swallowing the bird, tuxedo and all. But its most prized delicacy is whale tongue. It hectors a great whale in long thrilling sea chases until the whale's tongue is literally hanging out from exhaustion, then it darts in and chows up.

It is a sea-going equivalent of Mack the Knife. Once, in an English cove where whalers used to dump the tongues from their whale slaughter, a congress of killer whales soon appeared. In a few days these underwater racketeers had sized up the situation. They began ranging far at sea, rounding up herds of whales and steering them aground into the cove! They knew man would do their work for them and they just hung around and waited for their reward—the tongue.

I put the glasses on these marvelous creatures from the front yard of my house and I silently root for them to make it to their annual ball and back again. They are meaner, more peevish and less playful on the way back to the cold North like any other winter vacationers, but I know next January they will be coming back again to foal the calves conceived this year and start the life cycle all over again, the old bulls showing the way and keeping a not-so-sharp eye out for the wicked killers.

At least man now leaves them alone and he was worse than the killer whale. Nature keeps a balance but man is constantly tipping it the wrong way. In the old days, the natives of Africa and Japan used to catch whales by swimming out, climbing on their backs and plugging up their air holes. This may be where the expression "Rotsa Ruck" first started.

But while their great size has always terrified man, there is no evidence whales begrudge him in their life. The crew of the Kon-Tiki crossing the Pacific on a raft, encountered a few of the monsters and one of the crewmen wrote what might well be the way all of us should look at it. "It is strange and wonderful to hear something breathing at sea."

Pony Girl

Everyone knows how a lady picks winners at a race track. She sticks a hat pin in a program, an arm in her husband's pocket, or her fingers over her eyes, and points.

Occasionally—very occasionally—she will look at the field and if she sees a horse who looks like someone she knows—and dislikes—she will throw him out of the handicapping and go on to the next. "I like the 5 horse," she may say. If her escort wants to know why, she will explain, "I always did like fuchsia."

It's as good a reason to pick a horse as any.

She is not interested in bloodlines. A "hock" is something you make soup out of. A "morning line" has got wash hanging on it. She thinks horses are beautiful and smart and can tell Roy Rogers from a bank robber at a glance and will save little girls from drowning. People who know horses know they couldn't tell Roy Rogers from the Chinese ambassador, and wouldn't even know how to save themselves from drowning. As for being smart, there might be smart horses in the world—but they're not on race tracks.

Owners who are trying to set up killings on the track, the late Joe Palmer pointed out, scare women hunch bettors off by naming their animals things like "Ugly Sue," and "Zsa Zsa."

I bring this up because I ran into, down in Kentucky, a woman who knows so much about horses, she doesn't even bet on them. She just picks them. Joby Arnold is America's only woman handicapper of horses. She picked the order of finish of the Derby one-two. But that's nothing. She picked the order of finish of the day's second race—a field of cunning platers who make a habit of outwitting the bettors, which is not the toughest thing they have to do in a day.

Joby picks horses for a living—for newspapers. This is the toughest kind of tout work because you have to pick the same horse in the same race for everybody. You can't give 12 horses to 12 different people, like the guy in the checked suit in the grandstand, and then start all over again, so that, no matter who wins, one-twelfth of the people at the track will think you're a genius.

Joby was christened Betty Jo. Like the better horses, she was foaled in Kentucky. I won't tell you how long ago, but Roosevelt was President. Not Teddy, you cad! You can tell right away Joby (the "Betty Jo" got twisted and you have to understand Kentucky to understand why and that takes much too long for here) is a filly. Some women who hang around horses long enough begin to look like them—but not Joby. She looks like a woman all the way —fetlock, pastern, cannon and coronet, fine; muzzle, first-rate; tendons, definitely not bowed; withers, ship-shape; loin, U. S. Grade A; and these big brown eyes. It has complicated her life no end, because when she shows up around the barns for stories, she causes more eyes to roll than a syringe and her first request for an interview is usually greeted with "Sure, Baby, how about 5:30? For cocktails? Your place or my place?"

Joby, whose marriage broke down on the clubhouse turn and

had to be destroyed, has a 14-year-old son to raise as well as a number of horses of her own. She is as deadly serious about her business as U. S. Steel.

She rides around the track on her own pony in the mornings and puts her own clock on the steeds. She has shovelled manure in the stalls, walked hots, braided manes and tails, plated horses, and yet manages to look like Loretta Young in those old pictures where she came off two weeks crawling through an air raid without even her evening gown mussed.

Joby's biggest problem is discrimination. Horsemen like their women in mink, not on horseback. She can get into only every third press box in the country; so she has to write her story from observation, not handouts, a requisite which, if widespread, might have a lot of us driving a cab for a living at the end of a year.

Joby has only one area where she might be looking through the wrong end of the binoculars. She thinks trainers and jockeys give her valuable tips (which they do) because they have come to respect her so much they forget she's a woman. Only in a Warner Bros. movie with her curls underneath her cap and her curves underneath a shirt and overalls would you be asked to believe this. I may not know horses, but I know men.

Trainers who might not admit to me if one of their horses had just broken two clocks or three legs, lose all their reserve when Joby reins alongside and fastens those brown eyes on them. They come across like a guy whose fingernails are being pulled out with pliers.

"Joby, Baby," they sigh. "This beast of mine couldn't win this race with an electric cattle prod. Our only chance is that everything else in the race runs into a fence. Unless they repeal the law against syringes on the morning of the race, we may even have to van him into the paddock . . ."

Or, he may groan, "Joby, Honey, I wouldn't tell this to my best friend, but this horse ran so fast this morning that I thought we were going to have to shoot him to catch him. He'll be in the barns Saturday before the rest of that field finishes. Whirlaway would have gone to delivering milk if he had to run against this fellow. We're going to have to tie the jockey on——."

You can see, even without the handouts and the free lunch, Joby Baby is a 4–5 shot against the rest of us in this game.

A Pumpkin City Again

LOUISVILLE—This report is coming to you from the inside of a cut-out jack o' lantern. Louisville turned back into a pumpkin last night. The only visitors staying over are in jail. You could shoot a cannon off on Bardstown Road and not hit anybody that doesn't belong on it.

The hangover has moved on to Pimlico and the Preakness. The only accents you hear in the downtown hotels are southern, which is a welcome change from the Bronx and Bostonese. If you hear a sound of rattling on boards it's a woodpecker instead of a crapshooter.

What is a Kentucky Derby really like? Well, if you're a horse I expect it's a pain in the saddle cloth. But if you're just an ordinary lush like me, it's a ball.

I expect it's the only sporting event which really lives up to its form. The bloody horse race is never more than two minutes and five seconds and that's all right with everybody. Nobody bothers to watch it anyway except the jockey on the second horse. If you win the first payoff is hay fever because they throw a blanket of flowers over your head without bothering to brush all the bees out. The drinks make you sneeze, too, because of the heavy pollen count of the mint.

The whole town gets in the act. I bought a phony carnation off a kid that he and his sister had sat up all night weaving together out of boxes of Kleenex (and before those crummy trade-mark lawyers flash me another bulletin about capitalizing and spelling out "cleaning tissues" along with their name I got a flash for them—"drop dead"). The one I bought was in two colors, it only cost a nickel and it was the biggest bargain in town short of a ticket on Decidedly. "Hey, sis, make up some more in both colors," the kid shouted. "We're out of Kleenex," she answered. "Use the other stuff," he instructed.

Like I say, Dan'l Boone would be proud of these people. I'm glad they're on our side these last few wars.

The horse race, if you care for them, wasn't bad either. The winner was a Californian, the only one from there who showed up sober for the seventh race. He probably can't wait till he gets back and tells the crowd at Chasen's how he broke the track record. It was the fastest mile-and-a-quarter ever run in Kentucky, they say, but all I got to say is nobody clocked the guy the cops were chasing down Fourth Street the night of the race. He could have given Decidedly weight and run off and hid on him.

Of course, he had more incentive than Hartack. But not much. Hartack didn't give a hoot about the Derby and when they threw the roses over him he almost belted thc guy who did it. So far as Hartack was concerned the Kentucky Derby was a race between him and Ridan. The owner took Willie off Ridan and put the Panamanian Pistol, Manuel Ycaza, on him, and Hartack acted as if he'd just been deported.

I hung around the jocks' room all week to watch Hartack. I didn't introduce myself because if there's one thing Hartack hates worse than a horse it's a writer. But he paced daily outside the jocks' room, lips curling, smoking so much it looked as if he had two cigarettes going all the time, and talking to himself. The dialogue would have to be cleaned up to be put in a stag movie but when the race was run I knew Decidedly would either have to win it or defend himself from Hartack who would have strangled him on the backstretch. At the very least he would have to beat Ridan and the only way to beat him was win as Ridan ran third after he spent the whole race trying to escape to Indiana. Ycaza was so exhausted trying to keep him on the racetrack that he almost forgot how to curse in Spanish.

The winning trainer, Horatio Luro, is a delightful gaucho with liquid brown eyes and a gallantry of manner that makes him look as if he should be leading a samba line instead of a string of horses. He looks, if you know what I mean, like he's kissing a woman's hand even when he isn't, which ain't often. He's a lovely guy, as staid as an antimacassar, but you'd never trust him around your sister.

The new track record was inevitable. It came up hot and sunny and there's not enough sod on that racetrack for a kid to get dirty. You walk across most racetracks, you sink in to the top of your socks. At Churchill Downs you won't even need a shoe shine. I have seen more dirt in my Ricky's ears than they have on top of that racing strip. Even after a bath. It broke down so many horses they might as well run next year's Derby on the Harbor Freeway. If horses ever get a union, they'll picket this place. A chain gang would go berserk trying to chop it.

But as a show I have to rate the Kentucky Derby with the best I've seen—legally, that is. I have seen some shows I won't mention that it wouldn't run one-two with. I didn't puddle up when they played "My Old Kentucky Home" and I spent more time in a mutuel line in one day than I've spent at Santa Anita in my lifetime. But, honest, it's more fun than doing the twist with Jayne Mansfield (assuming, of course, she can do it which I don't make a short price, at all). It spoiled me so much I may start putting carnation leaves in my drinks when I get home.

You have to understand, of course, it was a great victory for us Californians. I mean, it even made up for Silky Sullivan. Decidedly is so much a native son of the Golden West he could get in the California Club. It only goes to show you not only don't need blue grass in your bourbon, you don't even need it in your horse.

But now, if you'll pardon me, I think I'll go downtown and get in a cab and go out to Churchill Downs. I can't believe it's really 100 miles from downtown Louisville even though it has been all week. It took so long I thought the last cab driver made a mistake and thought I said "take me to Winston Churchill."

I'd come back to California but I don't think I'll have time. I have to get in line at the $2 window for next year's Derby so I won't get shut out. If you need me, get in touch with your nearest local pickpocket. They post a winter book on people like me. Decidedly.

The Rite of Spring

LOUISVILLE—There are those who say the Kentucky Derby is just a horse race. But there are those who say the Taj Mahal is just a building—or Elizabeth Taylor is a woman. There's a little more to it than that.

The Kentucky Derby is a rite of spring, a time of the year when the whole slap-happy fraternity of racing comes together for its biggest binge of the year. Action is slow at every pool hall in the country because the hustlers have hot-footed it to Louisville with the old lady's rent money.

There are more pickpockets than there are pockets, preying on suckers in suede shoes and their mink-wrapped broads. They put weeds in the whiskey, which is such a bad idea this is the only day in the year they do it because of ante-bellum movies.

The blowout is held in a track that is such a jumble of buildings it's as hard to figure whether it's coming or going as an English sheep dog. It looks like it was nailed together on a dark night by two plumbers with a bucket of glue and their hair in their eyes.

Nobody counts the people who come to the Derby, they just call out the National Guard to keep them from being run over by the horses. The best guess is there's somewhat over 50,000 and somewhat under the announced 100,000. Even the jockeys can't find the finish line in this cockamanie park and Willie Shoemaker once missed it by a half furlong, which is still the freestyle record for this kind of thing.

Even the horses are imposters. A three-year-old thoroughbred in May is just a baby and has about as much idea what is expected of him as a boy on his first pair of roller-skates.

The track has been painted so many times it comes out on Derby day like an old strumpet with violets in her hat and enough rouge to dye a battleship. The next day she's back in her kimono with the rope around the middle and the floppy house-slippers again. As the old joke goes, they'd have to paint it to condemn.

They play "My Old Kentucky Home" as the horses come on the track and guys who don't even know how to spell "Kentucky" stand there with tears streaming down their cheeks. They are cursing five minutes later when they tear up their tickets and if Stephen Foster came up to them for a handout they'd kick him all the way to Ohio. The song is supposed to give even the jocks a clutch in the throat but, if so, it's not a patch on the throat clutches two of them were giving each other for real at the finish line one day. It was the first time a crowd got treated to a horse race and a murder attempt at the same time.

They hate to take a number down in the Derby but this may

be the year for it because the east has come up with an equine juvenile delinquent named Sunrise County who doesn't think it's a horse race, it's a rumble. He plays it like a fullback laying blocks all over the place and in his last he rode his competition almost all the way to the grandstand rail before Bill Shoemaker could steer him forward. He may rack up the field again. He doesn't need a bit, he needs a straight jacket.

Except for the Derby, Louisville is just a place where they make good whiskey before they spoil it with the parsley. It's a border town with a history of such violence that when the long knives walked they boasted you could canoe across the state in blood. It is more hospitable to strangers now. A Derby crowd drops four million at the track and spills more than that accidentally in the corridors of the hotels which could throw a mortgage burning every year on the dividends of room rents alone.

The cab drivers are so polite and friendly you scarcely notice they take the great circle route to your destination.

The natives are supposed to know everything about horses and the backstretch is popularly believed to be populated by a strange breed of leprechauns known as "hardboots" who can give you the winner's fractions without a watch-tick of error four days before the race. But all the natives I've seen were pin-stabbers like the rest of us. I don't think they know a girl horse from a boy horse.

I know I don't. I have about as much right to be at this rodeo as a mule has to be in the starting gate. But one lady horse may run, Cicada. If she does, I hope that ruffian, Sunrise County, doesn't clout her one in the coiffure. If he does maybe one of those nice little old ladies will hammer him over the ears with her reticule, the one she keeps her pickpocket earnings in.

I came down here only after I gave up on Michigan. I mean I didn't mind it when in one day the temperature there went from beastly hot to hail and sleet and high winds, then back to steamy heat again. But when the six o'clock news said this was only the beginning, that the tornadoes would be along momentarily, I quit on that state and lit out for Louisville, which you can recognize by the cloud of steam coming off the river.

It's quite a wrench to go from a state where they worship the auto to one where they worship the horse. Personally, I don't trust either one. The Ford people made a Lincoln Continental available to me in Detroit which I guess is a great automobile but which had so many buttons on the sides and front I thought for one minute they had given me an organ by mistake. It took me two days to figure out how to open the front window with that console and before that happened I had converted the front seat into a bed three times. I'm the only guy who disappeared from view three times in one block in traffic.

I'm hoping the horses are easier to figure. I'll go out to the barns tomorrow as soon as I learn what one looks like. That's known around the track as "going down the backside." That way I'll avoid the temptation of card games with kindly old strangers. If you need me, I'll be seining the poison ivy out of my drinks and trying to find where to buy a new pair of hard boots.

EPILOGUE

Now that this second book of the collected works of this student of the infield fly rule is completed, I am going to give myself over to a wider work to be called *The Power of Positive Drinking,* and, meanwhile, I reflect on a decade or more in sports and I find that little things stick out in my mind—like the time Orlando Cepeda told me his father died from cirrhosis of the liver; not from drinking alcohol, mind you, but from drinking the polluted water of San Juan's waterfront. I remember thinking what an extraordinary object lesson that should be to my wife the next time I rely on the deadly ten-to-one martini to draw a curtain over the day's worries.

I must remind myself also of the experience of the New York couple who had a tankful of tropical fish wherein their guests (they were very convivial folk) would dump all the cigarette butts, gin-soaked olives and even the aforementioned deadly ten-to-one'ers, and the fish thrived (throve?). Until finally remorse set in, or the doctor put the couple on the wagon, and suddenly their evenings were given over to thorough readings of Proust and bed before the witching hour. And one morning they awoke and found their little tropical fish floating upside down on top of the tank. They could not stand the pastoral life.

Neither can I. I don't necessarily like to be out where I can hear the roar of the crowd—but I do enjoy the roar of the partner who has just missed a two-foot putt. And I *like* to sit in a press box next to some old gaffer who remembers exactly how Matty threw the fadeaway and what the hell the fadeaway is or to hear again the story of how Lefty Gomez got eyeglasses one year, got a close look at Jimmy Foxx and threw them away at once.

I don't know where sports are trending or whether we will have many more of this eyewitness stuff in future. Because the day seems ever coming closer when the whole spectrum will just be a long-running TV series. A publisher's editor I know—in fact, *my* publisher's editor, who answers to the name Luther Nichols, but *not* if you call during lunch—reports he was so addicted to watching the weekend sports showings (which his wife refers to as "The Endless Summer") that his neglected fair lady came in the room to announce she had just shot to death her neighbors and their eight children and that everybody outside Colts' Stadium in Baltimore knew that war had been declared globally. Whereupon Luther rose to the occasion. "For God's sake, woman, be quiet!" he stormed. "Can't you see we're on the six-yard line?"

One of my own finest hours in athletics came the afternoon when we were watching the Braves and the Dodgers on the idiot tube and the network kept (momentarily) interrupting the between-innings banter of Pee Wee Reese and some other shortstop or announcer to say "We will bring you the latest reports on the Arab-Israeli War right after major league baseball." Cross my heart!

The day will come, of course, when television will no longer be able to contain itself over the bad scripting of major league ball games, fights, tennis, soccer, and so on. I can see right now where some non-star picks up a loose ball and runs 80 yards for a touchdown and the director comes thundering out of the stands holding his head and shrieking (probably in Hungarian): "No! No! No! How many times do I have to tell you?! *Sayers makes the touchdowns!* Sayers is the star on this show. Sayers is the man we're selling to the networks and syndicating on the smaller stations. What are you trying to do, No. 31—ruin us? Kill television? Now, run that over and this time, remember! Sayers! Right, *liebchen?*"

Wrestling adapted itself to the medium a long time ago with its rigid morality play but boxing continued to plod along with its succession of Bad Guys overcoming the white hats. Damn near killed the sport.

Of course, television has such a short tolerance for boredom that the playing of games, as we know it, may yet be saved in the nick of time and cut off the tracks just as the limited comes bearing round the bend.

Television is a great plunderer. It went through every able-bodied comic in America and left them limp and laughless. Then it exhausted The Old West. The Horror Story was emptied out till in the end they had to run japes of it.

It will take them longer to toss Sports out with the bath water. First, they will have to empty spontaneity, suspense. They have done this in some cases by having *delayed* telecasts (you heard me!) of major sporting events—like the 1960 Golf Open where I resolutely cut off every radio in my office and the one in my car, and rolled toward home at the appointed hour determined to turn on the Eye and watch the Open as if it were happening right before my eyes and was news, not history.

You guessed it. At the last stoplight before my home, there was a friend frantically wigwagging from another car and rolling down the window. I thought for one wild moment he was suffering a heart attack. He looked strangled. I rolled my window down. "ISN'T IT WONDERFUL ABOUT PALMER WINNING THE OPEN!" he screamed. I rolled my window morosely back up. The only suspense left was whether it was Johnny or Arnold. I went home and haplessly watched Ben Hogan trying to sneak a 2-stroke lead home, all the time groaning to myself, "Forget it, Ben. That guy back there with his shirt hanging out is going to get it all."

Videocracy is a despot we all have to put up with, I am afraid. It has already changed major traditions in sport—like the 36-hole final in the Open, match play in the PGA. It has put tennis to experimenting wildly with its game to suit it to the dimensions of the tube. It has caused timeouts to be called on a football team which had momentum going for it until they took time out to plug a deodorant or a hair tonic or just the upcoming fall shows on leave-blank-name-of-network.

Will it stop there? I think not. Like the creature that eats its young, it is systematically destroying itself and all around it. Some day, Fred W. Friendly may get his wish. Television may HAVE to televise all those boring Congressional hearings in their entirety. It will long since have consumed everything else. There will be nothing left but Senator Dirksen and test patterns. They will then be able to take a poll by phoning up just one man—Fred W. Friendly. He will be the only one watching.

But before that day comes, sport will have to be reduced to just another Playhouse 90 (a prehistoric program eaten by television in the winter of '55, children) with cues, prompters, marks for the actors between setups, directors, assistant directors, script crews, clapboards for scene-settings for the cutter and a guy in a megaphone and puttees overseeing the whole silly farce. Ready when you are, C.B.!